D1554485

Finding Meaning and Success

OTHER BOOKS BY CHRIS PALMER

Shooting in the Wild: An Insider's Account of Making Movies in the Animal Kingdom (Sierra Club Books, 2010)

Confessions of a Wildlife Filmmaker: The Challenges of Staying Honest in an Industry Where Ratings Are King (Bluefield Publishing, 2015)

Now What, Grad? Your Path to Success After College (Rowman & Littlefield, 2015)

Raise Your Kids to Succeed: What Every Parent Should Know (Rowman & Littlefield, 2017)

Now What, Grad? Your Path to Success After College, 2nd Edition (Rowman & Littlefield, 2018)

Love, Dad: Letters from a Father to His Daughters (Bethesda Communications Group, 2018)

College Teaching at Its Best: Inspiring Students to Be Enthusiastic, Lifelong Learners (Rowman & Littlefield, 2019)

Palm Chris, 1947-
Finding meaning and
success iving a ulfi
[2021].
3330524843 17
gi 08/12/

Finding Meaning and Success

Living a Fulfilled and Productive Life

Chris Palmer

ROWMAN & LITTLEFIELD
Lanham • Boulder • New York • London

Published by Rowman & Littlefield
An imprint of The Rowman & Littlefield Publishing Group, Inc.
4501 Forbes Boulevard, Suite 200, Lanham, Maryland 20706
www.rowman.com

6 Tinworth Street, London, SE11 5AL, United Kingdom

Copyright © 2021 by Chris Palmer

All rights reserved. No part of this book may be reproduced in any form or by any
electronic or mechanical means, including information storage and retrieval systems,
without written permission from the publisher, except by a reviewer who may quote
passages in a review.

British Library Cataloguing in Publication Information Available

Library of Congress Cataloging-in-Publication Data

Names: Palmer, Chris, 1947– author.
Title: Finding meaning and success : living a fulfilled and productive life
 / Chris Palmer.
Description: Lanham, Maryland : Rowman & Littlefield, 2021. | Includes
 bibliographical references and index. | Summary: "This book will help
 you design and create the best version of yourself. It will give you the
 chance to shape the kind of person you want to be and to articulate the
 goals you want to achieve in your life, both professionally and
 personally"—Provided by publisher.
Identifiers: LCCN 2021002923 (print) | LCCN 2021002924 (ebook) | ISBN
 9781475850536 (hardcover) | ISBN 9781475850543 (epub)
Subjects: LCSH: Self-actualization (Psychology) | Conduct of life.
Classification: LCC BF637.S4 P346 2021 (print) | LCC BF637.S4 (ebook) |
 DDC 158.1—dc23
LC record available at https://lccn.loc.gov/2021002923
LC ebook record available at https://lccn.loc.gov/2021002924

This book is dedicated to my nine precious and beloved grandchildren: Kareena, Neal, JJ, Max, Sammy, Aiden, Connor, Dylan, and Charlie.

~

Contents

~

Preface

This book explores an enormous and important topic: how to find meaning, purpose, and success in life.

It will teach you how to author your own life and how to make commitments to yourself and others that will transform your life for the better.

You'll learn to reflect on your life, think about what really matters to you, and how to create a personal mission statement.

You'll think about your values, articulate your goals, and manage your time effectively. You'll explore what it means to live an examined life.

Part I focuses on envisioning the future you want and capturing that vision in the form of a personal mission statement.

In part II, you will use your personal mission statement as the basis for creating your goals.

And in part III, you will learn how to take action on your goals and be highly productive.

These three foundational elements of your life—having a vision (part I), setting goals (part II), and taking action (part III)—are like the three legs of a stool. If one of them is missing, your life will not be a success.

Without a driving vision (leg one of the stool), there is no *why*, and without *why*, there is little meaning or purpose in life.

Without goals (leg two of the stool), there can be no progress.

And even if you have a vision and goals, without taking action (leg three of the stool), you'll be unable to achieve your goals.

All three legs of the stool are essential for a meaningful and successful life.

At the end of each chapter, there are questions to think about and actions to take that reinforce the key messages of the chapter. Consider gathering some friends and enjoying a friendly conversation about what you learned from this book using these prompts to kick off the discussion.

This book goes to press in the middle of the COVID-19 pandemic. The crisis has given many people a reason to think more deeply about what really matters to them. This book will help in that search.

Achieving success and finding meaning is a slow process, but it's also an exciting one. The best of luck to you as you embark on this challenging journey.

The following is an overview of the book:

Part I: "Create a Vision for Your Life"

Envision the future you want and capture it in the form of a personal mission statement.

Chapter 1: "Explore and Define Success"

Learn what success is and what it isn't, how others have defined success, why the pursuit of happiness is not enough, and the regrets some people have when they die.

Chapter 2: "Search for Meaning"

Learn how to find meaning in your life. The search for meaning entails creating an identity and character that reflects the best possible version of yourself.

Chapter 3: "Create a Personal Mission Statement"

Shape the person you'll become by writing, and deeply reflecting on, a personal mission statement that captures the vision you have for your life.

Part II: "Set Goals Derived from Your Vision"

Use your personal mission statement as the basis for creating a plan with specific goals.

Chapter 4: "Establish Goals"

Develop goals from your mission statement, then break them down into step-by-step actions.

Chapter 5: "Invest in Personal Development"

Learn what personal development is and why it's important. Explore the four dimensions of personal development: physical, social/emotional, mental, and spiritual.

Chapter 6: "Take Your Goals and Commitments Seriously"
Understand the impact of good planning and how to integrate it into your life.

Part III: "Act on Your Goals and Be Productive"
Work toward reaching your goals, and do so in an effective, efficient manner.

Chapter 7: "Create an Effective Daily Routine"
Find out how to use time and communications well to support your personal mission statement and goals.

Chapter 8: "Take New Actions Relentlessly"
Have a bias for action, learn how to deal with failure, and appreciate the importance of having a growth mindset.

Chapter 9: "Learn to Say No"
Learn the skill of saying no to help you keep your life on track.

Chapter 10: "Be Choosy about Technology and Social Media"
Avoid the traps of screens and social media. Recognize the problems and dangers of these addictive distractions.

Chapter 11: "Be a Successful Parent in Challenging Times"
Recognize and overcome the problems today's families encounter.

Chapter 12: "Be Organized and Live Simply"
Realize the importance of decluttering and being organized, and the benefits of a less acquisitive lifestyle.

Chapter 13: "Network and Find Mentors"
Explore the importance of networking and finding mentors as you endeavor to live a full life and become your best self.

Epilogue: "Design and Create Your Future"
Some final words on how to find meaning, purpose, and success.

Appendixes:
    A: "Personal Mission Statement and Life Goals"
    B: "Recommended Reading"
    C: "Syllabus for *Design Your Life for Success*"
    D: "Fifty Ways to Improve Your Personal and Professional Life, Increase Your Productivity, and Feel Fulfilled"

~

Acknowledgments

Writing a book is always a collective effort, and I am grateful to those who have helped develop and express the ideas presented here. I am indebted to the many experts, scholars, writers, thinkers, and activists who have inspired my thinking on meaning, purpose, and success. In particular, I want to laud the pioneering work of (in alphabetical order) David Allen, Dr. Albert-László Barabási, Joshua Becker, Dr. Arthur Brooks, David Brooks, Dr. Bill Burnett, Dr. Stephen R. Covey, Dr. Mihaly Csikszentmihalyi, Dr. Angela Duckworth, Dr. Carol Dweck, Dr. Dave Evans, Nir Eyal, Dr. Viktor Frankl, Anu Garg, Dr. Adam Grant, Dr. Mardy Grothe, Dr. Edith Hall, Dr. Yuval Noah Harari, Ryan Holiday, Arianna Huffington, Dr. Sue Johnson, Dr. John Kaag, Dr. Jane McGonigal, Greg McKeown, Cynthia Meyer, Caroline Adams Miller, Tara Mohr, Dr. Cal Newport, Dr. Dean Ornish, Dr. Scott Peck, Dr. Mary Pipher, Dr. Laurie Santos, Dr. Martin Seligman, Dr. Peter Senge, Dr. George Sheehan, Simon Sinek, Emily Esfahani Smith, Dr. Catherine Steiner-Adair, Brian Tracy, Dr. Irvin Yalom, and Dr. Benjamin Zander.

I'm deeply grateful to each of these luminaries, and I salute them for their research, insights, and expertise. Their wisdom is reflected on every page of this book, and I cite them frequently.

This book would never have crossed the finish line without the support of my family. My beloved wife, Gail, and my treasured daughters, Kimberly, Christina, and Jenny, gave me useful criticism and feedback. My family is a continual source of joy and inspiration. I'm deeply grateful to Gail, my three amazing and accomplished daughters, my three exceptional and caring sons-in-law (Sujay, CJ, and Chase), and my nine adored grandchildren: Kareena, Neal, JJ, Max, Sammy, Aiden, Connor, Dylan, and Charlie.

Heaps of gratitude to four special friends—Grant Thompson, Steve King, Kent Wagner, and Aditi Desai—for reviewing the manuscript and giving me constructive suggestions and comments that improved the book. They are all outstanding human beings, and I deeply value their friendship.

I appreciate the editing skills of Wendy A. Jordan, who did an excellent job editing the entire manuscript.

I thank all my friends in the Bethesda Metro Area Village (BMAV) for their support and friendship. I'm also grateful to my colleagues at MacGillivray Freeman Films (where I serve as president of the MacGillivray Freeman Films Educational Foundation) and to my colleagues at Montgomery Hospice (where I serve on the board and volunteer) for enriching my life, and thus this book.

Above all, I thank the hundreds of students I taught at American University and in my success classes. Without them, this book would not exist.

Finally, I'm grateful to the team at Rowman & Littlefield, but most especially to Tom Koerner, for believing in this book and publishing it.

Proceeds from this book will go to fund scholarships for students at American University, where I taught for fourteen years after my thirty-plus-year career in conservation and filmmaking at the National Audubon Society and the National Wildlife Federation.

~

Introduction

This book will help you design and create the best version of yourself. It will give you the chance to shape the kind of person you want to be and to articulate the goals you want to reach in your life, both professionally and personally. It will help you behave in ways that are true to your most honorable and generous self.

"Slow" Success

Don't expect rapid results or an epiphany. Achieving success is a slow process. Throughout this book, I use the word "success" to mean "slow success."

"Slow medicine"[1] means high quality care for patients. "Slow food"[2] means healthy, clean food for consumers. By "slow success,"[3] I mean a focus by individuals on relationships, character, and meaning.

I'm referring to a life not marked by accumulation of wealth and social status (although that might happen), but by love, growth, purpose, generosity, creativity, justice, accomplishments, and compassion.

Success is about character development, and that takes time.

Character Development

Retired navy admiral James Stavridis writes,

> In this postmodern era, we are witnessing the slow death of character, driven by a global culture that has turned increasingly away from classic values—honesty,

commitment, resilience, accountability, and moderation—to a world that moves at breakneck speed and refuses to slow down and consider what is right and just.[4]

Success is rooted in the values Stavridis cites—"honesty, commitment, resilience, accountability, and moderation"—as well as the values of love, truth, justice, empathy, kindness, generosity, and humor.

Success is undermined by arrogance, selfishness, cruelty, betrayal, bigotry, duplicity, greed, and hatred.

We forge character and achieve success through personal mastery. People with a high level of personal mastery accomplish results that are important to them. They sculpt and mold their own lives.

Personal mastery means living your life pursuing your highest aspirations through lifelong learning and not being distracted from what deeply matters to you. The process involves constantly clarifying your vision and goals.

Approach Life as a Creative Artist

Approaching your life as a creative artist means you're the author of your own life, as opposed to simply reacting to events and problems that are thrown at you. Japanese philosopher D. T. Suzuki said, "I am an artist at living, and my work of art is my life."[5]

We must approach life in a creative way because we're most alive and energized when we're engaged in a creative task, whether nurturing a child, growing a garden, painting a portrait, leading a team, cooking a new dish, or designing a new life. Creativity transforms us from observers into active participants.

We must spend more time creatively envisioning and planning our futures so that we achieve what we desire in life. Too many of us allow things like social media, toxic friends, or other negative influences to distract our attention from our goals and from realizing the lives we want. Author Dave Ellis writes,

> Amazingly, most people spend more time planning their next vacation than they do planning the rest of their lives.[6]

An Invitation

I warmly invite you to create a future you will relish, rather than leaving it to chance. Take charge, be creative, and make commitments that will transform your life.

Engaging with the ideas in this book is an opportunity to become your best self and to spend time designing your life afresh so that you won't live a life you dislike or regret.

How This Book Got Started

In my early twenties, I lived on the surface of life. By all appearances, I was successful. I had a well-paid job in the British military, and I was accumulating degrees from top universities. But deep down I felt unanchored, chaotic, and lost. I didn't know where I was going in my life or why I was doing anything.

I was set to pursue a career designing and building warships and submarines for the British Royal Navy, but it was not something I was deeply drawn to do. My father was a renowned naval architect, and I drifted into following his career path because I didn't have any other ideas.

I was both frenetic and bored. I was stressed, restless, and irritable. I had this vague sense that if I succeeded in the military or corporate world and earned a good salary, then happiness and contentment would materialize out of that worldly success. I knew I had much to be grateful for, that I was lucky and privileged, and I was baffled why I wasn't happier.

Shallow Thinking

The truth is that as a teenager and young man, I didn't think deeply about anything. I didn't question the life I was living, why I was doing whatever I was doing, or the choices I was making.

I gave little thought to developing a personal philosophy or a set of life goals. I existed. I drifted. I acted impulsively, without any framework except what I had grown up with.

I lived my life in a blur of frantic activity, most of it lacking purpose and connection. My life was both busy and empty. My connection to life felt shallow because most of the time I was simply finding ways to relieve my anxiety and discomfort. It was a recipe for suffering, anguish, and despair. I was unmoored and rudderless.

Caring about Nothing

I spent time on things that didn't matter to me. I didn't know what my life stood for. I didn't have the slightest notion of what I might be willing to die for or suffer for. My thoughts were fleeting and superficial.

Too much of my time was absorbed in useless worry and anxiety, in pernicious comparisons, and in destructive stress over frivolous matters. I devoted little time or thought to building relationships, pursuing goals I was excited about, and working on projects requiring creativity, compassion, and adventure.

I wasn't paying attention to things that mattered to me. In fact, I didn't even know what mattered to me.

A Glimmer of Optimism

While keeping up appearances that all was fine, one day in the late 1960s when I was about twenty, I had a simple idea that gave me a glimmer of optimism. Looking back, it seems like a slap-to-the-forehead revelation.

I realized I needed to create a vision for my life—an articulation of what I yearned to do, what excited and inspired me.

I began trying to describe my ideal life—the vision, goals, and behavior I wanted for my life—in the hope this would help answer the questions troubling me. What was I here for? How could I find meaning? What was my purpose? What kind of life did I want to live? I began to scribble primitive, inchoate, often incoherent and conflicting answers to these questions.

I called this document my "personal mission statement." It was a creed or credo. At first, I was dissatisfied and frustrated by what I produced. My ideas were dull, uninspiring, and confusing. They didn't make my heart sing.

I found it surprisingly challenging and difficult to articulate what I wanted out of life. I was a young adult, but I was naïve, clueless, and uninformed. I had a lot to learn.

But I persevered and, after several years and a lot of reflection and study, I eventually produced a draft of my personal mission statement that I was moderately pleased with. I found that the very act of grappling with this problem of purpose gave me some inner peace.

Trying to think deeply about my life and goals gave me some relief and serenity. The quest itself, regardless of the outcome, was beneficial.

My personal mission statement has continued to evolve over many decades. It's a work in progress. You can find the current version in appendix A. My goals, which grow out of my personal mission statement, are listed there as well.

Finding a Way

Articulating my vision and goals helped me find the life I wanted to lead, and that life had nothing to do with engineering or warships.

Instead, I pursued a career in environmental activism, conservation, wild-life filmmaking, teaching, writing, speaking, volunteering, and community involvement. Creating a personal mission statement helped me author my own life.

This experience started me on a journey of discovery and learning. I studied the lives of renowned people and tried to tease out what they did to create their success. I studied the work of researchers and others who investigated happiness, joy, and fulfillment. You can see their names in the acknowledgments, and appendix B lists books and authors I recommend.

My journey led to a lifelong quest for an understanding of how to make sense of the world. I started giving presentations and workshops on success, to teach others how to lead more fulfilling, meaningful, and successful lives.

This book is a summary of what I have gleaned from this journey, as well as what I learned from creating and teaching a college course on success.

A Class on Success, Fulfillment, and Productivity

At age fifty-six, after a twenty-five-year career producing wildlife films, I became a professor of filmmaking at American University (AU), where I was a full-time faculty member for fourteen years before retiring.

I routinely included a workshop in my classes designed to help my students gain a broader perspective on their lives and think about what they could do to create successful, meaningful, and fulfilling futures for themselves.

I was startled and disturbed to discover how many students, including the best and brightest, had given precious little thought to their life goals and the purpose and meaning of their lives. Reflecting deeply on their lives was something they had virtually no time for.

Many of them had no clear purpose. They found life puzzling, confusing, and full of activities that weren't a good use of their time and gave them little joy or satisfaction.

My workshop on success was greeted with enthusiasm by students, so eventually I created a stand-alone, noncredit class open to the whole university on how to live well, find meaning, and be successful.

Basic Problems of Existence

I created the class because I became acutely aware that students were often competent at particular subjects, such as law, geology, or French, but painfully ignorant about life—what it offered, how to find meaning and purpose, and how to live fully with few regrets.

Students were getting A's in their classes but were at sea when it came to basic problems of existence.

There are few opportunities in modern colleges and universities to ask big questions such as "What makes life worth living?" or to engage students as complete beings with longings for meaning and purpose. Many students yearn to ask questions about life and what they're supposed to do with it but rarely find an opportunity to pose such questions.

My new class quickly filled, and we had to turn away scores of applicants. I was surprised by the popularity of the class and how many students (as well as fellow professors and members of the public) wanted to take it. We constantly had to find bigger classrooms and tell ever larger numbers on the waiting list that they couldn't get in.

Thirty-Six Fundamental Questions

Behind the demand for the class was a craving for answers to life's fundamental questions. Students were troubled by questions that are rarely addressed in regular classes or their day-to-day lives, including the following:

1. Does my life have meaning and purpose?
2. Can I find ways to create meaning and purpose?
3. How do I make a difference in the world?
4. How do I leave a mark and a legacy?
5. How should I live?
6. What is a good life?
7. How do I live a fuller, better life?
8. What makes life worth living?
9. How can I find and express more agency and more control over my life?
10. How can I go from a life of drifting and being buffeted around by circumstances to a life of joy, fulfillment, direction, and design?
11. What do I want to accomplish and achieve with my life?
12. What are my life and career goals?
13. Whom do I want to become?
14. What values should I live by?
15. How can I bring more focus and less distraction into my life?
16. What is the best way for me to shape the person I want to become so I can contribute in a meaningful way to society and to helping other people?

17. What projects, goals, and relationships will lead me to live a life that will give me peace, joy, and fulfillment?
18. Is there a discrepancy between how I spend my time and what is most important to me?
19. Does moral, emotional, and ethical growth matter? Does character matter?
20. How can I take better care of myself (physically, mentally, morally, spiritually, socially, emotionally, and financially)?
21. What is the best way to draft a powerful and inspiring personal mission statement so that I can begin to see my life in a fresh, focused, and revitalized way?
22. What do the words *success, happiness,* and *fulfillment* mean? How are they distinct?
23. Is success tied to fame, visibility, income, status, or job title? Or does growth, morality, love, generosity, and giving relate to success somehow?
24. Why do many people seem to achieve worldly success, yet feel empty?
25. What are the best ways of integrating the vision I have for my life, my plan to achieve it, and the actions needed to make it a reality?
26. How can I be healthy and avoid illness?
27. How can I belong to some vibrant and welcoming communities, and how can I develop enduring and meaningful relationships with others?
28. How can I maximize my mental capabilities?
29. How can I resist the allure of materialism, overconsumption, acquisitiveness, and an excessive number of possessions and instead move toward frugality over opulence and the wise use of resources over thoughtless waste?
30. How can I find a career that will give me both a reasonable income and a sense of contributing usefully and constructively to society so that the world will be better off for my labors?
31. How do I make my job more than just a means of receiving a paycheck every week?
32. What are some daily habits and rituals that can make me feel more fulfilled and productive?
33. What are the benefits of taking more risks and getting outside my comfort zone?
34. How can I live a balanced life that doesn't neglect any important part of living fully?

35. How do I take on big, even scary, challenges that have a high prob-ability of failure, yet still come out on top?
36. How can I die happy, fulfilled, and at peace, with few regrets?

My success class was popular because people were searching for ways to answer existential questions like the ones above and to alleviate their suf-fering, whether it came from isolation, despair, loneliness, angst, depression, stress, fear, or some other malady.

If you're a professor, you quickly find out that many students are riven with anxiety and toxic stress, especially if they're intimately tied into social media, as virtually all of them are.

You can find the syllabus for my success class in appendix C. The three-part class encourages participants to actively design their lives rather than simply reacting to what happens to them.[7]

Appendix D is the class handout and a good overview of this book.

Finding the Right Direction

I taught the students in my success class that it's important periodically to quietly reflect and ask if your life is headed in the right direction. I taught them that it's healthy to look at the person you've become and ask if this is really who you want to be. We should all proactively shape our characters, visualize our futures, and create rewarding lives of meaning and purpose.

We all have a future we care about, including the future that will materi-alize after we die. We want our children and grandchildren and the organi-zations we care about to flourish even though we'll no longer be around to witness them. We should keep in mind the next hundred years, not just the next five years, as we create a future we'll be proud of.

This book is about not leaving the future to chance, but intentionally de-signing and choosing it. It is about making and implementing commitments consistent with our deepest beliefs and values.

Authoring Your Own Life

Figuring out our vision and goals is one the most important challenges each of us can take on. If we don't take it on, we'll have no compass and will get tossed around by the turbulent seas of life. We only have one chance to live, and we can't afford to misuse or squander our limited time.

With the help of this book, you'll develop the capability to create and design your own life so you'll have a meaningful and fulfilling future. I found from my success class that when people have the opportunity and time to consider their futures, their lives begin to improve and even flourish.

What future do you want to create for yourself? This book will help you plan the rest of your life and raise it to a higher and better level.

Disclaimers

It would be arrogant for me to suggest or imply I have all the answers. I don't. I'm struggling and learning like you. I consider myself a student.

There's little that's original in this book. It reveals no secrets or magic formulas. Nor does it espouse anything mysterious. It's largely common sense. I quote and cite a lot of people far smarter, wiser, and more erudite than myself.

Caribbean American writer Audre Lorde stated, "There are no new ideas. There are only new ways of making them felt."[8] Writing this book has involved borrowing ideas from psychologists, philosophers, and many others, then combining their thoughts with my own experience and attempting to make them, in some way, "felt."

When we aspire to be wise, much of what we discover are ideas humankind has known since antiquity but has forgotten. This book is grounded both in the wisdom preserved in literature going back thousands of years (often called the "wisdom literature"[9]) and in modern, rigorous, evidence-based research. You'll find many source citations in the notes section at the end of the book.

I describe in this book what has worked for me and allowed me to be more fulfilled and productive. You'll have your own ideas on what works for you, and they may differ from what works for me.

I don't presume to know what might make you successful. Your definition of meaning and success will likely be different from mine. I'm not arguing that everyone should make the choices I've made. I'm sure the advice in this book is not the only path to a fulfilling life of purpose and meaning.

Each of us is unique, with our own idiosyncratic and distinct goals, visions, and preferences. There's no one-size-fits-all definition. We all must figure out what's right for *us*. There's no single, simple answer to the question of how to live a meaningful, successful life with few regrets.

This book will help you uncover the reasons why some people live deeply satisfying lives and others do not. It's an exciting adventure to examine your life and to design and create your life's vision and goals.

My hope is that you will arrive at a new understanding of what life has to offer. The search for that understanding is not easy. It takes hard work, discipline, and diligence.

Making wise choices, living intentionally in alignment with your values, and taking action is an exciting and exhilarating challenge.

Avoiding Hell

Renowned science fiction writer Isaac Asimov loved to tell the following joke:

> A man died and found himself in a wonderful place of comfort and beauty. A servant waited on him and fulfilled his every need. He was a little surprised at finding himself in such bliss, for he had normally led a sinful life, but he accepted the situation.
>
> After a long, long time, however, he got tired of eating delicious meals, of listening to wonderful music, of indulging in sensual pleasures, so he said to his servant, "Isn't there any work I can do?"
>
> The servant shook his head. "Our people don't work. They merely enjoy themselves."
>
> "Well, frankly, I've had enough enjoyment. I would like to work. I would like to raise a sweat. I would like to feel tired. I would even like a little challenge and discomfort now and then."
>
> The servant shook his head. "Quite impossible. Such things take place only in the—uh—other place."
>
> "Well, damn it," said the man, "I think I would prefer to be in hell, in that case."
>
> "But, sir," said the servant, "you *are* in hell."[10]

This book is about avoiding hell. Thomas Paine, author of *Common Sense*, wrote in 1776, "We have it in our power to begin the world over again." This book will help you to begin your life over again, to describe your life's meaning, and to develop a set of goals that will fill your life with purpose and joy.

The goal is to help you create a life that is full of what the French call *joie de vivre*, which logophile and word expert Liesl Johnson defines as "your exhilaration from living a thrilling life, the pure happiness you feel by living your best life."[11]

Questions and Actions

Having read this introduction, consider the following questions and activities:

- Think about the concept of "slow success." Does it resonate with you?
- Do you agree with the importance of character development in achieving success?
- What does success mean to you?
- Peruse the thirty-six fundamental questions in this introduction and pick the ones most pertinent for you to deeply reflect on.
- If at times you feel unhappy, dissatisfied, restless, and melancholy without being able to pinpoint why you're experiencing this uneasiness and disquiet, what do you think is going on?
- Do you have a sense of what your best self looks like?
- How can you invest your life with more purpose and meaning?
- At what times in your life have you felt *joie de vivre*? Do these times give you clues as to how you might find more meaning and purpose?

~

CREATE A VISION FOR YOUR LIFE

Part I is about taking the bold and important step of creating a vision for your life and capturing it in the form of a personal mission statement.

~

CHAPTER ONE

Explore and Define Success

In this chapter, we'll discuss what success means—and doesn't mean—and how pursuing happiness may be less important than seeking meaning and purpose.

Most of us say we want to be successful. We eagerly want to avoid failure. Whether we succeed or fail in our lives matters to us. But what exactly *is* success?

What Is Success?

A successful life is one characterized by generosity, care, love, and gratitude. A successful person pursues what matters to them and lives a life of meaning, purpose, commitment, and joy.

Your life is successful if you have challenging work that matters to you, projects that help others, close family and friends who love you, and an enthusiastic desire to live fully and to be your best self.

Success is about character development. Slow success, mentioned in the introduction, is the only authentic success there is because character development takes time.

Success doesn't necessarily mean having a big house, a lauded career, and a large income. In fact, accumulating lots of things and spending lots of money on lavish cars, boats, and other possessions may be signs of failure.

Success isn't necessarily measured in income, visibility, or fame. For example, if one of your goals is to be an outstanding parent, then success is measured not by what other people think but by seeing your children grow up to create lives for themselves that have purpose and meaning and that make the world a better place.[1]

Success is living a life that matters, that has significance. Success is about bringing positive change to the world and the lives of others. Success means reaching for the highest that is in us and becoming all we can be.

Successful people overcome failures and setbacks. They stay focused on their goals and what matters to them. They don't get distracted. They have high ethical standards. They die with few regrets.

Success requires thoughtfulness. It requires that you design your own life and define your own purpose rather than existing and drifting passively, allowing yourself to be shaped by circumstances and the agendas of others. This requires a personal plan with goals for growth and improvement.

Success involves belonging to a variety of communities that you care about, of being a giver rather than a taker, of being conscious of what you owe future generations. It involves having a meaningful job and career (paid or unpaid) and living intentionally and generously.

A life well lived—a successful life—is a life of loving, caring, giving, sharing, and participating actively in various communities, from families to neighborhoods to bigger organizations and the world community.

Searching for meaning, enduring relationships, and engaging projects that put you "in flow," and pursuing worthwhile goals that help others will, in the long run, make you more fulfilled and satisfied than pursuing activities that put you into a temporary and fleeting good mood, such as eating junk food, shopping, playing video games, watching TV, and checking social media feeds.

To be successful doesn't mean you must attain the stature of Rosa Parks, Jimmy Carter, Nelson Mandela, or Gloria Steinem. We can't all save the world, but we can all strive to make a difference to our own family and friends. And by doing so, we can have a fulfilling, successful life that matters.

For life to be fulfilling and successful, we must succeed on multiple levels, including in our relationships, careers, and at home. A failure at any level makes it hard to claim success in life. You cannot consider your life successful if, for example, you are a highly paid entrepreneur but are estranged from your sixteen-year-old daughter.

The purpose of life is to make a difference, to have significance, and to help others. Success is to know that someone else is suffering less because of something you did. It's about becoming a better person and about making progress toward challenging goals that are rooted in good values.

Frank Capra's Film *It's a Wonderful Life*

In Frank Capra's classic 1946 film *It's a Wonderful Life*, George Bailey (played by James Stewart) mistakenly thinks the world would be better off if he'd never been born. He believes he's achieved little and that his life has been dull and unsuccessful. In his despair and misery, he almost commits suicide.

But with the help of his guardian angel, Clarence, Bailey discovers that he's lived a significant life. He sees that he's touched many lives and helped many people. He discovers that, far from being inconsequential and meaningless, his life has produced real benefits for others. He sees that the world is much better off because of the life he's led.

The message of the film is that we need to live lives that help others, and that to live honorably and generously and to treat others with kindness and consideration is what a successful life is all about.

Designing and creating a life full of meaning and purpose is the biggest challenge we all face.

Rethinking Your Life

The COVID-19 pandemic in 2020–2021 gave people across the world time to review their lives and reset their goals and priorities.

Rethinking and reimagining your life from time to time is a good idea. Achieving success involves ridding your life of such things as eating junk food, being in poorly run meetings, drinking too much, engaging in gossip, living with clutter, and relentlessly checking your social media feeds.

But it may also involve more radical changes, such as ceasing to pursue a job, contract, career, or relationship that's wrong for you.

It makes little sense to waste years of your life working at something you don't enjoy and that you think is basically trivial. If you are unhappy or feel unhealthily stressed, you may need to rethink your whole life rather than trying to make superficial improvements.

A good starting point is to ask yourself: What constitutes a successful life? Finding an answer to that question makes creating an inspiring vision for your life possible.

The rest of this chapter is devoted to exploring different takes on what it means to be successful in life.

The Mirror Test

A few years before World War I broke out in 1914, one of the most highly respected diplomats of all the great powers was the German ambassador in

London. He clearly was destined for great things—to become his country's foreign minister, at least, if not its federal chancellor.

Yet, in 1906, he abruptly resigned from his position rather than preside over a dinner given by the diplomatic corps for King Edward VII. The king was a notorious womanizer and had made it clear what kind of dinner he wanted. The ambassador is reported to have said, "I refuse to see a pimp in the mirror in the morning when I shave."[2]

Management guru Peter Drucker calls this the "mirror test." The German ambassador did not want to do something that was incompatible with his own values and that would leave him feeling disgusted with himself.

Success is more than doing well in society and receiving accolades from others. It is also about living decently and with good values.

A Troubling Definition of Success

But beyond having a moral code and living ethically, what is success? In his provocative book *The Formula: The Universal Laws of Success*, professor Albert-László Barabási proposes a definition of success that troubles me.

He measures success solely by public recognition and visibility. He suggests that performing well, such as winning a tennis match or doing well on a SAT test, doesn't necessarily mean you're a success.[3]

In Barabási's view, performance is what you do, whereas success is defined by how the community around you perceives what you do, acknowledges it, and rewards you for it. He acknowledges that skill, diligence, and persistence are needed to achieve high performance but contends they are insufficient to achieve success.

I attach less importance to public recognition than Barabási does when assessing success in life. The story about the virtuous German ambassador illustrates what I mean. The ambassador did the right thing and, in my view, led a successful life, but he would only be recognized as successful in Barabási's view if he had risen to higher office—which would have meant violating his conscience and presiding over that louche and dissolute dinner with the king in 1906.

How I Define Success

When I use the word *success* in this book, I'm not using it the way Barabási does. He defines success as the "rewards we earn from the communities we belong to."[4] For me, success is not about outside validation, accolades, fame, and approbation, but rather about the work you do. Success and outstanding performance are one and the same.

The problem with defining success with external rewards is that you can achieve it and still be friendless, stressed, and depressed, the very antithesis of success.

I see success as something far more personal than fame and worldly recognition. In my view, personal growth and mastery are more important than visibility and recognition. Success happens when you judge something you've done as well executed and worthwhile, regardless of what anyone else thinks.

Being a loving and capable parent, producing a verdant and beautiful garden, or visiting lonely and isolated elders to give them companionship are all things that may not be widely recognized or applauded. But they can provide enormous personal satisfaction and a sense of living a successful, worthwhile life.

Paradoxically, it's possible for people to receive public accolades ("success") but still feel they've failed because they know they've not authentically done their best. Consider a student who receives an A grade after doing mediocre work because her professor tends to inflate grades, perhaps to curry favor with the students. The student knows deep down that she should have received a B or B−, and her official A grade seems phony and undeserved to her.[5]

Barabási argues that overcoming adversity—like an injured athlete working hard with his coach to regain his former strength and performance—is not success because it's a private and personal accomplishment. Barabási only considers a person successful when audiences applaud and public accolades are awarded.

Endeavors such as playing the piano, enjoying grandchildren, writing a love letter, or rebounding from a failure can be richly rewarding even though they don't meet Barabási's definition of success. Overcoming adversity, for example, even without public recognition, should be considered achieving success because it leads to deep satisfaction and a sense of meaning.

Success versus Fame

Fame is a particularly insidious substitute for success. Social scientist Arthur Brooks writes,

> The truth is that, despite our prurient interest in celebrities, the overwhelming majority of people do *not* want to be famous, and the minority of people who truly desire fame are abnormal.[6]

Brooks reports that while most of us believe that other people see fame as central to personal success, only 3 percent say that fame is how they define their own personal success. Instead, 97 percent say that people are successful if they have followed their own interests and talents to become the best they can be at what they care most about. Brooks worries that social media and "the modern world is making it harder to detect fame's empty promises."[7]

In a similar vein, psychologist Dr. Catherine Steiner-Adair writes in *The Big Disconnect*, "Fame is the do-it-yourself dream of the digital era. We're all indie artists eager for an audience on YouTube or streaming videos to viral success through social networks, so it is hardly surprising that fame is the number one value of adolescence and young adults."[8]

Rather than fame, success is about being significant and bringing positive change to the lives of those around you. A purposeful life that makes a difference is a life that matters and is worth celebrating.

Success as Defined by Bill Burnett and Dave Evans

A useful definition of success comes from Stanford professors Bill Burnett and Dave Evans in their book *Designing Your Life*.[9] They write about success as a well-designed life and argue that a well-designed life results in a well-lived life.

They claim that true happiness and success come from designing a life that works for you and is meaningful, joyful, and fulfilling. "A well-designed life," they write, "is a life that is generative—it is constantly creative, productive, changing, evolving, and there is always the possibility of surprise."[10]

For Burnett and Evans, a successful life is one that makes sense because what you believe, what you value, what you devote your career to are all congruent and line up together.

A successful life is a rich amalgamation of discoveries, experiences, achievements, adventures, hardships, and failures that make you strong and teach you important life lessons.

Burnett and Evans also teach that five "mindsets" are needed to design a successful life: Be curious, have a bias to action, reframe problems, focus on the process, and ask for help (which they label "radical collaboration"). They don't stress diligence as much as I do, but their recommendations imply the need for a strong work ethic.

Teddy Roosevelt's Definition of Success

Another helpful definition of success comes from President Teddy Roosevelt. In 1899, he delivered a speech in Chicago in which he extolled the virtues of what he called the "strenuous life." He said,

I wish to preach, not the doctrine of ignoble ease, but the doctrine of the strenuous life, the life of toil and effort, of labor and strife; to preach that highest form of success which comes, not to the man who desires mere easy peace, but to the man who does not shrink from danger, from hardship, or from bitter toil, and who out of these wins the splendid ultimate triumph.[11]

David Brooks and *The Second Mountain*

Roosevelt's definition of success is vividly different from, but not inconsistent with, the theme explored by *New York Times* columnist David Brooks in his book *The Second Mountain.*

Brooks argues that the conventional and evanescent attributes of success, such as fame and fortune, need to give way, especially as we age, to more important goals such as service, wisdom, and humility.[12] He uses a metaphor of two mountains to describe his view of what it takes to live a full and satisfying life.

The first mountain is the one you climb as you clamber toward success in your career, try to make your mark in the world, and acquire money, status, and power. When you get to the top of that mountain, says Brooks, you realize it wasn't your mountain, and that there is another, bigger mountain out there with a less selfish worldview that's actually your mountain.

And so you begin a second mountain journey and a new life, one characterized by giving, caring, love, contribution, gratitude. On this journey, you pursue what really matters to you, and you live a life of meaning, purpose, commitment, and joy.

Brooks writes, "The central journey of life is to move from self to service"[13] or from the first mountain to the second.

The Founding Fathers' Definition of Success

Probably the best idea of what America's founding fathers viewed as success can be found in the Declaration of Independence. Thomas Jefferson wrote about the "pursuit of happiness," but when he wrote those words in late June 1776, he was thinking of happiness not just in the sense of good cheer, but of something more comprehensive.[14]

Historian Jon Meacham writes that to understand what the founding fathers meant by happiness (which is the nearest we can get to understanding what they meant by *success*, a word not used in America's founding document), we have to start where they did in their thinking, which is with Aristotle.[15]

In her book *Aristotle's Way*, Edith Hall, professor at King's College London, writes that Aristotle urged his followers to pursue *eudaimonia*, the Greek word for happiness or flourishing. He wanted his followers to strive for well-being and having a purpose.[16]

Happiness, Aristotle believed, is the whole point of life. It is an ultimate goal, worth seeking for its own sake. But by *happiness*, Aristotle meant having a sense of purpose and meaning that can help transform our lives from boring and humdrum to an adventure.

Aristotle believed we should live in accordance with universal and imperishable virtues, like courage, justice, determination, patience, temperance, kindness, humility, honesty, fairness, love, and gratitude.

He realized that man is a social creature whose life finds meaning in his relation to other human beings. Thus, Jeffersonian *eudaimonia* evokes virtue, good conduct, and generous citizenship. Happiness in both the ancient and foundational American traditions is much more than being in a good mood.[17]

By invoking the "pursuit of happiness," Jefferson meant that we have a right to pursue something far more substantive than having a good time. The point is to fulfill your potential and become the best you can be.

We'll discuss later in this chapter why there is more to life than being happy—as that word is commonly understood.

Martin Seligman and Positive Psychology

Another valuable definition of success comes from Dr. Martin Seligman, founder of the positive psychology movement. Traditionally, the goal of psychologists has been to relieve human misery, such as depression, addiction, trauma, and other disabling conditions.

In contrast, positive psychology is about increasing well-being and helping people to thrive and feel joy. Seligman suggests that understanding and alleviating misery is a very different task from understanding well-being and building the enabling conditions of life.[18]

Seligman's book *Flourish* explores what makes life worth living, including growth, relationships, love, meaning, gratitude, accomplishments, and engagement.[19]

He argues that to live a full and successful life, we need to have good relationships with others, to find meaning and purpose in our lives, to feel engaged and in flow, to feel positive emotions, and to accomplish whatever goals we set for ourselves.[20]

Seligman suggests that we'll get the most out of life and be most successful when we deploy our highest strengths and virtues to achieve our most challenging goals. He has summarized his findings with the acronym PERMA: positive emotion, engagement, relationships, meaning, achievement. Seligman argues that the person who flourishes and succeeds in life must excel in all five of the PERMA elements:[21]

1. *Positive emotion* refers to such emotions as joy, love, curiosity, pride, and passion. Research has shown that when we experience five positive emotions for every negative emotion, we are more likely to flourish and succeed.[22] Successful, contented people are more likely to notice and appreciate positive things that happen to them. They don't ignore them and take them for granted.
2. *Engagement* comes from doing things that are challenging and important and lead to a state of flow. When what we do is congruent with what we care deeply about and what our goals are, we are more likely to be engaged. Experiences that lead to growth are often challenging, but this makes them mentally absorbing and all the more rewarding.
3. *Relationships* are vitally important. Happy, successful people tend to have strong bonds with others. High-quality relationships are crucial to achieving success in life. I discuss this more in chapter 5.
4. *Meaning*, as we've discussed, is fundamental to a successful life. For people to feel successful and happy, they must perceive their life as having meaning and serving a higher purpose than the self.
5. *Achievement* is about reaching and fulfilling goals that are deeply meaningful. Both Seligman and Mihaly Csikszentmihalyi (see the following section) have found that successful people have well-articulated and challenging goals that are outside their comfort zones.

Seligman's pioneering work on success and happiness has much to teach us. He argues that you can plan and work your way toward a fulfilling and joyful life, a life where you'll have few regrets when you die, where you're engaged in pursuing worthwhile goals, and where you're committed to others and your own personal development.

Above all, a successful life is one in which you are involved in projects and activities you believe are serving some cause larger than yourself.

Mihaly Csikszentmihalyi and Flow

Seligman's second element for a fulfilling life through PERMA is, as we have seen, engagement. This factor is so important that I want to single it out for more attention. Engagement is about flow, and it requires your highest strengths and talents.

Psychologist Mihaly Csikszentmihalyi, who created the term *flow*, argues that flow is perhaps the most optimal psychological state. A flow state occurs when you have a clear goal, a challenging task, and sufficient skills to meet the challenge. In flow, you are in full control of your attention and find it easy to ignore distractions.

Winston Churchill provides an interesting example of flow. I'm guessing that when he indulged in his hobby of painting pastoral scenes, he was in flow because the activity apparently totally absorbed him.[23]

Csikszentmihalyi has found that people who seek out flow experiences in difficult but rewarding activities are happier and have more satisfying lives than people who pursue evanescent pleasures.

You are in flow when you become so engaged in a challenging activity that time seems to stop and you lose all self-awareness. You experience a deep and unrelenting focus.

Arianna Huffington's Ideas on Success

Best-selling author, columnist, and businesswoman Arianna Huffington argues that traditional measures of success have led to "an epidemic of burnout and stress-related illnesses, and an erosion in the quality of our relationships, family life, and, ironically, our careers." Huffington says we're losing our connection to what truly matters. She writes,

> We cannot thrive and lead the lives we want (as opposed to the lives we've settled for) without learning to go inward. . . . The timeless truth is that life is shaped from the inside out—a truth that has been celebrated by spiritual teachers, poets, and philosophers throughout the ages, and has now been validated by modern science.
>
> But remember that while the world provides plenty of insistent, flashing, high-volume signals directing us to make more money and climb higher up the ladder, there are almost no worldly signals reminding us to stay connected to the essence of who we are, to take care of ourselves along the way, to reach out to others, to pause to wonder.[24]

Huffington wants you to live "according to your own definition of success, so that all of us—women and men—can thrive and live our lives with more grace, more joy, more compassion, more gratitude and yes, more love."[25]

Bill Gates on Success

In his blog on December 29, 2018, Bill Gates wrote in "What I Learned at Work This Year":

> One thing that occurs to me is that the questions I am asking myself at age 63 are very different from the ones I would have asked when I was in my 20s. Back then, an end-of-year assessment would amount to just one question: Is Microsoft software making the personal-computing dream come true? Today of course I still assess the quality of my work. But I also ask myself a whole other set of questions about my life. Did I devote enough time to my family? Did I learn enough new things? Did I develop new friendships and deepen old ones? These would have been laughable to me when I was twenty-five, but as I get older, they are much more meaningful.[26]

We all need to ask these fundamental questions, and the earlier in life the better. There is far more to a full life that the common metrics for success: amassing money, prestige, power, or fame.

There Is More to Life Than Being Happy

You might expect a book about success to be largely about how to be happy, but *happiness* is a slippery word that has become virtually meaningless from being used in so many ways.

Success and happiness are often confused, as we saw in the above discussion on America's founding fathers. The distinction between them is important. True success in life requires considerably more than the pursuit of happiness as that word is commonly understood.

As psychologist Seligman points out, the problem with the word *happy* is that most people interpret it to mean merriment, cheerfulness, pleasure, lack of stress, and being in an upbeat mood—in short, a state of mind tied to hedonism, pleasure seeking, and even self-gratification, the feeling you have when eating ice cream, watching a movie, or drinking a glass of wine.[27]

But this understanding doesn't get at the deeper meanings of happiness related to friendship, love, meaning, purpose, gratitude, and achieving goals relating to helping others and helping society.

There is more to life than feeling content, upbeat, and free of stress and worry. For Ralph Waldo Emerson, being happy did not characterize the purpose of life at all. He wrote, "The purpose of life is not to be happy. It is to be useful, to be honorable, to be compassionate, to have it make some difference that you have lived and lived well."[28]

Focusing on happiness might lead people to think that failure, disappoint-ments, and setbacks (all of which naturally make people unhappy) mean that they've failed. But behavioral scientist Steve Maraboli says, "Happiness is not the absence of problems. It's the ability to deal with them."[29]

Negative emotions are a natural part of life. Setting a goal of being happy means that unhappy feelings are seen as failure. But feeling unhappy some-times is an important part of a full, healthy, and vibrant life.

I prefer to define being happy as living a rich and meaningful life with all the setbacks and disappointments that come with living fully. When we focus on the things that matter to us, clarify what we stand for, and act in accordance with our mission and goals, we experience a sense of autonomy, agency, and purpose.

Such lives will give us pleasure but will also give us occasional feelings of disappointment, rancor, and fear. If we are living well, we will feel all sorts of emotions as we strive to produce the most we can from our lives.

Happiness should be about more than pleasure, ease, or comfort. It should be about creating a life you are proud of because you've devoted it to goals that are important to you.

The conventional understanding of happiness doesn't capture enough of what we really want from life. As Seligman suggests, we want to flourish, not just to be happy. After all, we do many things (exercise, eat kale, hold a screaming grandchild, help our parents go to the bathroom when they're frail) because we know it's the right thing to do, even though it may not give us immediate pleasure or happiness.

Momentary pleasure, feeling good, and other positive moods are only a fraction of what we seek if we want to be our best selves. Success is more than achieving happiness. It's becoming the person you want to be and having the character you want to have.

Emily Esfahani Smith and *The Power of Meaning*

In her book *The Power of Meaning*, Emily Esfahani Smith argues that feeling happy is insufficient as a way of judging whether someone is successful.[30] She writes that there is more to life than feeling cheerful and feeling good, although those feelings are desirable.

A full life—a fully successful life—involves developing your character, pursuing worthy and challenging goals, contributing positively to society, living with integrity, and realizing your full potential.

When your life has meaning, it has purpose, significance, and a reason for being. As noted already, a meaningful life is part of something bigger than the self. Many organizations enable you to be part of something larger than yourself, including the armed services, Red Cross, scouts, nonprofit hospices, social-justice nonprofits, educational institutions, and so on.

Other members of society benefit from your involvement with such organizations. When you work with groups such as these, you are what psychologist Adam Grant describes as a "giver."

Smith makes the point that "takers," in contrast to "givers," may seek happiness by avoiding all stress, pursuing an easy, unchallenging life, being in a good mood, and prioritizing eating well and feeling well.

She argues that takers are often linked to selfish behavior. Happiness without a deeper meaning leads to a superficial, self-absorbed, even selfish life in which challenging projects and relationships are avoided.

Creating a life of meaning and success implies going beyond the simple goal of being happy and worry free. It involves being a giver.

All Joy and No Fun

Consider the issue of raising a family. This is often not an unalloyed happy experience. Research has shown repeatedly that having children reduces people's happiness.[31]

Conflicts, anxieties, worry, and the hard work of running a house full of obstreperous and occasionally defiant kids with irritating habits make for an exhausting grind. Changing dirty diapers, dealing with temper tantrums, and constantly cleaning up messes is an unpleasant way to spend time.

But raising a family can be an experience full of profound meaning because you have the opportunity, through your children, to help form generous, responsible, and conscientious human beings who will live honorable lives.

Parents put aside their own needs, desires, and concerns for the sake of their children. The often draining and enervating work of being a parent is performed for a purpose beyond the self—raising a child. Author Jennifer Senior calls parenting "all joy and no fun."[32]

Regrets

One way to take a long view of success is to ask, "What will you regret on your deathbed?" Designing a life that entails the fewest regrets is one way to make sure you create your best self and live a fulfilling, successful life.

Typical regrets include: I regret I wasn't kinder. I regret I wasn't more generous. I regret not speaking out more when I saw injustice. I regret not standing up more forcefully for what I believed. I regret not spending more time with my children and really listening to them.[33]

Thinking about regrets is a useful exercise when you want to improve your life and when you're brainstorming about the vision you want for your life. The risks not taken, the adventures not pursued, the opportunities spurned, the relationships neglected or damaged—all these and numerous other potential regrets come down to one thing: not living the life you wanted to live.

According to the book *The Top Five Regrets of the Dying* by Australian nurse Bronnie Ware, the biggest regret of people in hospice care is that they have done what other people wanted them to do with their lives and that their lives don't reflect their true values and are, in some sense, inauthentic.[34]

If used wisely, facing regrets (or anticipating them) can be used to help you live fully and well. We need to live in a way that minimizes the accumulation of regrets. Successful people are aware of their regrets, real and potential, and act to reduce them.

Questions and Actions

Based on the concepts and ideas explored in this chapter, consider the following questions and activities:

- Was there anything in the chapter that changed your mind about what success means to you?
- This chapter talked about various views of what constitutes a successful life. What is your definition of a successful life?
- How can you be successful without being rich and famous?
- Can you be successful yet still lonely, friendless, and depressed? Why, and what does this mean?
- Stanford professors Bill Burnett and Dave Evans write, "A well-designed life is a life that is generative—it is constantly creative, productive, changing, evolving, and there is always the possibility of surprise." Do you agree or disagree?
- How could you shape your life to invite the dynamic state Burnett and Evans advocate?
- How could you better balance immediate happiness and long-term purpose?
- Psychologist Martin Seligman argues that to live a full and successful life, we need to have good relationships with others, to find meaning and purpose in our lives, to feel engaged and in flow, to feel positive

emotions, and to accomplish whatever goals we set for ourselves. What can you do to achieve these qualities in your life?

- Psychologist Mihaly Csikszentmihalyi found that people who seek out flow experiences in difficult but rewarding activities are happier and have more satisfying lives than people who pursue evanescent pleasures. You are in flow when you become so engaged in a challenging activity that time seems to stop and you lose all self-awareness. You experience a deep and unrelenting focus and find it easy to ignore distractions. Have you ever experienced flow? If so, how has it affected you?

- Ralph Waldo Emerson wrote, "The purpose of life is not to be happy. It is to be useful, to be honorable, to be compassionate, to have it make some difference that you have lived and lived well." Can you capture in your own words the purpose of life as you see it?

CHAPTER TWO

~

Search for Meaning

The previous chapter explored different concepts of success. This chapter explores why it's important to search for meaning and how the quest itself confers success.

The Importance of the Search

In *The Moviegoer*, novelist Walker Percy wrote, "The search is what anyone would undertake if they were not sunk in the everydayness of their own life. To become aware of the possibility of the search is to be onto something."[1] The search is a quest to find an answer to the question: What gives meaning to your life?

It's more important to be engaged in the search than to achieve some end state of knowing the answer. The quest itself is what's important. The search itself gives life meaning and is itself a source of joy and fulfillment.

Rabbi Alvin Fine writes, "We see that victory lies not / at some high point along the way / but in having made the journey / step by step, / a sacred pilgrimage."[2] As someone once said, the road is more important than the inn.

Not enough people undertake the quest to find their life's meaning. Consequently, the world has far too many people who suffer loneliness, heartache, regrets, and entropy (Mihaly Csikszentmihalyi's word for disorder and randomness in life).

The search requires wisdom and courage, and it should be congruent with your values. It requires a commitment to self-discipline, reflection, introspection, solitude, and diligence. We should not live haphazardly and carelessly. Psychiatrist Irvin Yalom writes that we have a "fundamental human responsibility to construct an authentic life of engagement, connectivity, meaning, and self-fulfillment."[3]

Why don't more people undertake the search for meaning? The reason is that we're drowning in busyness (managing our jobs, families, finances, etc.), in distractions (watching screens, social media, the never-ending news cycle, etc.), and in suffering (from addictions, mental illness, anxiety, estrangement, etc.).

The search requires "productive solitude" and, as Professor Cal Newport of Georgetown University has shown, we are all subject to what he calls "solitude deprivation."[4]

To become aware of the possibility of this search for meaning is to experience, as Percy notes, a great insight. It is to realize the importance of searching for what makes life worth living.

Why Meaning Is Important

People have a compelling desire to find meaning and purpose in their lives. To find meaning is to make sense of things. As Albert Camus observed, "The meaning of life is the most urgent of questions."[5] And Rabbi Harold Kushner writes,

> Our souls are not hungry for fame, comfort, wealth, or power. . . . Our souls are hungry for meaning, for the sense that we have figured out how to live so that our lives matter, so that the world will be at least a little bit different for our having passed through it.[6]

Historian Yuval Noah Harari notes, "A meaningful life can be extremely satisfying even in the midst of hardship, whereas a meaningless life is a terrible ordeal no matter how comfortable it is."[7]

Some researchers, including Holocaust survivor and psychologist Viktor Frankl, believe our desire for meaning is stronger than our desire for power, prestige, and pleasure, and even stronger than our desire to avoid pain.[8] We are driven to understand and fathom the meaning and purpose of our lives. When we know the *why*, we can find fulfillment and peace even in the most hellish of conditions.

Frankl came to this conclusion after spending several years of unthinkable suffering in Nazi concentration camps. He found he couldn't control what happened to him—the starvation, brutality, and dehumanization—but he could control his response to what was inflicted on him. He famously wrote:

> Everything can be taken from a person but one thing—the last of the human freedoms—to choose one's attitude in any given circumstances, to choose one's own way.[9]

Frankl found that, in the camps, those who found meaning in even the ghastliest circumstances were more resilient than those who didn't.

The Search for Meaning

Nearly half of all Americans, according to writer Emily Esfahani Smith, do not have a satisfying life purpose. Their lives lack meaning.[10]

How do we find meaning? It can be found in our careers, in raising a family, in nature, and in love. It can be found in self-transcendence (serving a cause greater than the self), exemplified by the person who plants a tree in old age because of the benefits it will provide for future generations.

Most of the time, we seem to be oblivious to our need for purpose and meaning. And even if we have an inkling that something in our lives is missing, we don't know where to begin the quest to find our life's meaning.

We live shallow lives, barely aware that when we're on our deathbeds, we're likely to have aching regrets related to unresolved family relationships and missed opportunities for joy and love.

Searching for meaning transforms life into an intentional, mission-driven adventure. This is far preferable, as I explained in the introduction, to experiencing life as I did when I was a young man—confused, drifting, reacting mindlessly to events and happenings.

Life is puzzling and sometimes overwhelming, but searching for a life that's more than just a mishmash of experiences randomly imposed on us can help to make life more joyful and exciting.

Embedding the Search for Meaning in a Moral Code

Unfortunately, we're bombarded relentlessly by such things as advertising, texts, and email that distract us from our quest for meaning. These distractions make it challenging to think deeply about what we should be doing with our lives.

It's the search for meaning, embedded in a moral code based on love, kindness, and generosity, that can lead to the possibility of finding fulfillment and success.

We do a lot of things that fill our lives but accomplish little, including using social media excessively, binge-watching shows, overeating, being workaholics, abusing drugs, being glued to news channels, and succumbing to xenophobia, racism, or misogyny. These things typically don't help us to find satisfactory meaning in our lives.

Having a Self-Transcendent Purpose

Assumption College professor James Lang is eloquent on the value of meaning and purpose when it comes to teaching. He argues that infusing learning with a self-transcendent purpose can make a huge difference to students' progress. Students need to see that their learning can improve the world and make it less cruel, unjust, and harmful.

Lang argues that creating in students a strong sense of purpose and meaning through helping others, correcting social injustices, or otherwise making a real difference in the world will drive them to become more focused and attentive in class and more tenacious in their efforts to learn.[11]

This argument can be broadened from college students to all of us. Having a self-transcendent purpose is exhilarating because it gives our lives meaning.

In a review of Yuval Noah Harari's 2018 book *21 Lessons for the 21st Century* in the *New York Times Book Review*, Microsoft cofounder Bill Gates wrote,

> All three of his [Harari's] books wrestle with some version of the same question: What will give our lives meaning in the decades and centuries ahead? So far, human history has been driven by a desire to live longer, healthier, happier lives. If science is eventually able to give that dream to most people, and large numbers of people no longer need to work to feed and clothe everyone, what reason will we have to get up in the morning?[12]

Gates commented that no one has produced a satisfying answer to that question.

A common theme among those who have researched success is that to be successful means to have a purpose. For example, author and success expert Earl Nightingale remarked, "Success is gradual progress towards a worthy goal."[13]

But how do we find a purpose? There must be more to life than enjoyment. Why are we here? To what end? Philosopher Ludwig Wittgenstein wrote, "I don't know why we are here, but I'm pretty sure that it is not in order to enjoy ourselves."[14]

What Is the Meaning of Your Life?

So, I ask again: What is the meaning of your life? It's odd how infrequently we attempt to answer this fundamental question. The meaning of your life is tied to your having a purpose. If you can't confidently declare your life's purpose and meaning, then you're likely to feel a vague, uneasy restlessness deep inside you.

One of the many values of writing a personal mission statement is that it gives you the chance to answer the question "What is the meaning of your life?" There is no right answer, and your answer will be unique to you. What's important is wrestling with the question and searching for answers.

Religion and Meaning

Religion used to be the default path to finding meaning in life, but today, as author Emily Esfahani Smith writes, "It is one path among many, a cultural transformation that has left many people adrift."[15] For some, religion no longer carries the authority it once did.

Psychologist and Harvard professor Steve Pinker observes, "As people become better educated and increasingly skeptical of received authority, they may become unsatisfied with traditional religious verities and feel unmoored in a morally indifferent cosmos."[16]

This book does not judge anyone's beliefs or practices. It respects every person's certainty, ambivalence, or doubts. It takes no position on the validity of secular or religious beliefs. My goal is to support your search for meaning and purpose, wherever you stand on religion.

When religious authorities do not define *meaning* for us, it's up to us to create meaning in our own lives. Creating meaning involves creating a life that is adventurous, exciting, and honorable. Bill Burnett and Dave Evans write, "Designing your life is actually what life is, because life is a process, not an outcome."[17]

A good life is characterized by your becoming increasingly defined by the purpose you've chosen for yourself and expressing in blazing color who you are. Friedrich Nietzsche said, "Become who you are."[18]

Developing Character and Identity

The search for meaning inevitably leads us on a journey to shape and design who we are and who we want to become—our character.

Our character is the amalgamation of our values, behavior, experiences, suffering, love, work, projects, and creations. Our character is continuously in the process of becoming. It's a work in progress. Philosopher Thomas Szasz writes,

> People often say that this or that person has not yet found themself. But the self is not something one finds; it is something one creates.[19]

We are a rough draft of our future selves. As Johann Goethe wrote, "Life is a quarry, out of which we are to mold and chisel and complete a character."[20]

John Wooden, the famous UCLA basketball coach, advised, "Be more concerned with your character than your reputation, because your character is what you really are, while your reputation is merely what others think you are."[21]

Language expert Anu Garg writes about Baba Amte, a social worker and activist who lived from 1914 to 2008. Garg extols the successful life that Amte led:

> Baba Amte didn't wear a fancy hat or a black collar or any special clothes. He didn't call himself a pundit or a bishop or a pope. He didn't go around telling people how to be closer to Krishna or Jesus or Zeus. He didn't go on television or put his videos on YouTube. He didn't get his picture taken with presidents or prime ministers. He didn't rail against people who were gays or people who followed a different religion or those who thought differently from him.
>
> Baba Amte devoted his life to serving people with leprosy. His actions were his message. His wife Sadhna served with him. He had two sons, both studied medicine. After completing their studies, they too came back to serve with him. Their wives, both doctors, joined the family "business" as well. So with grandsons.[22]

What Garg is driving at is the importance of character over fame, power, wealth, and possessions.

We should be on a journey to invent ourselves and to create our identities and our characters. We are "pilgrims on the way to a new place of being."[23]

What Is Character?

I've elected to use the word *character*, but I could have chosen another word, like *soul*, *being*, *identity*, *essence*, *spirit*, or *light* (a Quaker word) to convey the same notion.

Character is what the search for meaning is fundamentally about: designing and creating who we are.

A major task you face as you go about improving your life is to create and design your character in a way that has meaning for you. This work is ongoing over a lifetime.

Your character embodies your personal values and philosophy, your sense of meaning and purpose, your sense of responsibility to your friends and neighbors and the society you live in, and your sense of what you want the world to aspire to in terms of equality, justice, and fairness.

Your character reflects who you are and who you want to become. Author Joan Didion notes,

Character—the willingness to accept responsibility for one's own life—is the source from which self-respect springs.[24]

Your character is one of the most meaningful things to survive when you die. It will be found in the communities and friendships you built and contributed to, in the creative projects you launched and engaged in, in the values you passed on to loved ones and others, and in the inspiring stories others tell about you after you're gone.

Good character does not require religious convictions, but it does require attaching importance to ethical behavior, integrity, keeping commitments, taking care of other people, and having an active conscience.

Character is formed and created through the steady application of focused and intense effort over many years. That's why in the introduction I call true success "slow."

It's formed in the commitments we make to other people we love and respect and to organizations that mean a lot to us. And it's formed in the keeping of those commitments and in the need we have to be trustworthy and reliable.

Character is affected and shaped especially by the experience of encountering and overcoming setbacks, disappointments, and failures. Author Stephen Covey wrote,

Just as we develop our physical muscles through overcoming opposition, such as lifting weights, we develop our character muscles by overcoming challenges and adversity.[25]

Character building is one of the pivotal challenges we face in life, and it's a crucial determinant of whether we will lead meaningful and successful lives. The famous marshmallow experiment by psychologist Walter Mischel in the 1960s provides some insight into character. Mischel found that children who mustered the self-control (a key component of character) to resist eating a marshmallow right away, in return for two marshmallows later, were more successful as adults.[26]

Motivational guru Jim Rohn wrote,

> Could creating your character be likened to an artist creating a sculpture? Character is the result of hundreds and hundreds of choices you make that gradually turn who you are, at any given moment, into who you want to be. Character is something that you must take responsibility for creating.[27]

Character is forged when we face challenges. For example, I'm currently learning to play the piano. I'm often tired, but I practice every day regardless of my mood. I'm not particularly good, but I'm getting better. Playing totally engages me. I can't think of anything else when I'm playing. I'm totally focused on learning how to play and sing a specific tune or song. I'm not thinking about my life's purpose and meaning.

Getting absorbed in the creative task of learning the piano puts me in flow, where I am absorbed in the task before me. I am exercising self-discipline and determination. My life feels worthwhile. It feels significant. I feel that I'm spending my time effectively. I feel a sense of satisfaction. I feel tranquil and at peace. The self-discipline helps to create my character.

What about Suffering?

Can a person be fulfilled and successful while also suffering? How does suffering and pain fit into the search for meaning and character?

Suffering and adversity come to all of us, whether as transitory pain from an illness or accident, prolonged psychological or existential anguish, or betrayal, addiction, financial ruin, grief, toxic relationships, or hardships of other kinds. No one is immune. As Nazi hunter Simon Wiesenthal said, "Suffering is the companion of every person from birth onward."[28]

One segment of the dark universe of suffering is the so-called deaths of despair, which describes the sudden rise since the year 2000 in deaths from suicide, alcohol, and drug abuse. Contributors to these deaths include the entangled causes of unemployment, underemployment, stagnant wages, drug abuse, mental disease, economic inequality, intense social media use, and the loss of meaning, purpose, hope, and optimism.[29]

People often say that their goal in life is to be happy and to avoid suffering, but paradoxically, in remembering the past, they often see their suffering, pain, and stumbling blocks as more significant than the happy times.

Suffering often brings personal improvement and even "post-traumatic growth" in terms of emotional maturity, formation of bigger goals, and committing to help others deal with suffering. For example, Franklin Roosevelt became more empathetic after being struck with polio.[30]

Living life with its inevitable suffering underscores the importance of offsetting the pain with loving relationships, purpose, and goals. Pursuing a search for meaning and character gives us the strength and resilience to handle pain and setbacks.

Life is about creating meaning and purpose amid pain, anxiety, stress, and suffering, and even to find meaning *in* the suffering. Meaningless pain causes existential anguish. Psychologist Jordan Peterson writes,

> The purpose of life, as far as I can tell, is to find a mode of being that's so meaningful that the fact that life is suffering is no longer relevant.[31]

There is no meaning in suffering itself, but we can ask if any good can be produced from pain and anguish to give it meaning. Having a heart attack or kidney disease is meaningless in itself, but the pointlessness of it can be offset by trying to find a silver lining, a benefit, or blessing that can emerge from the misery. Someone with heart disease attributed in part to eating junk food, for example, could devote time to helping others improve their health through better nutrition.

Viktor Frankl knew intense and prolonged suffering as a prisoner of the Nazis. Drawing from that experience, he wrote, "Suffering ceases to be suffering at the moment it finds a meaning."[32] For his part, Frankl helped a suicidal inmate realize he should fight hard to survive, rather than succumb, so he could be a father after the war was over to his young son who was still alive.

Perhaps we should be grateful for suffering. This idea is not as weird as it may sound. In a 1939 speech at Princeton University, the German novelist Thomas Mann said, "To be grateful for all life's blessings . . . is the best condition for a happy life . . . but this is not all. For there is another kind of gratitude . . . the feeling that makes us thankful for suffering, for the hard and heavy things of life, for the deepening of our natures which perhaps only suffering can bring."[33] I discuss this more in chapter 7.

Pain, fear, and suffering are a natural and unavoidable part of life. If we are lucky and smart, we can learn and grow from them and not just wilt and shrivel under their impact.

Questions and Actions

Based on the concepts and ideas examined in this chapter, consider the following questions and activities:

- Think about what success means to you.
- Generate ideas to go into your personal mission statement.
- Commit to designing your life instead of drifting haphazardly and to wrestling with life's most challenging questions about meaning and character.
- What are some of the challenging questions you have encountered in life?
- Develop some examples in which meaning and purpose could be enlisted to offset suffering.
- Does religion play a role in your life? In what ways does religious belief give your life meaning and purpose?
- Do you know people who seem to have fulfilling lives? What makes you think so?
- Think about how you would like to be remembered after your death.
- Our characters are not fixed. They are malleable. We can commit to be better and change the way we behave. We can change and improve our identities and characters. In what ways do you want to change and improve?
- I wrote, "The search for meaning and identity requires wisdom and courage and should be congruent with our values. . . . We are pilgrims on the way to a new place of being." Describe your pilgrimage.
- Historian Yuval Noah Harari wrote, "A meaningful life can be extremely satisfying even in the midst of hardship, whereas a meaningless life is a terrible ordeal no matter how comfortable it is." What does he mean? How can a life of comfort without meaning be an ordeal?
- Philosopher Ludwig Wittgenstein wrote, "I don't know why we are here, but I'm pretty sure that it is not in order to enjoy ourselves." How can he be so sure?
- Through our search for meaning, we give life our best shot, live joyfully, and die with few regrets. We avoid complacency, gluttony, lassitude, and indolence, and instead live with enthusiasm, energy, and verve. Do you agree or disagree?
- I suggested that designing our character, who we want to be, is one of the ways we find meaning in life, so at the end of life we can die with few regrets and not have our sense of fulfillment marred by having lived

a life that caused pain and suffering to others, or in which we were unproductive, uncreative, greedy, depressed, or solely focused on accumulating wealth, power, possessions, and fame. Your reaction?

- I wrote that suffering is unavoidable and a universal, ubiquitous experience. It's a fact of human existence. There's an enormous amount of pain in the world. Life will throw curveballs, including sickness, betrayal, addiction, financial ruin, grief, toxic relationships, and hardships of other kinds. No one is immune. Life is difficult and harsh, and we must accept it and deal with it the best we can. Do you agree that being stoic is a good thing?
- How did the pandemic of 2020–2021 influence your search for meaning and purpose?

~

CHAPTER THREE

Create a Personal Mission Statement

So far in this book, we've discussed what success means, the importance of finding meaning and fulfillment, and the need to search actively for the life you want.

Now it's time to sift through all these thoughts and draft a personal credo or creed—a personal mission statement—that captures in writing the vision you want for your life. This vision is the foundation of your future life.

A personal mission statement describes your core beliefs, your guiding principles, your most deeply held values, your key responsibilities, your character when you are at your best, and what you would like to accomplish in your life.

In this chapter, we'll look at why a personal mission statement is important, how to generate ideas for it, selecting roles and responsibilities, making personal development your first role, identifying the key relationships in your life, and understanding how your imagined eulogy can help you work out the kind of life you want to lead.

We must search for what we want to become. None of us has an immutable essence. Our character does not lie hidden somewhere, waiting for us to discover it. Rather, it's made in the creative act of living fully.[1] We are all malleable and able to improve.

One way to shape who we become—a way to rewire our brain's circuits and neurons to forge a bolder, more intentional, and more purposeful life—is to write a personal mission statement and deeply reflect on it.

Leadership expert Simon Sinek writes, "Most of us live our lives by accident—we live it as it happens. Fulfillment comes when we live our lives on purpose."[2]

A personal mission statement is something you can draft at any point in your life. It isn't just a good idea for young adults. Someone in mid-career, or about to retire, or in old age will find creating a personal mission statement to be a potentially transformative exercise. It's never too late to bring more intentionality—more purpose, character, and meaning—into your life.

Why a Personal Mission Statement Is Important

As a filmmaker, I would never greenlight a film without a script or treatment: something that captured in writing the vision for the finished film. Likewise, you shouldn't live your life without having a vision for your future (spelled out in a personal mission statement) to help keep you on track.

Writing a personal mission statement is an opportunity to define vividly what your life stands for and the kind of life you want to have. The statement expresses a clear and compelling vision of you at your best and flourishing. It's the governing document—like the Constitution is to America—that helps you live successfully and to your full potential.

Creating a personal mission statement is like painting an inspiring picture of your life. It can help you see new possibilities and increases your level of motivation and energy. It encourages you to set bold, audacious goals to get your life moving in the right direction.

By writing a personal mission statement, you are daring to take charge of your own life. The statement is like a letter of purpose to yourself. Without one, you are rudderless. As author and minimalist advocate Joshua Becker writes,

> Too many people live their lives without intentionality or thought. They rarely find a quiet moment to sit in meditation or solitude and examine their life—who they are and who they are becoming.[3]

Writing a personal mission statement will create a foundation for your life that will help you thrive. It will help give you sound values, such as empathy, diligence, tenacity, curiosity, resilience, self-control, perseverance, and fortitude.

I've always been puzzled by the fact that some people are concerned with money and getting a house and having a family (all of which are fine) but seem to stop their evaluation of life at that point. They don't seem driven to ask about the meaning and purpose of life.

This is the essential idea behind the personal mission statement. It gives you a chance to see the bigger picture and to think through the deeper issues underlying your day-to-day life.

When you encounter the challenge of a complicated situation—which designing your life certainly is—you need to devote time and attention to resolving it. Writing out your thoughts about your life's deepest desires requires you to be in a state of what Cal Newport calls "productive solitude."[4]

By this, Newport means getting away from distractions like social media and giving yourself the chance to think about your values, what matters to you, and what you want to achieve.

You benefit from struggling to *write* your personal mission statement as opposed to simply tossing ideas around in your head. You are contemplating the kind of life you want to design, create, and live, and then writing clear and inspiring answers to such big questions as: What is my best life? Where do I belong? What are my values? What deeply matters to me? What do I believe in? What is my purpose?

It is difficult and challenging to grapple with these questions, but the contemplation and struggle are invaluable.

The Eagle and the Barnyard Chickens

Author and Jesuit priest Anthony de Mello tells a story in which a man found an eagle's egg and put it in the nest of a barnyard hen. The eaglet hatched with the brood of chicks and grew up with them. All his life, the eagle did what the barnyard chicks did, thinking he was a barnyard chicken. He scratched the earth for worms and insects. He clucked and cackled. And he would thrash his wings and fly a few feet into the air.

Years passed, and the eagle grew old. One day he saw a magnificent bird above him in the cloudless sky. It glided in graceful majesty among the powerful wind currents, with scarcely a beat of its strong golden wings. The old eagle looked up in awe. "Who's that?" he asked. "That's the eagle, the king of the birds," said his neighbor. "He belongs to the sky. We belong to the earth—we're chickens." So the eagle lived and died a chicken, for that's what he thought he was.[5]

Before we can build the life we want to live, we must imagine it. This is the key lesson from de Mello's story of the eagle and barnyard chickens. A successful life starts by embracing new possibilities and creating a clear vision of the future. It is an exercise in creative imagining—if you like, a dream.

Inspiring dreams change the course of our lives. Author Gordana Biernat says, "Dream your life and live your dreams."[6] The only way to create a future that doesn't yet exist is to dream and envision it. Once we have a vision or dream for our lives, we can start making an operational plan with specific goals (which we will do in part II).

The story about the eagle underscores the importance of having an audacious vision for your life. But creating a clear and inspiring vision is challenging. It is much easier *not* to do it, to bounce along in reaction to whatever comes your way via genes, your environment, circumstance, and past programming.

I encourage you to get off autopilot and take command of designing and driving your life. I recommend that you develop a vision for your life and create a personal mission statement that captures that vision.

Determining a vision for your life, and encapsulating it in a personal mission statement, is the first step toward living with intention and purpose.

The Benefits of a Personal Mission Statement

Having an inspiring personal mission statement and reviewing it regularly can help to reshape your character and change who you are. It can reprogram how you react to things and help you behave in a way that's congruent with your values.

Acting in alignment with the vision you have for your life is deeply rewarding. We have a profound desire to behave in ways consistent with our highest aspirations. Actions that are out of alignment with your aspirations and values are likely to make you feel inauthentic, fake, and depressed.

By writing and using a personal mission statement, we're trying to reduce the influence of our genes, our upbringing, and the conditioning we receive from society—that is, the script written for us by culture and biology.

Instead, we're seeking to increase the influence of our own creative thinking about what we want out of life, what our deepest aspirations are, and what we want our legacy to be. We want to program ourselves, not be programmed by genetic instructions, social conventions, or other people's expectations.

It's common for organizations to have mission statements describing their values, vision, and goals, but sadly it's unusual for individuals to have them. The aim of a personal mission statement is to dig deeply into the "why" underpinning your life. The best way to take charge of your life is to articulate your own vision for your life.

As I've mentioned, a personal mission statement is like the U.S. Constitution but sets forth the guiding principles of an individual. A personal mission statement articulates the ideas, morals, and values that a person wants to live by. It expresses the person's "true north" and describes what is truly important to them.[7]

A personal mission statement is effective because, by writing down what you care about, you declutter your mind. If you try to hold in your head all of your thoughts about the future, the values and aspirations you care about, things on your to-do list, new projects to launch, commitments to keep, and so on, you will be overwhelmed.

As you draft your personal mission statement, you'll work through a confusing and tumultuous mix of ideas. You'll get your ideas on paper, where you can examine them more objectively, create an inventory of thoughts and hopes, rigorously edit the material, and get it organized.

I recommend you review your personal mission statement every week, especially if it contains detailed goals (see the next chapter), so you can revise it appropriately and keep it up to date, deleting commitments you've met and adding new ones.

Thus, your personal mission statement remains an accurate description of what matters to you and where you're planning to take your life. It constantly reminds you of your purpose in life and what gives your life meaning.

Having a purpose helps you persevere in the face of distraction, adversity, and failure. Nietzsche said, "To forget one's purpose is the commonest form of stupidity."[8]

Generating Ideas for Your Personal Mission Statement

Your personal mission statement should contain *everything* you think about when you contemplate ways to improve your life. You want to get all of these ideas out of your head and onto paper.

As noted already, you can ruminate on the possibilities more objectively when they are written down, and you can also worry about them less because you know you have captured them in a trusted place (that is key) and have no risk of losing or forgetting them.

The following are some questions to assist you in generating ideas for your personal mission statement. Brainstorming these questions can help you start generating ideas that will feed into your personal mission statement.

- *What does success look like for you?* What would have to happen for you to say on your deathbed that your life was meaningful and a success? What makes your life worth living?
- *How do you want to be remembered?* What do you want your legacy to be?
- *What are your values?* What values do you care deeply about and want to align your life with?
- *What would you do if you knew you could not fail?* What can you imagine doing if time, money, and fear were not obstacles? If you had all the money in the world, what would you do for free?
- *What do you want your purpose in life to be?* What are your goals? What would you like to accomplish?
- *What are the challenges you face in achieving your goals?* What things in your personal and professional life are stopping you from spending time on the issues, relationships, and projects that you care most about?
- *What is missing from your life right now?* Where do you sense a "hole" in your life? What is getting neglected or ignored while crying out for attention?
- *What are some of the steps you can take to begin overcoming the challenges you face?* Possibilities include: get a coach, identify a role model, stop smoking, eat more fruits and vegetables, combat anxiety, have a weekly date with your spouse/partner, exercise every morning, enrich your vocabulary, read deeply, be more patient with your kids, get home every night for family dinners, join a cycling club, clear the mess off your desk, be more loving, get out of debt, lose weight, watch less TV, spend less time staring at screens and especially social media feeds, be more curious and creative, speak up more in meetings, get more sleep, eat less junk food, volunteer for a local nonprofit, stop to smell the roses, spend more time outside, take art lessons, smile more, keep the promises you make, make more offers of help, and seek help more often.
- *What matters deeply to you?* Possibilities include: values such as kindness and generosity, relationships, your health, having enough money to support your family, feeling useful and appreciated, living to your full potential, finding a partner, increasing your knowledge, changing the world in some positive way, changing yourself in some way, working with decent, moral, and trustworthy colleagues, saving the environment for future generations, having more fun, being more playful, developing your sense of humor, feeling more joy in living, feeling safer and more secure, balancing your work and personal life, getting in bet-

ter shape, securing a qualification of some kind, being better organized, transforming an embittered relationship into a loving one, caring for someone you love dearly, getting out of the rut you're in, feeling less lonely and isolated, being more expressive and demonstrative, and feeling more grateful for all you have.

Thinking about the above questions can give you ideas for your personal mission statement.

Taking on Bigger Challenges

A vision helps us see the world as it can be and should be. Without a personal mission statement, we tend to see the world only as it is and as we know it. Having a vision helps to elevate our lives and reach for something bigger than we are.

It helps us to think ambitiously, to be more like eagles than barnyard chickens. One of the keys to this endeavor is to commit in a personal mission statement to undertake a big, even extreme, challenge.

This challenge might be launching a business, repairing a damaged relationship, becoming a more responsible parent, making a film, running a marathon, writing a book, defeating an addiction to opioids, creating a beautiful garden, reading biographies of all the American presidents, learning a language, learning to play a musical instrument, being more affectionate with your partner, running for public office, or being a more attentive and devoted grandparent.

The point is to intentionally undertake a difficult and meaningful challenge that creates significant and healthy stress. The challenge requires you to struggle valiantly toward achievement and, in so doing, to grow and reach a level of fulfillment and success that might otherwise have eluded you. In the next chapter, we will discuss setting audacious goals in more detail.

Singer and songwriter Bob Dylan wrote, "A man is a success if he gets up in the morning and gets to bed at night, and in between he does what he wants to do."[9] But a lot of people don't know what they want to do and end their lives with regrets.

This is where a personal mission statement can be helpful. When people talk and write about their futures and what they would like to accomplish, their lives improve. I've seen this happen repeatedly in my classes and workshops.

Your Personal Mission Statement, Like Your Life, Is a Work of Art

A personal mission statement helps you create the future instead of leaving it to chance. You're shaping and composing your future with intentionality, purpose, and creative energy, as if it were a work of art.

There is much at stake—no less than the quality and success of the life you're going to lead from now until your death. Designing and choosing your future is a far better option than drifting along passively waiting to see what happens.

As I've already noted, it's important thing to put your personal mission statement in writing. We have a lot going on in our heads, including various stories about ourselves that may or may not be helpful, and it's easy to live the life someone else wants us to live and adhere to someone else's map and compass.

We need to create our own map and compass and make sure it's in alignment with our values and what really matters to us. How we behave, what we do, what we care about, what we believe, and the character we want to forge must all be in alignment. Having a deeply felt personal mission statement helps this coherence happen.

Your Personal Mission Statement Reflects Your Moral Code and Values

A personal mission statement is a blueprint for designing, crafting, and sculpting your character. It describes the person you want to become, and it includes your values, ethics, social responsibilities, and the ways you want to give back to society.

Your mission statement should list the virtues and character traits you want to cultivate in yourself. It should describe your core values, moral vision, commitments, and the issues you care deeply about—the elements that make you a unique and valuable person.

We need a moral ecology, a moral vision, to guide us. A good start is the Golden Rule: "Do unto others as you would have others do unto you." But I like scientist and peace activist Linus Pauling's tweak to it. In 1960 testimony before the U.S. Senate Judiciary Committee, he offered his revised version of the Golden Rule:

> Do unto others twenty percent better than you would expect them to do unto you, to correct for subjective error.[10]

The point of a personal mission statement is to articulate your ideas on life and work and to make sure there's congruence between the life you're living, the career or retirement you're pursuing, the beliefs and values you have, and your sense of morality.

For example, it's damaging and highly stressful for you to believe in protecting the environment when the company you work for acts in a way that trashes coral reefs or rain forests.

A Personal Mission Statement
Helps You Find Meaning and Purpose

Don't expect an epiphany or a revelation as you create the vision you want for your life. It often takes time to find the words for a personal mission statement that inspire and excite you. But when you have articulated those important ideas, you'll gain a sense of purpose and meaning.

Your personal mission statement will help you identify what you want to do and then help you integrate that into your daily life and decision making.

In creating your personal mission statement, you are beginning to write the story of your life. It describes the kind of person you want to be and what you want to achieve in your life.

Your personal mission statement can be short, and it doesn't have to be perfect. There is no "correct" way of doing it, and you can revise it as often as you want. It is always a work in progress. But having it can be a life changer. The Stoic Epictetus wrote,

> What kind of person do you want to be? It's time to stop being vague. If you wish to be an extraordinary person, if you wish to be wise, then you should explicitly identify the kind of person you aspire to become.[11]

Your Personal Mission Statement
Explains the "Why" of Your Life

Your personal mission statement explains "why" you do what you do. And that must come before the "how" (which we'll come to in part II, on goals, and part III, on taking action).

"Why" explains the meaning and purpose of your life. It explains the guiding principles behind everything you do. It's your compass, helping you navigate tricky decisions, difficult relationships, and major life choices.

When you know your "why," it becomes easier to choose actions to take and what to spend time on. Articulating your "why" helps to bring your life into focus and makes it more likely you will live in congruence with your values.

I encourage you to do the work of uncovering your values and personal philosophy and capturing them in a personal mission statement. What are the highest priorities in your life? What does a well-lived life look like for you? What's important to you? What regrets do you *not* want to have at the end of your life?

For an example of a personal mission statement, go to appendix A to see mine. Just remember, it's a work in progress. It's neither good nor bad, but simply what works for me. Your personal mission statement will be unique to you as mine is to me.

Share Your Personal Mission Statement with Others

If possible, share your personal mission statement with someone you trust and discuss what you learned from drafting it. Finding an accountability friend, a mentor, or a group (like a "mastermind group") can help keep you on track. It can assist you in your struggle with any difficult challenges you want to take on.

Our lives are filled with so much busyness and distraction that we have little time to focus on what matters to us. We typically have negligible space in our day for creativity, listening, contemplation, and reflection.

Talking to a trusted mentor or colleague can help you reflect on such questions as: What commitments are you failing to live up to? Are you taking care of the people you love? What do you care most about, and are you focused on it? Chapter 13 discusses mentors and mentoring in more detail.

Don't Let the Pursuit of Passion Slow You Down

Sometimes people get stuck when writing a personal mission statement because they start by trying to answer the question "What am I passionate about?" They think that if they can answer that question, then the rest of the thinking and writing will follow more easily.

The trouble with this idea is that few of us know what we feel passionate about. Bill Burnett and Dave Evans think that 80 percent of people of all ages fall into that category.[12]

Instead of passion, focus instead on what *interests* you. As you work in areas that interest you, you'll develop skills that may eventually lead you to feeling passionate about a topic.

How can you get involved in areas that interest you? One way is to volunteer for an organization. Another is to shadow someone whose career you admire. Of course, you might also land a job in your area of interest.

Developing a passion for something often takes time. As Burnett and Evans put it, "Passion is the result of a good life design, not the cause."[13]

A Personal Mission Statement Will Bring Both Ambition and Serenity

Most of us get ambition and serenity wrong. Too often, our goals are small and picayune, while we are frenetically busy and anxious. We must reverse that. We want to pursue big, audacious goals while feeling tranquil and at ease, with just the right level of healthy stress.

Having a personal mission statement brings both ambition and serenity. It gives your life more intention, especially when it comes to the audacity of your goals. Without a written vision for your life, there's a risk that you'll sleepwalk through life and take on only insignificant goals.

A personal mission statement helps you to live more consciously and ambitiously and to take your priorities seriously. At the same time, having a personal mission statement helps you to stay on course. It encourages you to be more self-aware so that you know when you're getting off track and need to take course-corrective action. A personal mission statement helps you to live in accordance with your ambitions and values so that you can feel more serene.

Ambition is important because we don't have endless time. Life is limited. Death is inevitable. The more we can connect with what really matters as described in our personal mission statement, the more we can pursue goals that are important to us.

Personal Mastery

As I have already mentioned, a personal mission statement will help you sculpt your life and develop personal mastery. People with a high level of personal mastery achieve results that are important to them.

Personal mastery involves constantly clarifying the vision you have for your life and not allowing yourself to be distracted from achieving the goals anchored in that vision. It means living your life while pursuing your highest aspirations and goals through a process of lifelong learning.

Management expert Peter Senge argues that personal mastery starts with continually clarifying what is important so that we understand why we are living our lives rather than just responding to issues and incidents as they arise.[14] It's not helpful to have a confused, vague, or inaccurate perception of what is deeply important to us. Senge writes,

> People with a high level of personal mastery live in a continual learning mode. They never "arrive." . . . Personal mastery is not something you possess. It is a process. It is a lifelong discipline. People with a high level of personal mastery are acutely aware of their ignorance, their incompetence, their growth areas.[15]

Roles

Creating a personal mission statement that reflects the vision you have for your life requires you to organize and structure your life in a way that makes sense to you. Stephen Covey suggested using the "roles" we have in our lives as an organizing method. By *roles*, Covey meant much more than role-playing; he meant our key responsibilities and relationships.[16]

Personal development is one such responsibility or "role." Others might be sister/brother, husband/wife/life partner, mother/father, son/daughter, grandparent, friend, mentor, role model, employee/employer, team member, communicator, educator, volunteer, manager, advocate, community activist, learner, artist, athlete, entrepreneur, and so on.

By identifying your roles, you create a variety of perspectives from which to examine your life to ensure balance and to make sure nothing important in your life is neglected.

Covey recommended selecting seven roles, including personal development, to organize and examine your life. More than seven can become overwhelming, and fewer than seven may not be comprehensive enough. But there is nothing hard and fast about the number seven. If you pick six or eight, that's fine.

There are other ways to view and organize your life besides through roles. For example, retirement expert Cynthia Meyer, founder of Second Wind Movement, suggests using the categories of community, giving back, health, growth, and finance.

Others have suggested the domains of work, home, love, community, play, health, and self. Yet others have structured their lives around the mission to love, to leave a legacy, to laugh, to learn, and to live.

Author Nir Eyal suggests the three life domains of self, relationships, and work (work including community service, activism, and side projects). Researchers Richard Ryan and Edward Deci propose three elements—autonomy, competence, and relatedness—as the three drivers of humans who are flourishing.[17]

All of these are ways of viewing, framing, and organizing your life work effectively. They all accomplish the same goal of finding a way to view your life in its totality and to help you get to the heart of what you find meaningful.

For decades, I organized my personal mission statement using roles (for example, husband, father, friend and colleague, professor, author, and stand-up comic) and found it worked well. Now in my early seventies, I decided to organize my personal mission statement and life goals using Meyer's suggested categories of community, giving back, health, and growth (see appendix A). Whatever dimensions you use, they should capture the entirety of your life.

Roles and Your Personal Mission Statement

If you're new to creating a personal mission statement, I recommend you use "roles" as your organizing principle. I suggest, as already noted, that you select seven roles, and that your first role be personal development.

A healthy, balanced, fulfilling, and successful life requires full engagement in all of the roles in your life. They will likely overlap, and many activities carry over across multiple areas at once. They are interrelated and synergistic.

You must succeed in every one of the various roles and dimensions of your life. Not meeting any one of your key needs damages and reduces your quality of life. If one role is neglected or if you fail at one, you will feel unbalanced, unfulfilled, and stressed.

Remember, you're not playing a zero-sum game. Succeeding in your career does not mean you need to neglect your family. Making trade-offs between different domains of your life damages the relationships that matter to you and can lead to painful regrets and an overall sense of failure.

It's tempting to become so preoccupied with work that you lose sight of the importance of your home life. Keep your life in balance by being aware of the important roles in your life, not just your roles at work.

As Covey suggested, having a happy home life should be among your highest goals. However important your work is to you, there are things in your life outside of work that need a lot of your time, including your spouse/partner, your children, and your health.

If you are to lead a meaningful and successful life, you must pursue excellence in all the domains and dimensions of your life, in all your roles, and in all parts of your life mission.

Your Vision for Each Role

For each role, write a sentence or two (more if you like) about how you would like to behave and act at your best. For example, if one or your roles is "partner," you might write, "I want to be a kind and loving partner, saying many more positive things than negative, being helpful, and generously doing things for my partner to help them live a fulfilling and meaningful life."

The desired actions and behaviors you describe for each role will help to give your life meaning because you're envisioning your aspirations in all the important areas of your life.

Your Personal Development Role

As I mentioned, I urge you to make your first role personal development. Personal development is so important (and why I devote all of chapter 5 to the topic) because you must take care of yourself before you can take care of anybody else. Others depend on you to be strong and resilient.

Personal development is about putting yourself into a position where you are healthy and strong enough to help others. It is foundational because relationships are so important.

Key Relationships

Having selected seven roles, I now recommend you identify the key people in each role—in other words, the key relationships in your life. For the role of personal development, the key relationship is, of course, with yourself.

For your other roles, the key relationship is usually obvious. For example, if one of your roles is "spouse," then the key relationship is with your life partner. If one of your roles is teacher, then the key relationship is with your students.

For each of your roles, identify the people who are most important to you. This is an important step. Little is more important in our lives than the relationships we build with other people.

Eulogy Exercise

Out of all the key relationships you have identified, select the most, or one of the most, important.

Now imagine you are entering a big building. As you pull open the door and look inside, you see gathered in front of you about four hundred people, all with their backs to you. You strain to see what they are looking at. And then you spot it. They're looking at a casket, and you suddenly realize that you're witnessing a funeral.

As you try to fathom what's going on, you see the person that you just identified as being one of the most important people in your life standing up to give a eulogy. You realize, with great fascination, that you are witnessing your own funeral and your own eulogy.

What do you want to hear said about you? Assume you've led an honorable and successful life, what are the assessments you would like the eulogist to make about you? What character traits and behaviors would you like the person to praise and be grateful for? What have you accomplished? Were you compassionate, kind, and generous? What kind of friend or family member were you? Where did you excel?

One of the most useful exercises to come from positive psychology is to write an essay about your best possible future self. This is what the eulogy exercise is about—writing an essay describing the person you ideally want to be.

To write your own eulogy requires you to identify the most important components of your life. You must look ahead over the rest of your life to a time when your life ends. Fill in the blanks using your creative imagination and guided by the notion you have given life all you've got.

Assume you've lived according to your own values and worked hard to fulfill your dreams. Assume you've lived life on your own terms and marched to the beat of your own drummer. Assume you've had agency over your own life and have lived the life you wanted.

What do you want to have people say about you when you die? What kind of life do you want to lead? Your answers to these questions will help shape and inform your personal mission statement.

If this exercise is too emotionally painful for you (for some people, thinking about their own demise can be traumatic), then think instead of what you would like in a toast to you on, say, your eightieth birthday.

What did your life stand for? What were you admired for? What challenging missions did you take on and engage with? What did you strive for? This exercise creates a vision of who you would like to become and gives you raw material to add to your personal mission statement.

Creating a eulogy will help you think through your moral code. Your mind will become more sensitized to your responsibilities as a citizen and the importance of social responsibility. You'll generate the ability to act against your more thoughtless impulses for the sake of moral aspirations. This is the essence of having a good character.

Use your eulogy to help you write your personal mission statement. Writing your personal mission statement will help you rewire your brain so you start to live the life you want to live rather than being driven by habits and genes.

We have come to the end of part I where we focused on creating an ambitious and inspiring vision and capturing it in a personal mission statement. In part II, we'll look at setting goals and planning—in other words, making your personal mission statement operational.

Questions and Actions

Here are some questions and activities to help you further explore the ideas covered in this chapter:

- Improving your success involves more than ridding your life of time wasters like poorly run meetings and gossip. Major gains in success and productivity come from ceasing to pursue a course of action (a job, a contract, a career, or a relationship) that is wrong for you. What choices have you made that you regret and need to change?
- Your personal mission statement helps you decide at critical moments in your day what to do with your time and energy. Think about key decision points that occur during your daily life and describe what you might do differently.
- Having a personal mission statement that is deeply meaningful to you will give you a sense of purpose. In creating it, you are beginning to write the story of your life. What gives your life meaning? Who do you want to become? What matters deeply to you?
- Have you picked out seven roles (your key responsibilities and relationships) for yourself, including personal development? What roles did you choose, and why?
- Share your personal mission statement draft with someone you trust and ask for feedback and comments. Ask the person to tell you what is missing, what is overly ambitious, and what needs more clarity.
- Can you find ways to connect to a cause larger than yourself and thus give your life a transcendent sense of purpose? Meaning and fulfillment come in large part from giving back and helping others.
- You want congruence between how you spend your day and what matters most to you. Are you spending time on projects and relationships that in the long run matter to you?

- Keep your life in balance by being aware of all the important roles and responsibilities in your life (not just your roles at work). Do you agree that having a happy home life should be among your highest goals in life?
- A personal mission statement articulates the guiding ideas, morals, and values that a person wants to live by. It expresses the person's "true north" in the same way that the U.S. Constitution lays out guiding principles for the nation. Do you have a sense of your own "true north"?

~

PART II

SET GOALS
DERIVED FROM YOUR VISION

In part I, you began creating your personal mission statement to give you an energizing and inspiring vision for your life. In part II, you'll use that vision to generate and commit to goals you can act on. One reason people are reluctant to set goals is that they dread the pain they imagine goes along with failing to reach them. If they don't set goals, then the threat of that pain is removed. But so is the possibility, as I wrote in the introduction, of beginning "your life over again."

CHAPTER FOUR

~

Establish Goals

A personal mission statement doesn't get you that far if it never gets translated into specific, concrete goals. Let's look at how to put your personal mission statement to work by developing goals from it.

In her book *SuperBetter*, game designer Jane McGonigal tells the story of how she overcame being bedridden and suicidal following a severe concussion. In 2009, McGonigal had an accident, experienced a brain injury, and didn't heal properly. After thirty days, she still had relentless headaches, nausea, mental fog, memory loss, and vertigo.

She could do none of the things that she loved to do, like running, writing, playing video games, and working. Suicidal thoughts can result from traumatic brain injuries, and this is what happened to her.[1]

Then, thirty-four days after she hit her head, McGonigal had a crystal-clear thought that changed everything. She realized, "Either I am going to kill myself or I'm going to turn this into a game." She had a conviction, based on the research she had done to get her PhD in game theory, that when people play games, they tackle challenges with creativity, determination, and optimism.

So she created a simple recovery game called *Jane the Concussion Slayer* and invited her twin sister, Kelly, to call her once daily to give her a quest for the next twenty-four hours.

The first quest that Kelly (a PhD psychology professor at Stanford University) gave her suffering sister was, "Look out of the window near your bed, and tomorrow, tell me at least one interesting thing you saw."

McGonigal felt she had a purpose. She found that taking purposeful action every day sparked her motivation and expanded her sense of what she was capable of achieving.

She writes, "Every time you set your mind to do something—and then do it—you remind yourself of the power you have over what you do, think, and feel."[2] The quests from Kelly helped her to heal. Within days, her anxiety and depression vanished. Her cognitive symptoms took longer to heal, but today she's fine.

This story about McGonigal underscores the power of setting specific and measurable goals. Making your personal mission statement operational by establishing actionable, specific goals is a powerful step to take.

Without goals, our important work (as opposed to low-priority work) tends to get postponed or even neglected. Without goals, our days are often marked by procrastination, missed deadlines, and a sense of pressure and chaos.

Setting goals can help us deal with feeling burned out and overwhelmed, pulled in scores of different directions by other people's requests, and deluged with distractions.

Make Your Personal Mission Statement Operational

Make your personal mission statement operational by using it to generate specific goals and actions. The idea is to get so specific that you can plug the actions into your calendar when you do your weekly and daily planning.

In her book *Bird by Bird*, author Anne Lamott gives a vivid example of the value of setting specific goals and tasks. When she was a child, her older brother, who was ten years old at the time, was trying to write a report about birds. He'd had three months to write it, it was due the next day, and he was panicking.

He was sitting at the kitchen table close to tears, surrounded by binder paper, pencils, and unopened books on birds. He was immobilized by the hugeness of the task ahead.

Then Lamott's father sat down beside his son, put his arm around his shoulders, and said, "Bird by bird, buddy. Just take it bird by bird."[3] As her brother broke the big job down into smaller, specific, and doable tasks, his panic subsided, and he completed the report.

As Lamott's story makes clear, breaking big goals into doable subgoals or chunks is the key to moving forward. In fact, motivational guru Tony Robbins calls this process "chunking."[4] Cynthia Meyer calls it creating "micro steps" and says creating micro steps achieves four things:[5]

- It keeps you less overwhelmed by the big-picture goal.
- It makes your goal more achievable and realistic.
- It shows you exactly what to tackle next.
- It builds up your momentum and nurtures a habit of working consistently toward your goal.

In short, breaking large goals into smaller ones gets you moving. So subdivide each of your long-range goals into more manageable shorter-range goals or tasks. Begin to think of these short-range goals as commitments; that is, things you promise yourself to achieve by a certain deadline.

SMART Goals

Consider your relationship with your spouse. Let's call her Gail. You might write in your personal mission statement, "I will regularly convey my profound love for Gail by always thinking of her first, caring about her feelings, respecting her opinions, and by expressing appreciation, love, and care."

That's lyrical, expressive, rarefied—the language of vision and personal mission statements as discussed in part I, not the more granular language of setting goals we're focused on here in part II.

As you move toward setting goals, you might instead write, "Spend time with Gail from 10 p.m. to 11 p.m., communicating with her without interruptions. Go dancing together every Monday at 7 p.m. Go on a lunch date together every Friday at noon, leaving our phones in the car."

These pledges meet the SMART test for goals—that is, they're expressed in such a way as to be specific, measurable, achievable, relevant, and time bound.[6] Here's how to meet each of these five criteria when setting goals:

- *Specific*: Set goals that are concrete, clearly defined, and detailed. The goal of going dancing every Monday at 7 p.m. is a good example.
- *Measurable*: Whatever the goals, find ways to measure progress toward meeting them. It is easy to measure how often you go dancing or go out on dates.
- *Achievable*: Aim high but don't be unrealistic. Your goals should be challenging and a stretch, but ultimately achievable.
- *Relevant*: Find goals that matter enough to you that you'll be motivated to stick with them. The goals should be congruent with your values and with each other. If there is incongruity between a goal and the vision described in your personal mission statement, then the goal will be nearly impossible to achieve. For example, going dancing weekly is

unlikely to work if weekly dancing lessons are not broadly compatible with your personal mission statement.

- *Time bound*: Set a reasonable time line for achieving each goal. Time-management expert Brian Tracy says there are no unrealistic goals, only unrealistic deadlines.[7] Once you have set a clear schedule and deadline for a goal, you can work toward it. Suppose, for example, that one of your long-range goals is to write a book on your family history. Then a few of your subgoals (or commitments) could be to interview your mom and dad by June 1, to find a coach who can help you by July 1, and to find all the photos in your parents' home relating to your grandparents and their parents by August 1. If you don't achieve a goal by the deadline, set another deadline and work toward that one until you finally succeed. In other words, don't overcriticize yourself if you miss a deadline; just regroup and carry on.

Setting goals means getting specific about what you want to accomplish, how you're going to do it, and when you want to accomplish it.

As you commit to financial, career, personal-development, and other goals, be savvy about acknowledging success. What happens as you pursue a goal can be as valuable as the end result. You don't want to be so focused on the final goal that you neglect to relish small successes that materialize along the way.

There is great opportunity for growth and joy long before you reach your final goal. Celebrate the small victories.

Why Goals Are Important

Goals flesh out the vision encapsulated in your personal mission statement. They have the power to transform your vision into reality and to give your life purposeful direction. Goals allow you to stretch and grow. As a mentor once told me, what you *get* by achieving a goal is less valuable than what you *become* by achieving it.

Without goals, life quickly becomes disorganized, haphazard, and superficial. Without goals, your life lacks purpose. You may sink into unhealthy stress and even anxiety.

Having goals focuses your attention and gives your life significance. With goals as guideposts, you can shape the kind of person you become and the character you develop.

Goals help you to achieve flow. As we saw in chapter 1, Mihaly Csikszentmihalyi defines flow as the peak experience of intense living, when your mind and skills are fully involved in overcoming a challenge, usually when working on a favorite activity.[8]

The highly desirable, richly fulfilling state of flow happens only when we're making a strong effort to pursue a goal we care about and that demands a lot from us. People achieve flow when they're focused on pursuing a clear, challenging goal that requires their full effort and concentration.

Goals matter because they help define us and give meaning to our lives. They focus our attention on what matters to us. And they give us a way to measure our progress. They also fill us with enthusiasm and energy. They engender perseverance, especially when the goals are hard to achieve and push us to the limits of our capabilities.

Lives change in extraordinary ways when people accept the challenge of taking on big and difficult goals that are important to them.[9]

Avoid Paltry Goals

In *The Heart Is a Little to the Left*, clergyman and peace activist William Sloane Coffin wrote, "Everyone is in danger of succumbing to what de Tocqueville called 'paltriness of aim.'" As author Dr. Mardy Grothe notes, Coffin captures in this sentence a pervasive and dismaying reality.[10]

Many of us have goals that are paltry and insignificant. But, as I noted in chapter 3, we must be ambitious and set lofty and audacious goals to help us achieve the most out of life.

It's far better to have bold goals and fail to reach them than to have inconsequential goals and achieve them. In his 1868 poem "For an Autograph," American poet James Russell Lowell noted, "Not failure, but low aim, is crime."[11]

High and inspiring aspirations that demand our best are essential for a successful life. They pull us toward the life we want.

Commit Your Goals to Paper

Your goals are of little help unless they're in writing. Putting them on paper makes them concrete, meaningful, and real.

It's more likely you'll fulfill the promises you make to yourself and to others if they're in writing. This is a critical step if you are to align your daily activities around what is most important to you.

Express on paper your long-range and short-range goals. Organize them into the roles you've selected for your life, including the four personal development areas (physical, social/emotional, mental, and spiritual).

You can incorporate your goals into your personal mission statement or put then in a separate document. Either way is fine. I have put mine in a single document. Both my personal mission statement and goals are in appendix A.

Your Financial Goals

Your personal mission statement almost certainly includes roles relating to financial security and to succeeding in your career, so let's give setting goals in those two areas some attention.

In listening to politicians, whether on the left or right, you get the impression that the highest goal we have as a nation is material prosperity. However, as Martin Seligman has pointed out, what matters most to us as individuals is not wealth but well-being.

Once a certain level of income is reached, other issues, including loneliness, isolation, pollution, depression, anxiety, and mistrust, become increasingly important.[12]

Why do some wealthy people keep working to acquire ever more money, more than they can possibly spend? Their whole identity is yoked to the pleasure of amassing a fortune, but Eastern philosophy and many religions warn that concentrating on accumulating money for selfish reasons is unlikely to lead to a fulfilling life.

Of course, some effort must be made to acquire money and skillfully manage it, because without financial security, life can be miserable. There are many excellent books on this topic, so I won't dwell on it here.

But I do encourage you to include in your goals the following types of personal directives, modified for your own situation: stay out of debt, don't buy stuff you don't need, don't overspend on online shopping, save 20 percent of your income every month, avoid credit card debt, don't get behind on taxes, and maintain a budget to enable you to track your finances.

Debt is a corrosive burden that drains the color out of life and threatens people with poverty. Debt forces people to work at jobs they hate just to pay bills. Debt shackles people with stress, misery, and dread.

Being debt free is liberating and opens new opportunities to achieve the vision described in your personal mission statement.

Many people work long hours and multiple jobs to earn enough money to survive. You need a financial plan that reduces spending, increases saving, pays off debt, and brings in enough money to give you financial security.

Income relates to employment, and that bring us to jobs and careers.

Your Career Goals

Finding happiness and success in your career is challenging. Professor Edith Hall notes the appalling dystopia in many people's working lives. She cites a 2015 report compiled for the British government that revealed that 37 percent of working adults believe their jobs are pointless and not making a meaningful contribution to the world.[13]

Business psychologist and Harvard professor Frederick Herzberg argues,

> The most powerful motivator in our lives isn't money, but rather the opportunity to learn, grow in responsibilities, contribute to others, and be recognized for achievements."[14]

We all need work that encourages us to use our skills and strengths, allows us to continually learn and develop as professionals, and gives us a sense of agency and autonomy over our work lives.

We also want to work in an organization and community where we feel connected, recognized, and respected—where we feel we belong. And we want the organization to espouse a purpose consistent with our values.

Every job worth having is going to need significant skill and that means lifelong learning. We can't go to college for four years and expect to learn everything we need to know for the next forty or more years.

The most important quality to have, if we want to stay employed, is a commitment to never-ending learning and improvement. Having an agile, flexible, supple mindset is crucial to sustained success.[15]

A good place to start when looking for a job or launching a career is to ask yourself: Can you find a link between the work you'd like to do and your values? If you can, positive psychology says you'll find the work more satisfying. I was always interested in conservation and the natural world, and only started to get glimmerings of satisfaction with my career when I started working in those areas.[16]

If you are unhappy with your current job, think about the skills you want to build and the daily tasks you want to do. What parts of your life make you feel satisfied? What kinds of jobs call upon the skills you enjoy using?

Talk to trusted colleagues about what they think you're good at. Think about the projects that might make you excited to work on. What activities do you find absorbing and put you in flow?

Ideally you want to find a job that involves tasks as similar as possible to the activities you find engaging and compelling. If this leads to job ideas that are new to you, then find a way to try them out without making a big commitment.

Ask to shadow someone in a job you are interested in, or meet with someone who holds a position intriguing to you. People love to help others with their careers.[17]

Look for what might give you satisfaction and follow that path.[18] As Stanford professors Bill Burnett and Dave Evans point out, what makes work satisfying and fun is not office parties, getting paid a high salary, or receiving generous benefits; it's when you're building on your strengths, are frequently in flow and highly engaged, and are energized and excited by what you do.[19]

The average full-time professional will spend about eighty thousand hours at work over the course of their working life. This is most of their waking hours. If you're in a career that leaves you feeling unfulfilled or even miserable, that means you're spending thousands of hours on projects and tasks you don't care about or dislike.

No one should accept this level of torment and deprivation without a fight. The best way to better your work life is to think about your values. We'll delve more into values in the next chapter.

For now, focus on articulating your values in your personal mission statement as an aid to identifying which job or career would be a good fit for you. You'll want to do work that aligns with your values, even if it means accepting a lower income.

New York Times columnist Nicholas Kristof notes that when he speaks at universities, he's sometimes asked if it's wrong for graduates to work in finance or consulting. He always says, "No, not at all—but keep your moral compass and make sure you connect with a cause larger than yourself." Kristof adds:

> Alas, companies have a remarkable ability to lose that compass: Consider the way pharma companies recklessly peddled prescription painkillers and helped cause a wave of addiction and overdose deaths across America.[20]

Positive-psychology research has shown that people who live meaningful lives—lives lived with purpose—are most likely to find fulfillment and die with few regrets. The secret to finding fulfillment in your career is to bring meaning to it. You do that by connecting what you do in your job to ideas and values that are important to you.

The ideal career is the one in which you work for a cause you deeply believe in, and you feel that what you do makes a difference.

Bumps in the Career Road

Even if you have found a fulfilling job, you may sometimes make mistakes at work or even face reprimands. Use this as an opportunity to improve at what you're committed to doing well.

If, for example, you receive a bad performance review, use it to identify the weak spots in your work and strengthen your performance. Undoubtedly, you'll be dismayed and demoralized that your faults have been brought up for discussion. But you don't have to let it eat at you. The goal is to turn negative feedback into an opportunity to grow.

Try to keep from getting defensive or angry. Instead, pay attention to your manager's emotions. Is the feedback being delivered with optimism and a genuine wish for your success? Or is your manager in a pessimistic mood, projecting negative or even rancorous feelings?

This can tell you a lot about how much your boss expects of you and whether they're angling to eventually fire you or they sincerely want to help you become a star performer.

Be sure to ask your manager for specific examples of the areas in which you need to improve. Make sure you understand exactly what should change.

At the end, thank your manager for taking the time to review your performance, then really examine their comments. Suggest a follow-up meeting to go over the comments if you want more guidance on how to change. Develop an action plan with your manager. This will show you are engaged and ready to improve—and will help you make the improvements happen.

Walk away from the performance review—or from your own realization of mistakes or missteps—with the objective of setting new goals to help you do better.

My Own Goals

I have included my personal mission statement and goals in appendix A.

The way I view it, I have only one chance at life, so it's crucial that I have an accurate map and compass that can guide me to live fully and successfully. Appendix A is that map and compass. I have tried to make my goals clear and specific. I review and update this document several times a week and plan my day and my week based on it.

My goals are inspired by my personal mission statement, which describes my true north. The level of detail in my goals may strike you as unusual, but they reflect who I am and who I want to be. They capture the totality of my life.

Getting these goals out of my head and onto paper declutters my mind and gives me peace. As productivity guru David Allen says, "Your mind is for having ideas, not holding them."[21]

Someone once said that the purpose of life is a life of purpose. Living with purpose makes the world a better place, while it also helps me feel fulfilled.

My personal mission statement and goals document is organized into five sections. First, my personal mission statement. Second, my core values. Third, my daily routine. Fourth, my goals. And the final section describes new goal possibilities that I am mulling over (more on that below).

As noted in the preceding chapter, my goals are organized into four core categories: community, giving back, health, and growth. I could have selected other ways to view the whole of my life. For example, I could have organized the goals by *roles* (husband, father, grandfather, writer, speaker), *life domains* (work, home, community, self), or *mission* (to love, to leave a legacy, to laugh, to learn, to live). All of these approaches work equally well and accomplish the same goal of finding a way to structure and organize my life.

As I indicated in part I, the structure that appeals to me most at this stage of my life is the four core categories of community, giving back, health, and growth:

1. *Community* includes relationships, social life, a sense of belonging and engagement in community. My "community" goal is to be an engaged and loving family member and a warm and active community member.
2. *Giving back* includes having a sense of purpose, finding meaning, creating a legacy, volunteering, and contributing. My "giving back" goal is to live a life brimming with purpose and enthusiasm and to leave a legacy.
3. *Health* includes diet, exercise, sleep, and lifestyle. My "health" goal is to be in the best health possible and to invest significantly in personal development.
4. *Growth* includes lifelong learning, new experiences, overcoming challenges, and adopting a growth mindset. My "growth" goal is to embrace challenges and to devote myself to lifelong learning.

A healthy, balanced, fulfilling, and active life requires full engagement in all four of these core categories. Note that the categories overlap. They are interrelated and synergistic. Many activities help me to accomplish goals in more than one category. Not meeting a goal reduces the quality of my life.

I constantly tweak and edit my personal mission statement and goals, enriching them with new ideas and fresh, inspiring language. The document in appendix A, which is organic and always a work in progress, inspires me to lead the best life possible and to keep me in alignment with my values and goals. It helps me be less distracted, more focused, more intentional, and more purposeful.

Of course, I frequently stumble, make mistakes, and use poor judgment, but my personal mission statement and goals help me get back on track.

New Goal Possibilities

At the end of my personal mission statement and goals document, I have a section called "New Possibilities and Aspirations." This is where I collect ideas for goals I haven't thought through completely and am therefore not yet willing to commit to. I write them down because I don't want to risk forgetting them. I review them periodically and mull them over.

Periodically, I'll decide to start pursuing one of my "possible goals." I move it from being something in development to being an active goal.

I urge you to capture your "possible goals" in writing so they won't bounce around in your brain as unfinished thoughts and open loops, causing confusion and distracting you from your current task.

Once captured in a trusted system where you know you won't lose them, you can stop worrying about them and put them aside until you're ready to give them your full attention.

Questions and Actions

Based on the concepts and ideas examined in this chapter, consider the following questions and activities:

- Brainstorm about goals that will challenge and stretch you.
- Identify concrete, specific, and detailed goals derived from your personal mission statement and establish a reasonable time frame for them. Be as specific as possible.
- What is the best way for you to organize your goals? By roles? Or some other way?
- Put your goals into a written draft. Revisit the draft several times over a week, revising and adding to it.
- Now revisit those goals and see if you can break them down into doable, actionable steps.

- Make a supplemental list of potential goals (new possibilities) that appeal to you but are, as yet, vague or undeveloped. Work to refine them over time.
- Have you made a misstep at work or been called out for performance that needs improvement? If so, how did you react? How might you have responded to achieve a more positive result?

~

CHAPTER FIVE

Invest in Personal Development

Why is personal development so important? Because how well you take care of yourself determines, to a large degree, your level of success in life and whether you find life meaningful and fulfilling.

You must take care of yourself so you'll be able to take care of others. You have a role to play in the world and thus you have a responsibility to take care of yourself so you can fulfill that role to the fullest.

What Is Personal Development?

There's no one more important than you in determining the kind of life you want to live. Personal development is about putting yourself in a position where you're strong, healthy, and robust enough not only to invest in your own life and career but also strong enough to help others through service and compassion.

Personal development equips you to contribute to society. It's hard to have a flourishing career if you are exhausted or anxious. It's hard to have a loving family life if you're irritable and impatient. If you don't allocate time for personal development, then your work, career, health, relationships, and family will likely suffer.

Personal development is not about personal gain or spending hours focused on excessive self-pampering. Personal development is different from self-indulgence.

Taking care of yourself is not selfish or pleasure seeking. Nurturing yourself so that you can be strong for others is not mindless self-gratification. Simon Sinek says,

> The ultimate value of personal development is not to feel better about ourselves but to contribute to how those around us feel about themselves.[1]

Your physical, social/emotional, mental, and spiritual health should be a top priority because you must take care of yourself to be able to help others. When your health is compromised, you undermine your ability to fulfill your personal mission statement and goals.

Personal Development versus Generosity

Is there a conflict between devoting time to personal development and spending time helping others? After all, both endeavors are good.

Behavioral scientist Aline Holzwarth has grappled with the issue of how personal development fits into a model of generosity.[2] Giving to ourselves and giving to others can conflict, she explains, if they are taken to extremes. Excessive personal development can become selfishness, and excessive care for others can lead to burnout.

When people become extreme givers and excessively altruistic, they can become exhausted. And when people become obsessed with personal development, they can neglect other people's needs. We need to give to others without sacrificing ourselves. We need to take care of ourselves without neglecting our loved ones and friends.

We all have limited time, attention, and energy, so we must decide how to allocate our resources. Even generous people sometimes have to say no. Holzwarth argues that we need to find the right balance between giving to ourselves and giving to others. Both are important. One should not be sacrificed for the other.

As already noted, personal development helps us to take care of other people. It's good to be good to others, and it's good to be good to ourselves. We must do both.

Don't Take Personal Development for Granted

Personal development won't happen automatically. It takes time and effort. You need a plan, otherwise you won't reach your full potential and become your best self. Leadership expert and author John C. Maxwell says it's vital to set aside time for personal development and growth.[3]

Personal development can be uncomfortable because it requires you to push beyond your comfort zone, learn new things, and make changes.

The Four Dimensions of Personal Development

Leadership expert Stephen R. Covey described personal development as the vital process of enhancing your capacity to make you a more effective and capable person.[4] He identified four dimensions (or frames of reference) of personal development: *physical, social/emotional, mental,* and *spiritual.* These are the four fundamental domains of our nature, and they define a person's basic needs and capacities.

As Covey pointed out, these foundational dimensions can be found in all philosophies.[5] For example, in his book *Running and Being,* philosopher and runner George Sheehan described the four fundamental components as being a good animal (physical), a good friend (social/emotional), a good craftsman (mental), and a saint (spiritual).[6]

- *Physical* includes health, fitness, exercise, strength, flexibility, endurance, posture, balance, eating healthfully, getting enough sleep, and stress management.
- *Social/emotional* includes love, friendship, empathy, service, connecting with others, community building, volunteering, helping others, and having a sense of belonging.
- *Mental* includes adopting a growth mindset, learning, studying, reading, writing, visiting museums and science centers, planning, visualizing, solving puzzles, and developing intellectually.
- *Spiritual* includes finding purpose and meaning in your life through a wide range of pursuits, such as giving back, service to others, art, contemplation, poetry, going on a personal retreat to reflect on your life, creating your personal mission statement, clarifying your values, being at one with nature, identifying your goals, studying your family history, leaving a legacy, being guided by a sense of honor, and, for some people, having religious convictions.

Note that few items in these four dimensions involve quick fixes or immediate gratification. Rather, they involve working for long-term and enduring results. They all bring you closer to being the person you want to be rather than acting impulsively in ways you may regret. They all fit into the "slow success" concept mentioned earlier. They all involve building character.

Let's examine the four foundational dimensions of personal development in more detail.

Physical

It isn't easy to exercise regularly. We're deluged with job and career demands, commuting can be time-consuming and stressful, and raising a family is exhausting. Harvard Medical School reports that two out of every three of us are overweight or obese.[7]

But without regular exercise, you can feel even more tired, stressed, and overwhelmed. This doesn't mention the fact that, as fitness expert Aubrey Reinmiller says, "You can't care for others if your health is not where it needs to be."[8]

If you haven't been active for a long time, check in with your doctor to be sure you have guidelines for how to start exercising safely. This is especially important if you have heart disease or breathing problems.

Why do you want to get fitter? When you understand your "why," you are more likely to stick to a regular exercise schedule. Take a few minutes to think about why you really want to get into better physical shape. How would you feel? How would your loved ones feel? Do you want to have the strength and endurance to take on new responsibilities? Do you want to be able to wrestle and play with your kids or grandkids?

Research shows that exercise has a powerful beneficial effect on our minds by reducing anxiety and low moods. And exercise, or any fitness-based movement, increases our vitality, circulating blood and oxygen throughout the body.

The research of Dr. Dean Ornish. One of the pioneering doctors in the field of health is Dean Ornish. His 2019 book *Undo It!* is based on multiple, randomized, double-blind studies that are the gold standard. He describes his landmark research showing that simple lifestyle changes—eating well, moving more, loving more, and stressing less—can *reverse* (undo) the progression of the most common chronic diseases, including severe coronary heart disease, early-stage prostate cancer, high blood pressure, elevated cholesterol levels, and type-2 diabetes.[9]

The nine-week Ornish Lifestyle Medicine program is now available in hospitals, physician groups, health systems, and clinics around the country. It is the only lifestyle program scientifically proven in randomized trials to reverse heart disease, and it is covered by Medicare and many insurance companies. By following this lifestyle program, many people have been able to avoid bypass surgery, stents, prostate cancer surgery, and even heart transplants.

In practical terms, this means that when we visit our primary care physicians, they should be spending a lot of time asking us about our diets, exercise regimens, stress levels, relationships, work, finances, and purpose and meaning in our lives. Unfortunately, most doctors spend just ten to fifteen minutes with patients during an office visit, and most of that time is not spent asking lifestyle questions.

Ornish's program has four major components, each a healing mechanism on its own and synergistic when done together with the others:

- *Eat well.* Nutritionists such as Ornish emphasize the need for a whole-food, unprocessed, plant-based diet that is naturally low in animal protein, fat, sugar, and refined carbohydrates. This diet features primarily fruits, vegetables, whole grains, legumes, seeds, and nuts in their natural, unprocessed forms. Rabbi Moses Maimonides wrote, in 1190, "No disease that can be treated by diet should be treated with any other means."[10] One of my tricks to staying healthy is to eat *before* I go to a party or other event. Before leaving home, I eat a healthy meal with cancer-preventing fruits, vegetables, whole grains, nuts, chickpeas, and a glass of water. When I get to the party, I can focus on the people there and am not hungry for the candy, cookies, cakes, or other highly processed, unhealthful, sugary, fatty, or high-salt foods that might otherwise tempt me. The less processed your diet, the better.[11] Diet is medicine.
- *Move more.* Moderate exercise, such as walking, stretching, and strength training, is part of the regular routine in a healthy lifestyle. There's growing evidence that prolonged sedentary behavior is as bad for health as smoking. Sitting too much instead of moving fosters cardiovascular disease and early death. The shocking fact is that more than eighty million Americans over age six are entirely inactive.[12] Do phone calls while standing or doing squats. Hold small meetings while standing or walking. Incorporate exercise or physical activity into other daily activities. Exercise is medicine.
- *Love more.* Ornish writes that people who feel lonely, depressed, and isolated are three to ten times more likely to get sick and die prematurely from virtually all causes than those who have strong feelings of love, connection, and community. More on this in the "social/emotional" section.

- *Stress less.* Meditation, mindfulness, and other mental-focus techniques reduce stress levels. More on this later.

Neuroscientist Daniel Levitin, in his book *Successful Aging*, argues that Dean Ornish is not as rigorously scientific as he (Ornish) claims.[13] But Levitin concludes that plant-based foods like cruciferous vegetables, flaxseed, and beans are healthy, and he endorses author Michael Pollan's famous phrase: "Eat food. Not too much. Mostly plants."[14]

The bottom line is that Levitin, Ornish, Pollan, and many other experts are pretty much on the same page when it comes to what constitutes a healthy diet: eat mostly unprocessed, plant-based foods.

Meditation and mindfulness. Meditation strengthens our physical as well as emotional well-being. Andy Puddicombe, cofounder of the popular meditation app Headspace, writes persuasively about the benefits of meditation, including stress reduction, better concentration, being present and in the moment, being less bothered by minor irritations, improved moods, and improved relationships with loved ones and colleagues.[15]

Meditation involves concentrating on one object, such as your breathing. It allows you to stay calm as you observe your consciousness and what appears in it. It's difficult not to get distracted by stray thoughts, emotions, or sensations, but, with practice, you can learn to meditate and become less distracted.

Mindfulness is a form of meditation. It is a loving, moment-to-moment awareness that gives you the opportunity and space to cultivate wisdom. Mindfulness is about paying attention, holding that attention in the present moment, being fully engaged but not judgmental. It is a conscious effort to be completely present and to be fully aware of the current moment without longing for something else or something better.

There are many apps and websites to help you learn how to meditate and be more mindful. I have found the app Waking Up, created by neuroscientist Sam Harris, to be one of the most thoughtful and effective.[16]

One key to reducing stress is to be conscious of what you allow your mind to dwell on. You may need to steer clear of distressing news programs, pessimistic colleagues, trolls on social media, and other stress-inducing experiences that can sabotage your efforts to find serenity and joy. Be careful what you feed your mind.

Those who think about life's meaning and purpose deal better with daily stress because they have goals that engage them and bring them into flow. They are also more likely to have other habits and projects that promote well-being, good health, and deeper self-understanding.

Get enough sleep. Sleep experts recommend going to bed and getting up at roughly the same times each day. Having enough sleep is crucial for high productivity. Lack of sleep interferes with your ability to think clearly. Research shows that almost everyone needs seven to eight hours of sleep a night, so if you get up early, you need to go to bed early.[17]

Psychologist Angela Duckworth says that sleep is a miracle drug with no side effects. She says everything in our body and mind is compromised when we don't get enough sleep.[18]

She also cites a suggestion from neuroscientist Matthew Walker: set an alarm to get ready for bed at the same time each night. Doing so reliably can, over time, help you to put going to bed at a reasonable hour on autopilot.[19]

Social/Emotional

One of the important challenges we each face is to make our lives worth something—to be significant and purposeful in some way. This is possible only by connecting to others. Meaning and community are intimately tied together. If we fail to make our lives meaningful and significant, we are inviting pessimism and even despair into our lives.

A major goal for each of us should be to take responsibility for intentionally designing our relationships. Forging relationships with other people is a major force in improving our lives.

Warren Buffett says his measure of success is, "Do the people you care about love you back?" Lewis Carroll wrote, "One of the deep secrets of life is that all that is really *worth* the doing is what we do for others." Author and philosopher Sinek says, "Success is a team sport." And Leo Tolstoy said, "Joy can be real only if people look upon their life as a service and have a definite object in life outside themselves and their personal happiness."

The importance of relationships. We are hardwired to connect with others. Our need to belong is powerful and basic. We like to live in groups that have strong and enduring relationships among members. Research studies, especially in positive psychology under Dr. Martin Seligman, have shown again and again that relationships are pivotally important to people and have a major impact on whether we consider our lives successful.[20]

Seligman asks: When was the last time you laughed uproariously? When was the last time you felt indescribable joy? The last time you sensed profound meaning and purpose? The last time you felt enormously proud of an accomplishment? Seligman points out that these high points almost always take place around other people.[21]

The power of doing a kindness. What Seligman and other scientists have found is that doing a kindness produces the "single most reliable momentary increase in well-being," compared with any other action or exercise.[22] Poet William Wordsworth wrote about "that best portion of a good man's life, his little, nameless, unremembered, acts of kindness and of love."

Communities and families are fraying. Senator Ben Sasse writes, "Most Americans just don't have community cohesion like we used to. We don't feel we are connected to our neighbors in any meaningful way." The bonds that join people together, that give their lives meaning and richness, are fraying, Sasse says.[23] He tells the shocking story of the 1995 Chicago heat wave, when neighbors and city personnel began discovering the decaying corpses of people—generally men—who had died alone. Sasse writes, "They sometimes found next to them stacks of handwritten letters to estranged children." The letters asked for forgiveness for their lack of involvement, for events they missed, and for the neglect of long ago.[24]

In a *New York Times* article, author Bruce Feiler describes what happened at a public lecture on forgiveness.[25] About halfway through the discussion, Rabbi Joseph Telushkin posed the following question to the audience: "In how many of your families, at the level of first cousin or closer, are there people not on speaking terms?" An astonishing two-thirds of the four hundred or so people in the room raised their hands. The rabbi pointed out that the figure was staggering, adding that, when you ask people to explain the origins of such family fights, they often sound ridiculous. When I read this story, it hit home. I have relatives who are not speaking to each other, and it breaks my heart.

The scourge of loneliness. According to Stanford University social scientist Dr. Emma Seppala, loneliness has become frighteningly widespread; nearly half of Americans feel lonely. Seppala says this causes great suffering because of our deep-seated need for social connection.[26] Some observers think that loneliness—not obesity, cancer, or heart disease—is the nation's number one health crisis.[27] Mother Teresa said, "The most terrible poverty is loneliness, and the feeling of being unloved."[28]

The woes of being a workaholic. Many research studies have shown that our level of satisfaction with life is directly tied to the relationships we have. If you have an unbalanced work life—in other words, if you are a workaholic like I was for many years—you will inevitably neglect the deeper relationships that can provide protection against the suffering and pain that life has in store for each of us.

The people around you. Jim Rohn urged his audiences to do the following:

Constantly ask yourself these questions: Who am I around? What are they doing to me? What have they got me reading? What have they got me saying? Where do they have me going? What do they have me thinking? And, most important, what do they have me becoming? Then ask yourself the big question: Is that okay?[29]

True friendships. True friendship has little to do with Facebook or other social media platforms. I urge you to identify the people in your life you respect and who have admirable characters. Reach out to them. Invest time in them. Let them know you value and appreciate them. These are the people you want to witness your life and have as friends.

David Brooks writes that we need to develop a "moral ecology" or creed acknowledging that "we are formed by relationship, we are nourished by relationship, and we long for relationship."[30] Life is a process of forming attachments. It's not a solitary journey. Brooks abhors hyper-individualism that puts the individual in the center instead of the relationship.

Building quality relationships. Developing and maintaining quality relationships takes effort. To have good friends, you must be a good friend, even to people in your own family. According to the Mayo Clinic, good friends have the following qualities:

- They like, respect, and trust each other.
- They accept each other, even though they don't always understand each other.
- They allow space for each other to grow, change, and make decisions, even if there's disagreement.
- They listen and share freely, without judging or criticizing.
- They respect each other's boundaries.
- They don't take advantage of each other.
- They accept and give help as needed.
- They don't reveal private information about each other to others.
- They have each other's best interests in mind and help each other make good choices.
- They are there for each other but not obsessed with each other.
- They have individual and mutual interests.[31]

Remember that there are different levels of friendship. Some are close, others are more casual, but all can be beneficial.[32] To establish and maintain relationships, people must be fair, honest, generous, and loyal. They must be perceived as good partners. In other words, they must behave morally. What underlies these moral traits is the ability to put something else ahead of our immediate desires and interests. David DeSteno notes in the *New York Times* that when we feel gratitude and compassion, we are more likely to exercise self-control and be there for others.[33]

Marriage. If you are married or in a marriage-like relationship, your relationship with your spouse or partner is the foundation of your family's happiness. I encourage you to build a strong family whose members love each other, enjoy meaningful relationships with each other, respect each other, have fun together, and grow together.

Obviously same-gender marriages or partnerships can brim with love, caring, and mutual support just like traditional marriages or partnerships can.

Author Carl Walter wrote,

A great marriage is like two trees standing tall, side by side. Their branches intertwine so beautifully, so gracefully, they almost become one, yet they remain two. Standing together, they are strong, beautiful, and better able to withstand the high winds of storms that come now and then. They are separate living things, yet so interdependent, growing more beautifully entwined year after year. Providing shade, comfort, and safety for each other and all who walk their way.[34]

Aphorist and quotation expert Dr. Mardy Grothe also finds a nature analogy helpful when describing marriage. He writes,

Falling in love [is] like stumbling into the most magnificent garden, a sanctuary filled with strange and beautiful specimens, dazzling colors, and sweet fragrances. If that garden is to remain a haven for years to come, though, it must be given the loving care a special place deserves. To tend it properly, weeds must be picked, invading pests controlled, and nutrients added. Falling in love is a bit of a mystery and has all the characteristics of a happy accident. Staying in love is less mysterious, and brings to mind words like will, effort, skill, and commitment. Now, whenever I meet people who continue to be "in love" after many years of marriage, I view them as Master Gardeners. They've worked diligently, for the most part, and they've continued to work at it even when occasionally tempted to slack off or even pack it in. But they've never given up, and their reward is a beautiful garden that is deeply satisfying to them and a model for others.[35]

A safe, emotional connection. In her pioneering book *Hold Me Tight*, psychologist Dr. Sue Johnson argues that each of us has an innate need for safe emotional connection and bonding with those closest to us. We all need to have someone in our lives to depend on for trustworthy emotional connection and comfort.

Being responsive, open, loving, kind, and in harmony with another human being can make life worth living and protect us from despair and loneliness. Johnson says that love "has an immense ability to help heal the devastating wounds that life sometimes deals us." She writes, "Loving responsiveness is the foundation of a truly compassionate, civilized society."[36]

In his book *Bowling Alone*, academic Robert Putnam showed what Sasse also observed: Most of us have few opportunities to develop close ties with others. We tend to live in social isolation, without the benefits of sympathy, help, and the camaraderie of neighbors and supportive communities.[37]

Thus, a love relationship, as Johnson points out, "has become the central emotional relationship in most people's lives."[38] As the Celtic saying goes, "We live in the shelter of each other."[39]

Close bonds with a few key people. We need to be emotionally bonded with a few key people to flourish and find emotional protection from the vicissitudes of life. Suffering is more easily tolerated when we're not also suffering from isolation and loneliness.

Having close ties with a small number of people is crucial to our well-being. Meaning in life comes from mattering to a few people and making a difference in their lives rather than from being known to many, for example, on a social media platform.

Extensive research has shown that positive, loving, kind, and trusting relationships with others help us to keep stress at bay and deal more capably with the challenges and setbacks of life.[40]

Johnson writes, "Contact with a loving partner literally acts as a buffer against shock, stress, and pain."[41] And the loss of loving connection—the severance of a bond because of betrayal, conflict, or death—can be terrifying and cause us to feel panic.[42]

We need a community. We all need a community to belong to where we feel welcomed, understood, supported, and valued. Without such a community, people become lonely and isolated.

As already noted, many studies have shown that chronic loneliness leads to acute suffering, poor health, and early death. There is a reason solitary confinement is among the most feared and painful of punishments.[43]

Warm relationships are essential for living a fulfilling life. We all need to receive and give affection and love. It is through working with others that we often discover meaning in our lives. Finding meaning often starts by reaching out to colleagues, friends, family members, or neighbors.

Maslow's hierarchy of needs requires tweaking. Psychologist Abraham H. Maslow famously proposed that people have five categories of human need, which he ranked. First is the need for food, water, and shelter. Second, the need for safety. Third, the need for social acceptance and a sense of belonging to a group. Fourth, the need for recognition and prestige. And finally, Maslow asserted that if those four needs were met, then people need what he called "self-actualization," a feeling that they could create their best selves and accrue achievements, confidence, and competence.

We all understood—or so we thought—that the goal in life is to climb Maslow's hierarchy of needs and reach self-actualization, but I've come to believe that Maslow's hierarchy of needs may need tweaking. In my view, his third need, a sense of belonging to a community and having meaningful commitments to other people, is inseparable from the actualization of our selves.

I believe that community may be our highest and most challenging human need. Belonging to a community in which people care about each other and are committed to each other's welfare, and where there are shared values and genuine communication, may be the only real way to find meaning and purpose, and, ultimately, to find self-actualization.

Families. The importance of community underscores the importance of families and how deeply committed we should be to their care. It's tragic when families are riven and broken by abuse, alcoholism, distrust, workaholism, estrangement, selfishness, betrayal, self-absorption, narcissism, excessive screen use, and other destructive behaviors.

The Losada ratio. As a young father, I was guilty of being grumpy with my family members and of viewing my main responsibility to be correcting their weaknesses. From positive psychology and Seligman, I learned that my real responsibility was to build strengths and catch other family members doing something right.

Research has shown, for example, that the "Losada ratio" (named after Brazilian psychologist Marcel Losada), which is the ratio of positive to negative comments, needs to be five to one for a strong and loving marriage. A ratio of one to three in a couple is disastrous.[44] I hate to think what my Losada ratio was when I was younger.

The story of J. R. Storment. If you're a parent, then spending time with your children and building a strong connection with them is vital. Hard-charging tech executive J. R. Storment discovered this in the worst way possible in August 2019 when his eight-year-old son Wiley suddenly died of complications from epilepsy.

Storment was filled with regret for his workaholic tendencies and wished he had a better balance in his life. He wrote a wrenching LinkedIn post urging others to avoid his mistake of not spending enough time with their children. Storment still values work—he quotes the poet Kahlil Gibran who said, "Work is love made visible"—but now believes that he missed out on things that mattered and his life was not sufficiently in balance.

He encourages parents to hug their kids, get home in time for family dinner, straighten out their priorities, and schedule one-on-one meetings with their kids, just as they do with work colleagues.[45]

Social media. Social media is not helping because, as professor and author Cal Newport has shown, it tends to take people away from the real-world socializing that is far more valuable. The more people use social media, the less time they tend to devote to offline interactions with friends and family.[46] I discuss social media in more depth in chapter 10. **Conversation versus connection.** Newport quotes MIT researcher Sherry Turkle who writes that conversation (as opposed to the superficial connections we make in our online social lives) "is the most human—and humanizing—thing we do."

It's where we relish the joy of being heard, of being understood, and of having a sense of belonging and community.[47] It's also where we receive the encouragement to pursue our quest for a successful and fulfilling life.

Listening. Listening is crucially important in developing relationships that are rewarding, warm, and full of trust and empathy. Smartphones and other devices undermine our ability to listen to others because we get distracted so easily.

We need to listen attentively and actively to other people. Stephen Covey observed that most of us have never learned how to listen in a way that lets us deeply understand another human being from that individual's own frame of reference. Such listening is hard work. It means, as Covey said, "listening with the intent to understand rather than reply."[48]

Good listeners are rare. We tend to think of ourselves first and spend most of our conversation time appearing to listen but actually thinking about what we're going to say next.

Here are ways to listen more skillfully. Lean slightly forward to show you are alert and paying attention. Be totally engaged in the conversation and not distracted in any way. Make and keep eye contact. Be approachable, and don't cross your arms. Adopt an inviting, gentle tone of voice. Be attentive to the other person's feelings and emotions. Don't interrupt when the person is talking.

Ask the person to clarify points that confuse you. Invite details. Gently ask for more information. Be curious. Say, *tell me more.* Say in your own words what you think you heard to see if you have correctly understood the person. Be calm. Try not to judge but to understand. Pay close attention. Be totally present. Make the person feel supported and respected.

Make a real human bond with the person. Be present and live totally in the moment. Show through your eyes, body language, and voice that the person is really being heard and listened to and that there is nowhere else you'd rather be. For that person, it will be a rare and precious experience.

Listening empathetically doesn't necessarily mean you agree. It means simply that you understand. And, as Covey pointed out, when the other person's need to be understood is satisfied, you are more likely to be listened to and understood in return.

Be intentional about your relationships. As mentioned earlier, I encourage you to identify in an intentional way the people who are most important to you and to add their specific names to your personal mission statement and goals.

In other words, in the part of your personal mission statement relating to relationships, list the people you want to have as your friends. You can see how I have done this in appendix A. Nothing is more important in our lives than the relationships we build with other people. Grothe writes, "When I think of the people I've most admired, it is not those who've achieved success or fame, but those who've been most willing to lend a hand to people in need."[49] Author and philosopher Simone de Beauvoir wrote, "One's life has value so long as one attributes value to the life of others, by means of love, friendship, indignation and compassion."[50]

Mental

Robust personal development entails exercising and expanding your mind throughout your life. It's important to keep using your mind in challenging ways and to continue learning even after you finish your formal education. Isaac Asimov said, "The day you stop learning is the day you begin decaying."[51]

Lifelong learning is a necessity. Make a commitment to not let your mind atrophy and to continue learning new things despite not having the external discipline of college. Serious reading, exploring new subjects, thinking critically, and writing clearly are things we need to do throughout our lives.

People now change jobs and careers so often that they must continually learn new skills. Four years at college is just the start. As knowledge and skills become obsolete, people must continuously update their competencies to remain competitive in the workforce.

But learning for work purposes is only one reason to grow your mind. If you are continually learning, then you are, says author Peter Senge, getting to the heart of what it means to be human. He writes,

Through learning we re-create ourselves. Through learning we become able to do something we never were able to do. . . . Through learning we extend our capacity to be part of the generative process of life.[52]

By "generative," Senge means learning that increases our capacity to create and shape our own futures. Generative learning continually expands our ability to create the results in life that are deeply meaningful to us.

Be an avid reader. It's vital to be an avid reader. Extensive reading does not guarantee success in life, but people who read a lot are more likely to be successful. Never go anywhere without a good book in case you find time to read a few pages—whether you're waiting in line at the post office or sitting on a train commuting to work. Books can change your life. Capable readers read books not just to finish them but to expand their knowledge and enrich their lives.

Work hard. When I was about twelve years old, I read Samuel Smiles's famous 1859 book *Self-Help*.[53] A quarter of a million copies were sold in his lifetime. His thesis was that hard work and energy accomplished far more than genius. This is in line with the recent research of professors Carol Dweck and Angela Duckworth. Smiles celebrated patience, courage, perseverance, and, above all, assiduous and tireless effort.

Smiles argued that the joy of success was in the effort, not the achievement. And he linked the glories of hard work to moral character and integrity. The book made a big impression on me when I was young, and I've been a strong believer ever since in the importance of hard work.

I believe that hard work is a basic building block of every achievement. This may sound quaint in an age of instant gratification, but whether you are talking about writing a book, getting a PhD, creating a beautiful garden, raising a successful family, or landing humans on the moon, a key element of any major accomplishment is hard work over a long period of time.

And a great work ethic is a far better life strategy than shortcuts and quick fixes. Writer and film producer Shonda Rhimes says,

Dreams are lovely. But they are just dreams. Fleeting, ephemeral, pretty. But dreams do not come true just because you dream them. It's hard work that makes things happen. It's hard work that creates change.[54]

Critical thinking. In an age of fake news and faux videos, we all need to become better critical thinkers. Author Grace Fleming says the following skills are important:[55]

- *Recognize assumptions you carry with you.* Have you ever wondered why you believe the things you believe? Is it because you've been told to believe them? Step outside your own beliefs to observe them from a neutral viewpoint. Be aware of assumptions and learn to self-reflect.
- *Process information honestly.* People sometimes pass along misinformation, such as a false news story, without having checked its truthfulness. It is prudent to take a few minutes to verify things, especially with headlines and stories coming at us so fast, in such great numbers, and often with unclear and hazy sourcing.
- *Recognize a generalization.* Girls don't like math. Old people are useless. Screens are bad for kids. These are generalizations and not always true. Judge for yourself, and without succumbing to sweeping generalities.
- *Evaluate old information and new ideas.* There was a time when doctors thought leeches and bloodletting could cure us. Recognize, says Fleming, that just because something is commonly accepted, doesn't mean it's true.
- *Analyze a problem and recognize the complex parts.* A mechanic must understand how an entire engine works before they can diagnose a problem. Sometimes it's necessary to take an engine apart to figure out which part isn't working. You should, says Fleming, approach big problems the same way. Break them down into smaller parts and observe carefully and deliberately. That is what we are doing in this book as we try to work out how to live a meaningful and successful life.
- *Use precise vocabulary and communicate with clarity.* The truth can be blurred and obfuscated by fuzzy language. It is important to develop your vocabulary so you can communicate truths accurately. I recommend Merriam-Webster's Word of the Day (https://www.merriam-webster.com/word-of-the-day), Anu Garg's A.Word.A.Day (https://www.wordsmith.org/awad/), and Liesl Johnson's daily newsletter about words (http://hilotutor.com/).
- *Manage emotions in response to a situation or problem.* Don't be fooled by overwrought, emotional pleas or angry speech. Stay rational, says Fleming, and keep your emotions in check as you encounter new information.

- *Judge your sources.* Learn to recognize hidden agendas and bias when you collect information. This is particularly important when using the internet, where there is an abundance of bad sources.

New York Times columnist Thomas Friedman writes, "The internet is an open sewer of untreated, unfiltered information" where students especially "need to bring skepticism and critical thinking to everything they read."[56] Of course, developing effective critical thinking skills is important for everyone, not just students.

Battling pseudoscience. Nowhere is it more important to use critical thinking than in identifying and outing pseudoscience. Pseudoscience, characterized by extravagant, suspicious, and even fraudulent claims, includes such fake sciences as astrology, phrenology, witchcraft, and the study of alien abductions.

These ideas are based on nonexistent scientific "evidence" and have no empirical support. The only bases for them are anecdotes, stories, and unsupported testimonials.

Author Kendra Cherry lists four key things to probe to determine if something is a science or a pseudoscience:

- *Consider the purpose.* Science is focused on helping people develop a fuller, richer understanding of the world. Pseudoscience tends to do the opposite.
- *Consider how challenges are dealt with.* Science welcomes challenges and attempts to disprove or refute different ideas. Pseudoscience tends to reject or ignore any challenge to its dogmas with hostility and resentment.
- *Look at the research.* Science is supported by a deep and ever-growing body of knowledge and research. Pseudoscience, Cherry points out, is static and involves little rigorous research.
- *Can it be proven false?* Falsifiability is a key hallmark of science. This means that if something is false, researchers can prove that it's false. Cherry writes, "Many pseudoscientific claims are simply untestable, so there is no way for researchers to prove these claims false."[57]

Astrophysicist Carl Sagan wrote perceptively about the difference between the myths of pseudoscience and the testable hypotheses of science in his book *The Demon-Haunted World:* "The method of science . . . is far more important than the findings of science."[58]

Spiritual

Spirituality is about finding meaning in your life. Spirituality is whatever brings a sense of transcendent meaning, purpose, and connection to you. For some that is religion, for others, a love of nature, music, or art. Or it can be expressed through relationships, involvement in a community, or personal achievements that benefit others. Spirituality can also be found in designing a full and flourishing life and in leaving a vibrant legacy.

Both religious and nonreligious people can be spiritual. A person's spiritual life consists of the most foundational values and beliefs relating to the meaning and purpose of life. It's impossible to live a truly fulfilling and successful life without feeling that you are connected to something bigger than yourself. This is why religions have given meaning to people for eons.

Devotion to spiritual matters—to values, to the common good, to helping others—is fundamentally important. The key to spiritual strength is turning attention away from yourself and your own preoccupations and toward something—a cause or a community—bigger than yourself, something that gives you a sense of purpose and direction.

As we discussed in the last chapter, a fulfilling and successful life is one with meaning and purpose, and one of the most effective ways to find meaning and purpose is to work for more than your own prosperity and advancement. Your goals should involve thinking of others, how we can care for them, and how we can help them grow and flourish.

This can be done in the context of raising a family, helping a neighbor, volunteering at the local library, or reading to kids in class. Or it can be something more far-reaching, such as fighting climate disruption, stopping animal abuse, helping teenagers with depression, improving the health care system, encouraging voter turnout, or supporting immigrants.

Almost everyone, religious or not, has spiritual needs and concerns.[59] Religious people will likely be concerned about their relationship with God or some other spiritual entity, as well as with religious doctrine, rituals, traditions, prayers, and sacred writings. All this and more will deeply matter to them.

Both religious and secular people will be concerned with morality, ethics, and conscience. They will grapple with the meaning of life, suffering, and evil, and what they can do to contribute to society to leave the world a better place for their journey through it.

Values. One way to start thinking spiritually is to think about values or self-evident truths as Thomas Jefferson did when he wrote the Declaration of Independence.

In one sense, such values will be unique for every individual, but I'm betting most of us have shared values, in the same way we likely have shared ideas about freedom of expression, freedom of the press, and equal justice under the law.

As already mentioned, spirituality includes clarifying our values.[60] You need to know your values because they illuminate the direction in which you must travel to experience a fulfilling life. Your values shape your character and behavior.

Don't confuse values and goals. A value describes how you want to live. It's permanent, and it infuses every hour of every day of your life. Goals change and evolve. Values are guidelines for the actions we take when pursuing our goals.

Values are what we want to stand for and how we want to be. Values are never achieved (like goals are). Values are more like guiding lights that help us reach our goals. The best way to live a meaningful life is to align your actions with your values.

It is easy to neglect values. People tend to allow their values to be shaped by pop culture, the media, and the influence of others instead of doing the hard work to find out what values really matter to them.

Spelling out your values in your personal mission statement can help you to live consistently with them. Without keeping your values in focus, you can feel diminished, inauthentic, and adrift.

Articulating your deepest values can help answer the question of why you want to achieve a goal, and as we've already noted, understanding the "why" behind a goal can release enormous motivation, perseverance, and energy.

Values from religion. We can gain insight into values by looking at the values espoused in the books of Judaism, Islam, Buddhism, Christianity, Hinduism, and other religions. They all recognize the importance of honesty, patience, generosity, kindness, endurance, diligence, tolerance, courage, justice, and helping others, especially those less fortunate.

Earlier, I mentioned Linus Pauling's tweak to the Golden Rule: "Do unto others twenty percent better than you would expect them to do unto you, to correct for subjective error." All religious books espouse a golden rule, and they also espouse professor and social reformer Felix Adler's definition of the supreme ethical rule: "Act so as to elicit the best in others and thereby in thyself."[61]

Live according to the values that matter to you. Having a sense of what values matter to you—your own true north—can be pivotally helpful.

Martin Seligman identified the following twenty-four guiding values, which he organized into six groups:

1. *Wisdom and knowledge*: Curiosity, love of learning, judgment, ingenuity, social intelligence, and perspective
2. *Courage*: Valor, perseverance, and integrity
3. *Humanity and love*: Kindness and loving
4. *Justice*: Citizenship, fairness, and leadership
5. *Temperance*: Self-control, prudence, and humility
6. *Transcendence*: Appreciation of beauty, gratitude, hope, spirituality, forgiveness, humor, and zest

"Résumé virtues" and "eulogy virtues." *New York Times* columnist David Brooks distinguishes between "résumé virtues" and "eulogy virtues."[62] Résumé virtues, he explains, are focused on professional success. In contrast, eulogy virtues are what your loved ones talk about at your memorial service, where the focus is more on character and values.

When you die, you want the people who know you best to say, "She was a thoroughly decent and honorable person, completely trustworthy and devoted to her family and friends," rather than, "She was the top sales agent for her real estate company for five years in a row and frequently was awarded the biggest bonus."

Having moral purpose. You want to be highly capable and accomplished and also equipped with moral purpose. You want to know the difference between right and wrong.

How do you pursue a decent and moral life when contemporary culture shows little interest in that topic, and indeed is in large part an assault on such values because of its frequent lionizing and feting of social ills like violence, misogyny, and consumerism?

It's hard to be morally grounded and have good character when you're surrounded by a popular culture filled with advertising, social media, films, music, and video games that regularly violate boundaries of civility, truth, and decency. Some of this is artistic license, but some of it is nihilism. If nothing else, all the noise and clutter militate against your finding the time and solitude to reflect quietly on your values and what deeply matters to you, a prerequisite for creating a personal mission statement, goals, and a life of significance.

Living a morally awake life. Living a morally awake life comes about by working on personal development every day, the way Ben Franklin did when he wanted to cultivate virtues.[63] It's a person's daily practice and actions, however small, that aggregate over time to make an honorable life.

Be careful of moral certainty. Morality and ethical conduct are areas rife with danger for those who write about them, especially if the writing is infused with zeal and conviction. As writer, editor, and critic H. L. Mencken put it,

> Moral certainty is always a sign of cultural inferiority. The more uncivilized the man, the surer he is that he knows precisely what is right and what is wrong. All human progress, even in morals, has been the work of men who have doubted the current moral values, not of men who have whooped them up and tried to enforce them. The truly civilized man is always skeptical and tolerant, in this field as in all others. His culture is based on "I am not too sure."[64]

In discussing how having a moral purpose is related to meaning and success, I want to be, in Mencken's words, "skeptical and tolerant." Surely, though, we can say that for a life to be assessed as meaningful and successful, that life must be consistent with honesty, kindness, integrity, gratitude, generosity, and other similar foundational values. To oppose that view is to risk nihilism and having a dearth of moral direction or conscience.

Being a person of honor and character. In his illuminating weekly online newsletter, "Dr. Mardy's Quotes of the Week," Grothe once outlined what he believes are some enduring constants surrounding a person of honor. The things he mentioned make up a good list of what each of us should want to hear in our eulogies.[65]

Grothe wrote that a person of honor is not careless with the truth or the reality of things; has a moral compass; attempts to live life on the heights and not in the gutter; can be trusted to keep confidences and commitments; tries to listen—in Abraham Lincoln's memorable phrasing—to "the better angels of our nature"; is respectful of the rights and sensibilities of others; will not attempt to use or manipulate people for selfish or devious purposes; fights hard for core beliefs and values; views adversaries and opponents as fellow human beings (not enemies to be demonized); stands up for the less fortunate; believes in fairness and fair play; and will not lie or cheat.

Of course, we all stumble and blunder—I certainly have—but these are the ideals to aim for.

A fulfilling and joyful life is not shaped by having money and fame. It comes from having a good character, good values, good friends, meaning, purpose, and goals. This, in turn, comes from making personal development a top priority.

Questions and Actions

Based on the concepts and ideas examined in this chapter, consider the following questions and activities:

- How can you take good care of yourself so you are strong, healthy, and resilient?
- Is it possible to take care of yourself and still be generous to others? How?
- Describe the vision you have for your personal development in the four domains of physical, social/emotional, mental, and spiritual.
- In the physical domain, is there one particular area (e.g., sleep, diet, exercise, stress levels) where you feel you need to improve?
- In the social/emotional domain, do you think of yourself as a good listener? If so, why?
- In the mental domain, do you attach a high enough priority to lifelong learning? What can you do to improve?
- We all have spiritual concerns, whether we are religious or secular, because spiritually at its core is about the search for meaning and purpose in our lives. Do you feel well equipped in this area? If not, what can you do to gain stronger spiritual grounding?
- Values are not goals but rather guidelines for our actions. What values are most important to you?
- The thrust of this book is consistent with what Dr. Martin Luther King Jr. said on February 4, 1968, at the Ebenezer Baptist Church. His words were, "Everybody can be great, because everybody can serve." That is, success is not the ability to outshine and gain status and power over others. Real success is achieved by being part of something greater than ourselves. What can you do to fold this interpretation of success into your approach to life and personal development?

CHAPTER SIX

~

Take Your Goals
and Commitments Seriously

We've discussed creating a personal mission statement, establishing goals, and investing time in personal development. Now let's focus on why you need to take your commitments, goals, and promises seriously. In other words, why is it important to live with intentionality? Living with intentionality can lead to a transformation in your character and in your life.

Moreover, when enough people live with intentionality, they can change the world. As John C. Maxwell writes, "One person is a start. One person can act and make a change by helping another. One person can inspire a second person to be intentional, and then another. They can become a movement. They can make an impact."[1]

The Pilot and the Flight Plan

I wish I could credit the person who came up with the following metaphor, but I don't know who it was. It involves a plane and a pilot, and it explains why goals are important. A pilot takes off from Dulles International Airport outside Washington, DC, to fly to Los Angeles International Airport. They have a flight plan to follow (a set of goals).

But the plane often gets off track because the pilot flies around storms, avoids turbulence, and gets distracted. Rather than getting upset or anxious, the pilot calmly brings the plane back to the flight plan, eventually landing safely in Los Angeles.

Your goals are like a flight plan keeping you aware of your progress (or lack of it), and eventually landing you where you want to go. Just like that pilot, when you get off course in your life or make a mistake, you review your personal mission statement and your goals and take steps to get your life back on track.

Rocks and Sand

Another useful metaphor, which I first heard from author Stephen R. Covey, involves a pile of sand and a pile of rocks. The sand represents the zillion little unimportant things that can easily fill your week, and the rocks represent the important things you want to do, which are described in your personal mission statement and goals.

Your upcoming week is like a large empty bucket. If you fill the bucket with sand, there's no room for any rocks. To succeed, you must put the rocks in first, before the sand goes in and leaves no room for any rocks.

You may be familiar with the distressing feeling of coming to the end of a hectic, exhausting day and having a baffling sense that you've accomplished little. It's been all sand and no rocks.

During the day, you got caught up in the minutiae of urgent, inessential activities and distractions—meetings, phone calls, email, social media, interruptions—and lost sight of your goals. Working on your rocks can help you avoid the feeling that the day has been squandered.

As you plan your week, put the rocks on your calendar first and block out time for them before the sand fills your schedule. I talk more about "time blocking" in the next chapter.

Planning Weekly

I recommend that you have a regular time once a week (I do it on Sunday evening) when you review your personal mission statement and goals and block off time on your calendar to work on your rocks. Fill your upcoming week with activities and tasks that support your personal mission statement and goals.

The point is to create a daily schedule that reflects your goals. The only way to create the future you want is to constantly work on your goals.

So put your rocks on your calendar first, so they don't get squeezed out by the unimportant grains of sand. For example, if one of your goals is to repair a strained relationship with a colleague, then you might schedule time to meet with that person (perhaps for lunch) someday in the coming week.

Through weekly planning, you are more likely to spend time on the relationships, projects, and goals that matter to you.

Keeping a Time Journal

Every so often, especially if you have a vague feeling of unease about how your life is progressing, it's useful to track your time for two weeks to see how you're actually spending it, compared with how you would like to spend it.

People are often dismayed to discover that they spend large amounts of time on low-priority activities.

Always Think on Paper

It's a challenge to match how you spend your time with your values, goals, and what's important to you. One way to begin to solve this problem is to write things down and not rely on your memory.

Productivity expert Brian Tracy urges people to always think on paper. Work from written lists and not from your mind. Whenever you have a new task, add it to your list. Tracy says this will sharpen your thinking and increase your effectiveness and productivity.[2] Besides, crossing off items one by one as they're completed will motivate you to keep going, give you energy, and elevate your mood.

Plan for Spontaneity

One argument people use against planning and setting goals is that they think it might prevent spontaneity or serendipity. (Serendipity is finding valuable things when you least expect it.) They worry that planning will in some way curtail their freedom and limit their lives.

It isn't always necessary to follow a plan rigidly. A plan is there to keep you headed in the right direction, like a flight plan, not to deprive you of all spontaneity and serendipity.

Setting goals gives you a clear sense of the times when you are focused and in flow and the times when you are taking a break to explore some new idea, get a snack, chat with a friend, go for a swim, enjoy watching a bird, absorb some sunshine, or admire a sunset.

That said, it's true that spontaneity can be a sinkhole. What you thought would be fifteen minutes looking through the latest videos on YouTube can too easily end up being two hours.

When you are deviating from your planned day, make a habit of setting some kind of reminder of time passing so you make a conscious decision to deviate from your plans rather than let time slip away mindlessly.

Focus on the Task in Front of You

Being totally focused on the task in front of you enhances your effectiveness. Multitasking is never a good idea. It's easier to not multitask when you're supported by a personal mission statement and a set of goals.

It's easier to focus 100 percent on the task in front of you when you have an inspiring vision for your life and goals that help you move toward a life that is fulfilling and meaningful for you.

Pay Attention to Your Commitments

Commitments are vitally important, whether they are made to yourself, your work colleagues, your spouse/partner and family members, or your friends.

Productivity expert David Allen, famous for his Getting Things Done philosophy and programs, correctly points out that many people carry around a lot of free-floating, gnawing anxiety because they have open loops (that is, open commitments or unfinished business) that are haunting them and not letting them relax. Allen says they need to process their interactions with others to close those loops.

Allen writes, "It seems that there is an unconscious part of us that hangs onto all of those incomplete creations" and open loops. This unfinished business will haunt you and slow you down until you know you can trust that those promises have been kept or managed.[3]

Whenever you have conversations or communications with others, pay attention to the promises, requests, and offers made on both sides. Make sure you capture and process all the commitments so you know exactly who is to take the next action, what documents must be delivered to whom and when, and who is responsible for what and by when.

A key to being effective, productive, and less anxious is to capture in writing in a safe place everything that needs tracking and follow-up. When you know that all the commitments made by you, your colleagues, and your coworkers have been taken care of, you can relax and turn your attention elsewhere.

Take Your Commitments Seriously

David Brooks built his book *The Second Mountain* around the profound notion of commitments or promises. He asks that we "surrender to a life of commitment" and put commitment making at the center of our lives.

He argues that the best life is marked by meaning, purpose, and moral joy, and that these are achieved when we take our commitments seriously.[4]

Brooks is talking about commitments to our spouses, family, colleagues, neighbors, and community. He writes, "The second mountain is . . . about making commitments, tying oneself down, and giving oneself away."

A commitment, writes Brooks, is different from a contract. A person entering a contract assesses the advantages and disadvantages of the deal but remains essentially the same person. By contrast, when you make a commitment or promise, your character and identity are affected in a deeper way. You are involved in a new relationship, not just a new transaction.

When you make a commitment, you are giving your word and should do everything possible to keep it. Your commitments shape the kind of person you become and the character you develop. Your commitments show how serious you are about achieving your goals.

An honorable, successful life is about caring and giving. Your ability to make and keep promises and commitments reflects your character and how much you care about others. As Brooks notes, "Character emerges from our commitments."

He argues that "if you want to inculcate character in someone else, teach them how to form commitments."[5] You want your life to be defined by commitments you are determined to fulfill.

When you keep your commitments and promises, you become a person who can be trusted and who has integrity. You have integrity when your daily actions are consistent with your personal mission statement and goals and when you are keeping the promises you make to yourself and to others.

Incorporate your commitments (including those relating to personal development) into your weekly schedule. As you do your weekly planning, what commitments do you want to add to your schedule? Select commitments from your personal mission statement and goals and resolve to make significant progress on the tasks, relationships, and projects that matter to you.

Strengthen your self-respect and integrity by making and keeping promises to yourself and others. Making promises that are kept (or, at a minimum, effectively managed) is a characteristic of successful people.

Take all your commitments seriously, however small. When you agree to do something, advises Tracy, do it; do it when you said you would do it and in the way you agreed to do it.

To help you keep your commitments to yourself and others, keep a planner or notebook (or a simple manila folder) containing your personal mission statement, roles and key relationships, goals and commitments, and schedule. Label your notebook or planner "My Life Plan" or some other title that juices you up when you see it.

Share Your Goals

Gail Matthews, a psychology professor at Dominican University, has shown through her research that writing down our goals helps us achieve them and that we have even more success when we share our goals with others.[6] Choose friends or mentors you trust and ask them to review your goals and commitments and provide honest and supportive feedback.

Doing this makes you more accountable and helps you to take your commitments seriously. You won't want to appear flaky, unprofessional, and immature to mentors and friends, so you'll be motivated to carry through on your plans and goals. I write more about finding mentors in chapter 13.

Questions and Actions

Based on the concepts and ideas examined in this chapter, consider the following questions and activities:

- What is an example from your life when you acted spontaneously? How did you feel about it afterward? Was it beneficial? Was it hard to get back on track? If so, how would planning have helped?
- As you go through a typical day in your life, do you pay meticulous attention to the promises, requests, and offers you make to others and that others make to you? How could you do a better job of capturing and processing all the promises and commitments you make and are made to you?
- *New York Times* columnist and author David Brooks argues that the best life is marked by meaning, purpose, and moral joy—and that these are achieved when we take our commitments seriously. Do you take your commitments seriously?
- Why is it important to you that others recognize your trustworthiness and reliability?

- How might you incorporate an important goal into your weekly planning?
- Will you commit to regular weekly planning in which you review your goals and block off time on your calendar to work on your "rocks"? What day and time?

~

PART III

ACT ON YOUR
GOALS AND BE PRODUCTIVE

In part I, we focus on envisioning the future you want for yourself and capturing it in the form of a personal mission statement. In part II, we use your personal mission statement as the basis for creating a plan with specific, actionable goals. In part III, we will work on how to act on your goals and get things done efficiently and effectively.

CHAPTER SEVEN

~

Create an Effective Daily Routine

Successful people manage their lives so they're focused on what matters to them. They're good time managers and well organized.

Successful people don't just have good intentions. They take action to make a difference in their own lives and in the lives of others. Taking action, when coordinated with specific and inspiring goals, leads to a more accomplished, meaningful, and fulfilled life.

Success is the natural consequence of consistently acting in accordance with the values and vision expressed in your personal mission statement and in accordance with your goals.

Pay Attention to Daily Micro Steps

You must take action steps daily toward your goals so that over time you will make major progress. Big change is the result of hundreds of small action steps.

Life depends on the little things and on paying attention to micro steps. Books get written one word at a time. Gardens get created one plant at a time. Homes get built one brick at a time.

Ben Franklin said, "Little strokes fell great oaks."[1] And pastor and author Robert H. Schuller wrote, "Spectacular achievement is always preceded by unspectacular preparation."[2]

Failure in life often results not from one major mistake but from scores of unwise micro decisions we make daily. These small choices accumulate and eventually lead us to assess our lives as failing.

Motivational speaker Jim Rohn said, "Success is nothing more than a few simple disciplines, practiced every day, while failure is simply a few errors in judgment, repeated every day."[3]

You are what you spend your time on. Your life is what you pay attention to. In historian Will Durant's formulation, you'll become what you repeatedly do.[4] From Heraclitus: "Day by day, what you choose, what you think, and what you do is who you become."[5] Author Annie Dillard notes, "How we spend our days is, of course, how we spend our lives."[6]

If every day we work on unimportant things instead of spending time with a loved one, or we eat junk food instead of something healthful, or we binge watch something frivolous instead of reading a challenging book or going for a jog, then all those small, careless actions will lead us away from finding a fulfilling and meaningful life.

It isn't disastrous if you occasionally make an ill-advised choice, but making unwise choices day in and day out inevitability leads to negative long-term consequences and poor life outcomes.

Plan Each Day

Remember that each day is important and shouldn't be wasted. Each day that passes means you have one day less to live. The secret of your future lies hidden in your daily routine. You will not improve your life until you improve something you do daily.

A study by Promotional Products Association International found that only a third of Americans keep a daily schedule, which means most people wake up with no formal plans.[7]

Before you go to bed every night, you should briefly review your goals and plan the next day. Jim Rohn advised, "Never begin the day until it is finished on paper."[8]

Derive what you are committed to do on a daily basis from your goals and personal mission statement rather than from the flood of emails, meetings, social media feeds, interruptions, and requests that tend to distract you from what matters most.

You must focus on what matters most to you in both your professional and personal life. Is there alignment between how you spend your time and what is important to you? Or are you spending time on projects and relationships that in the long run don't matter to you?

When there is congruence between how you spend your time and what matters to you, you increase both your inner sense of peace and your productivity. You feel more fulfilled, more effective, and more successful. Your life will have more meaning.

Doing Something Hard

As we've seen, University of Chicago professor Mihaly Csikszentmihalyi discovered through his research on flow that a fulfilling and successful life can be achieved only by pursuing challenging goals.

Stretching ourselves, applying a high degree of skill, taking on hard tasks and projects, and getting outside our comfort zones, makes us ultimately feel better about ourselves and puts us on the road to success.

By taking on meaningful challenges, we author and sculpt our own lives rather than letting our biology, circumstances, or other people dictate the life we lead. We march to our own drummer.

If you're living well, you'll always be doing something hard. Philosopher and activist Bertrand Russell said, "When striving ceases, so does life."[9] And Nietzsche believed that embracing difficulty is essential for a fulfilling life. He famously asserted, "What does not kill me makes me stronger."[10]

Goethe said, "If you want to make life easy, make it hard."[11] Psychologist Angela Duckworth recommends that everyone should do at least one hard thing every day.[12]

Having a Daily Routine

To take on hard tasks, it's helpful to have an effective daily routine so you spend your time well. You can see my daily routine in my goals document in appendix A. Yours will be different and unique to you, as mine is to me.

In his book *Daily Rituals*, author Mason Currey examines how scores of famous and successful artists, scientists, and philosophers get their work done. He describes the daily routines they use to overcome distractions and procrastination.[13] Their daily routines help them to be creative and productive and to get their work done. Virtually all the successful people Currey describes organize their daily lives according to repetitive, disciplined routines, and this helps them stay in alignment with the vision they have for their lives.

Author Gretchen Rubin says, "Habits are the invisible architecture of everyday life."[14] Annie Dillard writes, "A schedule defends from chaos and whim. It is a net for catching days."[15]

Diligence

I wrote about the importance of diligence and hard work in chapter 5 in the "Mental" section, and I want to emphasize it again here. Rohn argued that results are always in direct proportion to effort. He wrote, "Those who rest in the spring do not reap in the fall, regardless of need and regardless of desire."[16]

The people Currey features in his book *Daily Rituals* are diverse, but it's striking to see how many of them have a strong work ethic. They are conscientious and self-disciplined about imposing daily habits on themselves.

It's impossible to exaggerate the importance of self-discipline and hard work and how they are manifested in our daily rituals and routines. Poet Henry Wadsworth Longfellow wrote: "The heights by great men reached and kept / Were not attained by sudden flight, / But they, while their companions slept, / Were toiling upward in the night."[17]

Time Blocking

The leadership organization Monday.com recommends "time blocking," and I recommend it, too.[18] Time blocking is a scheduling format that helps boost productivity through focused work done in specific blocks of time.

It is the opposite of multitasking. Using this approach, tasks—derived from your personal mission statement and goals—are outlined and slotted for different dates and times.

Time blocking is like the concept we discussed in chapter 6 of putting your "rocks" (your most important projects and relationships) on your calendar at the start of the week.

Time blocking adds clarity, intention, and important boundaries to the day. You work for set "sprints" of fifteen to sixty minutes (or longer) at a time and then take a short break to recharge before picking up work again.

Monday.com argues that the time-blocking approach to scheduling allows you to get away from the defensive approach to work in which you're constantly fielding tasks, emails, and requests as they crop up throughout the day. Instead, time blocking creates a more deliberate and intentional structure for the workday. It enables you to get into flow and "deep work" with minimal distractions. Deep work, according to productivity expert Cal Newport, is when you're focusing without distraction on a cognitively demanding task.[19] Newport has an excellent website on time blocking at timeblockplanner.com.

Time blocking helps you protect your time and your focus. It enables you to guard against distractions, which otherwise can take over your workday and diminish your productivity.

Effective Daily Habits

No specific daily routine is effective for everyone. But there are certain things you can do, such as time blocking, to help make your days more productive, fulfilling, and successful.

Having a routine matched to your goals makes it easier to get started on tasks and stop procrastinating. A daily routine also helps you exert more self-discipline and have more focus.

Getting to your desk at roughly the same time each morning, regardless of your mood or how you feel, stopping for a light lunch at about the same time each day, and so on, can get you into a rhythm that helps you to be productive and to make steady progress toward your goals.

I have found the following eleven daily habits to be useful:

1. *Get exercise every day.* As we discussed in chapter 5, getting your body moving is crucial. Build exercise into your day by using stairs instead of elevators, walking short distances instead of driving, and holding meetings while walking or standing instead of sitting. Research shows that sitting too much causes poor health.[20] I suggest exercising early in the day, before breakfast, so it doesn't get forgotten.

2. *Plan your day.* I've already described how beneficial it is to plan the next day before going to bed. It's a habit that can help you relax, knowing you've captured in writing everything that needs to get done the following day. And as already noted, you should plan your day based on your personal mission statement and your goals.

3. *Make your bed.* This advice comes from Admiral William McRaven, a distinguished Navy Seal. He says that making your bed means you start your day with one task accomplished.[21] This can inspire you to keep going. It gives your day a foundation of conscientiousness and care that helps as you approach other tasks.

4. *Eat the frog before getting into social media and your emails.* This advice comes from Mark Twain, who felt that people should start their day by tackling the most important and strategic (and often most challenging) task first.[22] You may feel obliged to quickly check your email at the start of the day to make sure your boss, child, or another important person in your life isn't trying to reach you. Beyond that, the more you can postpone attending to your email, the better. Email and social media tend to be major distractions that trigger procrastination and drain mental energy. Author Susan Moon writes, "I've made a rule for myself that I mostly keep: no appointments, no

telephone calls, and no email before noon. Mornings are for writing and study."[23] See below for more on how to deal with emails.

5. *Delete useless apps and turn off notifications.* Whenever our phone or laptop emits a beep or a ding, we get distracted from the task at hand, and the more apps we have on our home screens, the more likely we are to get sidetracked. Delete useless or no-longer-used apps and turn off notifications. We'll talk more about screens and social media in chapter 10.

6. *Make productive use of travel and waiting time.* Too many of us squander travel and waiting time. On a plane, train, or bus, make every minute count by preparing for any upcoming presentations or meetings, working on a high priority strategic goal, or reading a substantive book. As I've already noted, always have a book or other reading material with you so that if you suddenly have spare time (for example, while waiting for a colleague to join you for lunch), you can use the time well. Turn your car into a learning machine (i.e., a college on wheels) by playing audio programs that teach skills and knowledge you need to succeed.

7. *Keep meetings short and on schedule.* Almost everyone dislikes meetings because they're tiring, time-consuming, and often an unproductive use of time. Your colleagues will appreciate it if you start meetings on time with a clear, detailed, and worthwhile agenda and finish on time after defining a specific set of actions to be taken by specific people with explicit deadlines.[24]

8. *Eschew multitasking.* As already noted, multitasking is far less productive than doing one thing at a time. There may be a couple of minor exceptions to this rule. For example, it makes sense for me to simultaneously brush my teeth and stand on one leg for exercise. Ditto for when I exercise while listening to podcasts. But what I can't do effectively is answer emails while participating in a meeting. Most of us can only focus cognitively on one thing at a time.[25]

9. *Clear your desk at the end of the day.* If you don't organize your desk at the end of the workday, you'll arrive the next morning to a messy, disorganized work area. Clutter not only looks bad to others, but it's distracting and slows your progress. We'll talk more about clutter and how to be organized in chapter 12.

10. *Meditate.* Meditation is another daily ritual that helps many people to be less stressed and more focused. As mentioned already, I find Sam Harris's mindfulness app, Waking Up, to be helpful.[26] If meditation

isn't appealing to you, then try to find the time to look out of the window at birds or trees or flowers. Connecting to nature can help to calm you.[27]

11. *Stop looking at screens an hour before you go to bed.* Research shows that unplugging an hour before you plan to fall asleep and disconnecting from your phones and screens will help you to get to sleep and to sleep better.[28] As noted in chapter 5, I recommend setting an alarm an hour before your bedtime so you can start to finish up your work and activities. An alarm will help you to take your sleep more seriously.

Time Poverty versus Time Affluence

We must be stewards of our time and husband it carefully. You hear many people talk about how short of time and busy they are. Csikszentmihalyi argues that this complaint often is unfounded and simply reflects that people haven't exercised agency and control over their own lives. He asks,

> How many of the things we do are really necessary? How many of the demands could be reduced if we put some energy into prioritizing, organizing, and streamlining the routines that now fritter away our attention?[29]

If we manage our time well, we can turn "time poverty" (the feeling that we never have enough time to spend on the projects and relationships that matter to us) into "time affluence" (a feeling that we have plenty of time to spend on our highest priorities).

The Best Use of Your Time Right Now (and the 80/20 Rule)

Brian Tracy recommends asking yourself the following question again and again as your day progresses: What's the best use of my time right now? This is a key question if you're interested in improving your productivity.

Discipline yourself to work only on the answer to that question. Remind yourself that the answer is not "refreshing my Facebook newsfeed" or some other time-wasting activity.[30]

Remember, too, the 80/20 rule, which says that 20 percent of the things you do will account for 80 percent of the value of all the things you do. Your job is to identify those few activities that are vitally productive and spend more time on them.

I recently noticed my car was dirty and covered in bird droppings. I wanted to wash it, so I got a bucket, filled it with water, and then in less than five minutes, washed the whole car quickly using a big sponge. It wasn't a perfect job, but then what would be the point of spending another thirty minutes doing a perfect job? That would be a poor investment of my time.

I got 80 percent of the results with 20 percent of the effort. To complete the remaining 20 percent of the job and get perfection (a perfectly clean car) would take 80 percent of the effort and would be highly inefficient.

This is the 80/20 rule or Pareto principle. Voltaire had the same thought when he talked about "the best" being the enemy of "the good."

Use Email Effectively

At the start of each workday, check your email quickly to identify anything that needs an immediate reply. Then put your email and social media feeds aside so that you can select the most important and valuable strategic task you are facing (the aforementioned "frog") and work on that until it's finished.

This will energize you for the whole day and make you feel like a winner. By starting the day tackling your biggest challenge, you'll set yourself up to storm through the rest of the day with self-confidence and enthusiasm.

Try to check email only once or twice a day. Productivity expert Kara Cutruzzula asks, "What's the most efficient way to fill a water glass? Turning the tap one centimeter and letting a slow drip fill it? Of course not. You crank that faucet and let the water flow."[31]

Cutruzzula says that's what "batching emails" feels like. Instead of responding one at a time to the forever trickle of your inbox, email batching—responding to as many as possible during a time you have specified—is more effective.[32] She answers emails twice a day, first around noon and then again at 6 p.m. She says knowing she must get through dozens of important messages makes her replies quick and crisp, and she can also delete the ultimate enemy (junk mail) all at once.

Of course, this idea doesn't work if your job requires you to provide immediate responses, but it's still possible to jump on urgent messages and corral less important ones for later in the day. The point is to somehow make sure you have time during the day to think creatively and do deep work without email or social media interruption.[33]

With so much work conducted virtually, it is important to use email effectively and efficiently. Here are eleven suggestions for how to manage your emails:[34]

1. *Answer in a timely manner.* Each email is different, but it's courteous to respond soon after receiving one (within eight hours and preferably sooner). This shows you care about the person and are taking care of their concerns, whatever they are. Some emails will warrant an immediate response.

2. *Keep your inbox clean.* To maximize efficiency, your inbox should be organized and uncluttered. Don't let hundreds of messages pile up. Attend to messages regularly to avoid being overwhelmed. Delete all unimportant emails and those you have dealt with. Clear your inbox within eight hours or less. Keep emails in your inbox only as a reminder of something important to you. File or archive messages that you might need in the future.

3. *If you find yourself in email—or on Facebook or YouTube—when you weren't planning to be, make a conscious decision to close it and return to your work.* Refer to your to-do list or your plan for the day to recall what you should be doing.

4. *When you do attend to your emails, be focused.* Make the message clear and succinct. Your goal is to respond so effectively that you end, if possible, the exchange of emails. Cover one topic per email and place that topic in the email heading. If it's necessary to touch on more than one topic, make the reader aware of the broader nature of the message by using the subject line "Four issues to discuss," for example.

5. *If you can't respond fully to a significant email, send a quick message acknowledging this so the sender knows you have received it and are working on an answer.* If you're not the right person to handle a question, direct the sender to someone who is.

6. *Include a "calling card" with your telephone number and other contact information at the bottom of all emails.* This will enable recipients to contact you easily via other avenues if needed.

7. *Review your emails before sending them.* Remember that every email represents who you are to the world. Your emails should be free of typos, misspellings, grammatical errors, and other mistakes. Use spell-check if necessary and reread your message before pushing the "Send" button.

8. *Use clear, informal, and personal language.* Don't use exclamation points in professional emails and avoid the passive voice. It's clearer to write, "Fred has made a film about toxics," than, "A film has been made by Fred about toxics." And don't write in all capital letters. It looks like you're yelling.

9. *Always be courteous and professional.* Don't send an email written in anger. Calm down, and then, if possible, talk to the person with whom you're angry. If you cannot talk, try not to be negative or aggressive in the email. Poorly handled emails are likely to come back to haunt you.

10. *Use "Bcc" when sending an email to many people.* Put your own name in the "To" box and the addresses of the recipients in the Bcc section. Your recipients don't want their email addresses sent to strangers.

11. *When saying thank you, don't copy everyone on the email.* Respond just to the person you're thanking.

Email is one of the greatest tools of the digital age. It's easy to use, saves paper, allows you to contact people without creating the potential interruption of a phone call, enables them to respond when it fits their schedules, and produces a written record of your correspondence—something a phone call doesn't do.

But it can also turn into a major time consumer if you don't approach it with awareness of what you're trying to accomplish. The suggestions outlined above will help you make email a powerful tool in your professional and personal repertoire, as well as enhancing your focus and productivity.

Don't Waste Time Stopping and Starting a Task

The most important task (the task that will make the biggest difference to your life and career) will be listed first on your to-do list. Focus on it with energy and concentration. Keep that task, and nothing else, in front of you. Discipline yourself to stay with it until it is complete.

If you break your concentration (for example, to check your email or a social media feed), then you are squandering time because of something Newport calls "attention residue."[35]

Attention residue represents the extent to which a person's attention is only partially focused on a current activity (or task or social interaction) because a prior activity is still holding part of their attention.[36] Every time you stop concentrating on a task, you waste time and lose cognitive focus.

Use Your To-Do List Effectively

Too often in the past, I would arrive home from work exhausted, struggling to recall one thing I had accomplished, dissatisfied because none of my projects had made any progress, and convinced that my day had been wasted despite the frenetic rush of meetings, phone calls, and emails.

Although I had a to-do list, I was making mistakes in using it. For example, I would list too many tasks, the tasks would be nebulous and unrealistic, or they were things that deep down I knew I had no intention of doing.

Here are nine suggestions on how to manage your daily to-do list:[37]

1. *Derive your daily to-do list from your personal mission statement and goals* so that every day you are moving your life in the direction you want to go, not simply reacting to someone else's agenda. See chapter 4 for more on goals.

2. *Write down your daily tasks (i.e., your to-do list).* Don't rely on your memory.

3. *Capture all of your tasks for the day and put them on one to-do list.* This gives you a comprehensive list that includes everything you need to accomplish. Add any new task to the master list. Don't use sticky notes or scraps of paper.

4. *Practice the two-minute rule.* If a new task takes less than two minutes, do it immediately, without adding it to your to-do list.

5. *Draw up your to-do list first thing in the morning, before distractions begin (or, even better, before you go to bed the night before).* Are there any tasks that can be delegated or deleted? Don't procrastinate on important (but perhaps not urgent) jobs critical to your success. Try to give priority to important tasks over urgent (but unimportant) tasks. More on this below.

6. *Make your desired outcomes specific.* Instead of "Contract for Barnes," write, "Review contract for Barnes, especially the deliverables, then send it to Fred in HR." Start each item on your to-do list with an action verb.

7. *Arrange your to-do list items in order of importance.* You can work effectively on only one task at a time. Work on the first task until it's complete, then move on to the second. This allows you to work with total concentration on the task at hand without worrying that you might be forgetting to do something important.

8. *As the day progresses, keep asking yourself*: Of all the items remaining on my to-do list, which one is the most important right now? The answer to that question constitutes the best use of your time. Reorder your priorities as appropriate.

9. *When you complete a task, put a check beside it* or draw a line through it to give yourself a satisfying sense of accomplishment. Brian Tracy says that when you complete a task, you will feel a rush of good feel-

ings—high self-esteem, joy, and optimism. You will feel rewarded for your self-discipline.[38]

Adhering to these guidelines will boost your productivity, help you make steady progress toward your goals, and help you feel more fulfilled.

Leisure-Time Activities

We've been talking mainly about daily routines as they apply to work, but self-discipline and the effective use of time are equally important for non-work, leisure-time projects.

You might argue that after a hard day at work, all you want to do is go home, get a drink, and veg out in front of various screens with a total absence of effort, commitments, schedules, and goals.

You may well have experienced the negative impacts of making this type of choice. As you eventually haul yourself off to bed at night, you feel nothing but lethargy, dismay, torpor, and regret.

Csikszentmihalyi has found that, through "inattention, ignorance, and lack of self-awareness," people often bounce between two extremes: They are stressed, overwhelmed, and anxious from all the professional and family pressures on them, but during their leisure moments, they live in passive boredom doing things like mindlessly watching screens. He wants people to find flow and the joy of complete engagement in all areas of their lives, including their leisure time.[39]

Newport has written perceptively on this topic in his book *Digital Minimalism*. He argues, as does Csikszentmihalyi, that in your free time, you should prioritize demanding activity over passive consumption.[40] I can return home from a long, tiring day and feel too exhausted to do anything. But if my wife and I go out dancing, that fatigue quickly vanishes and is replaced with energy and enthusiasm.

The value you receive from a leisure-time activity is often proportional to the effort and energy you invest in it. Newport's research shows that your vitality and sense of fulfillment will be enhanced by choosing leisure activities that are hard and strenuous and involve cognitive struggle rather than activities that adhere to the more traditional idea of relaxation, such as binging on Netflix, playing video games, watching sports on a screen, drinking for long hours at a bar or pub, surfing the web, or mindlessly swiping and tapping.

Newport distinguishes high- and low-quality leisure activities. High-quality activities include things like carpentry, gardening, playing tennis, playing a musical instrument, drawing, hiking, or spending in-person social time with people.

Low-quality activities include passive pursuits like answering email, checking your social media newsfeed, and watching a screen. It's virtually impossible to live a fulfilled, successful life if you fill your leisure time with low-quality activities. The point is to be intentional and strategic about *every* domain of your life.

Urgent versus Important Actions

Having an effective daily routine requires you to distinguish urgent from important actions and tasks.

Important things—but usually not urgent—include creating a personal mission statement, setting goals, seizing new opportunities, strategizing, anticipating challenges, preparing, preventing crises, learning, and working out ahead of time how to deal with potential problems.

Other important things include reading, writing, taking professional-development courses, helping a struggling child, rehearsing a presentation well ahead of schedule, spending time listening to people who matter to us, getting feedback, and acting on personal development goals.

All of these should be top priorities, but none of them are urgent. They can all be done next week or even next month, but it would be far better not to postpone them.

Time-management expert Roger Merrill points out that many of the things that are important to us—things that contribute to the richness of our lives and give us meaning and purpose—are not urgent. They don't press us for our attention the way a ringing phone, an interruption, or the arrival of a new email does.[41]

Important matters that *are* urgent, such as the unexpected resignation of the CEO of your company, get attended to for obvious reasons. But important matters that lack urgency are easy to ignore or postpone. Putting them aside in this way is a mistake. Nonurgent, important issues should not be neglected or postponed. Successful people spend time on important things, even if those things have no urgency attached to them.

Don't let urgent things displace important things. Having a personal mission statement, a set of goals, and an effective daily routine help prevent this from happening. Unimportant but urgent things should never be given priority over important yet not urgent things.

Keep a Personal Journal

Keeping a personal journal daily will help you become a more skillful observer of yourself and more aware of the identity you create for yourself with other people. If you are unhappy about something or pleased by something you have accomplished, write about it. When you gain an insight, put it on paper.

Keeping a personal journal encourages you to improve, to raise your standards, to live more purposefully, and to observe how much of your behavior is automatic rather than intentional. Keeping a journal helps you to have more agency and autonomy over your life.

One benefit of keeping a journal is that you can become more aware of which activities improve your mood and *joie de vivre* and which are a drain on your sense of fulfillment. What are you doing when you feel in flow, engaged, and energized? What are you doing when you feel restless, bored, irritated?

Expressive writing can be healing. Social psychologist James Pennebaker of the University of Texas has discovered that traumatized people who write about their suffering heal faster than those who keep it all in.

Pennebaker has found that when people write about their experiences, they're not just expressing their fury, frustration, or whatever powerful emotion they were feeling but are actively working to make sense of the experience and create some meaning from it.[42]

Writing gives them insight, understanding, perspective, and new interpretations that lead to better health outcomes. Pennebaker says that sustained and thoughtful writing, whether in a daily journal or in some other form, has been shown to be highly beneficial because it draws order and meaning into our lives. That has certainly been my experience.

Expressing Gratitude

Keeping a journal also gives you the chance to express gratitude on a regular basis. I keep a daily gratitude journal and find it helps me think about and savor all the blessings in my life (to offset my natural tendency to take them for granted and to focus on what might be going wrong).

But there are other ways, beyond keeping a journal, to fill your life with gratitude. Make a list of what you're grateful for and share it with your friends and colleagues. Thank other people when they do something for you. Express gratitude in a sincere way as often as you can.

Don't take for granted little acts of service from others. Instead, notice and express appreciation for them. Extend thanks even for small things, such as the extra effort a hairdresser or waitress puts into their job.

Neuroscientist Christina Karns has conducted research on the link between gratitude and altruism and found that the practice of gratitude makes people "more supportive of others and improves relationships." Expressing gratitude encourages "more optimism, less anxiety and depression, and greater goal attainment."[43]

Throughout the day, observe the things that make your life a pleasure and that you might take for granted, such as a gentle wind, puffy clouds in a blue sky, majestic trees, running water, clean clothes, the love of your family, and living in a democratic society.

Demonstrate gratitude to your family and to other people in your life. Author and political commentator E. J. Dionne Jr. writes,

> A genuine sense of gratitude is rooted in the realization that when I think about all that I am, all that I have, and all that I might have achieved, I cannot claim to have done any of this by myself. None of us is really "self-made." We must all acknowledge the importance of the help, advice, comfort, and loyalty that came from others.[44]

It's important not to take good fortune for granted. We can easily slip into a sense of undeserved and pernicious entitlement. None of us is entitled to anything. We all have a lot to be grateful for. Many of us, including me, lead lives of unearned privilege but are blind to it. We were born with social advantages over others and take them for granted.

Comedian Stephen Colbert's father and two brothers were killed in a plane crash when he was ten. He would never suggest he was grateful for the tragedy, but many decades later, he was able to say in an interview, "It would be ungrateful not to take everything with gratitude. It doesn't mean you want it. I can hold both of those ideas in my head."[45]

Colbert was saying that he approaches every aspect of life with an overall attitude of gratitude. Gratitude equips us to handle failures, disappointments, and setbacks in a more resilient way. As I suggested at the end of chapter 2, perhaps we should be grateful for everything life throws at us, including, paradoxically, even suffering.

Expressing gratitude is one of the most effective ways to generate good feelings and closer connections with others. We must grasp how much we depend on others for the life we lead.

The important thing is not only to *feel* grateful but also to *express* it. When you thank someone, you become socially stronger and better connected.

Dr. Martin Seligman's Gratitude Visit

In his book *Flourish*, psychologist Dr. Martin Seligman describes a brief but powerful exercise called the "gratitude visit," which will do good, increase your well-being, and help you feel more fulfilled.

He says to close your eyes and recall the face of someone still alive who, years ago, did something for you that changed your life but whom you did not properly thank at the time. Perhaps you said a brief thank you, but it was quick, pro forma, and not very thoughtful.[46]

Seligman says to write this person a letter of gratitude. The letter should be specific and concrete, describing what this person did and how it influenced and shaped your life. Speak from the heart. Open up about your feelings of appreciation. Explain how the person you have become was shaped by what that individual said or did for you.

Once you have written the testimonial, call the person and say that you'd like to visit. Then, when you are together, read the letter aloud—slowly, so the person can savor and absorb it. Seligman says a gratitude visit will give you a strong sense of fulfillment and joy.[47]

Take Responsibility

When we make excuses or try to blame others for setbacks or disappointments, we are failing to take responsibility. I have seen this in myself repeatedly.

For example, I remember as a young father coming down for breakfast with my three little daughters, yelling at them to hurry up and get ready for school and causing a lot of unnecessary tension in the family. I was frantically trying to get myself ready for the upcoming day as a struggling wildlife filmmaker.

Then one of my daughters spilled milk all over the floor, and I went nuts blaming her for her carelessness. I know now, in retrospect, that I should have taken responsibility because it was my grumpiness that caused the tension in the room that, in turn, caused little hands to slip and spill the milk.

I've learned that, when things go wrong, it's a mistake to immediately blame others. Instead I need to focus on how I contributed to the breakdown. This is called "taking responsibility." Rather than make excuses or look for someone to blame, I've come to realize a better first step is to ask myself, "What did I do to help bring about this state of affairs?"

As life coach Jeff Durham writes, "In shouldering responsibility ourselves, we are giving ourselves the power to shape the outcome ourselves and are therefore taking an active and not a passive role in how the outcome turns out."[48]

You need to accept that you are responsible for every action you take and every decision you make. The more personal responsibility you take, the more agency you have over your life, and the more likely you will achieve the vision described in your personal mission statement.

Durham writes, "In accepting responsibility, you are accepting a willingness to develop your character and in doing that, the stronger your character will become and your life will be improved as a consequence."[49]

Questions and Actions

Based on the concepts and ideas examined in this chapter, consider the following questions and activities:

- You are about halfway through this book. You may be feeling overwhelmed by the volume of ideas and advice. Does it feel as though you are drinking from a fire hydrant? If so, take a deep breath and look at appendix D ("Fifty Ways to Improve Your Personal and Professional Life, Increase Your Productivity, and Feel Fulfilled"), where you will find a step-by-step guide.
- Motivational speaker Jim Rohn said, "Success is nothing more than a few simple disciplines, practiced every day, while failure is simply a few errors in judgment, repeated every day." Identify some examples in your life where Rohn's observation might apply.
- Robert H. Schuller wrote, "Spectacular achievement is always preceded by unspectacular preparation." What does he mean exactly?
- Do you have a daily routine you like? Does it help you achieve your goals? How can you improve it?
- Do you produce a daily to-do list? Are you satisfied with the way you currently do this? In what ways might you improve and strengthen your use of your daily to-do list?
- Does the distinction between urgent and important tasks make sense to you? How do you feel about unimportant and nonurgent tasks? Should you delete them entirely from your daily activities?

- How many emails are currently unanswered in your inbox? If it is zero or very few, good for you. If it is hundreds, are you okay with this, or do you find it stressful and exhausting? Do you waste a lot of time scanning them again and again? If so, might the suggestions in this chapter help you?
- What is your reaction to the notion that success is tied to doing something hard and challenging?
- I argued in this chapter that in your free time, you should prioritize demanding activity over passive consumption. If you agree, how would you put this into action?
- Professor Cal Newport distinguishes high- and low-quality leisure activities. What are some examples of these two types of activities in your life, and what changes would you like to make in your choices of how to spend your leisure time?
- Could Dr. Martin Seligman's "gratitude visit" idea apply to an experience in your past? What would you hope to gain from making a gratitude visit?
- What do you think of the two-minute rule? (If a new task takes less than two minutes, do it immediately, without adding it to your to-do list.)
- How do you feel about the advice in this chapter on using travel time productively?

CHAPTER EIGHT

Take New Actions Relentlessly

To achieve success in any field, you must relentlessly take new actions. Your enthusiasm can energize you to take action, but taking action can also increase your enthusiasm.

Many of us are stuck in "inaction" because of fear or some other emotional barrier. Overcoming fear and reluctance and taking action can change our mood from resignation to resolve.

Taking action, even if it is only calling a friend for advice or visiting a website, gets you out into the world where good fortune is more likely to happen. The more diligent people are, the more luck they seem to have.

Taking Action Gives You Feedback

Taking action is also an effective way to obtain feedback on a goal. Hurdles and stumbling blocks are often revealed that may not have been apparent when you established your goal.

Taking action will enable you to sharpen the goal further, clarify the next steps, and identify where you'll need help from others.

Have a Bias for Action

Highly productive people are action oriented and continually taking new initiatives. They have a bias for action. They are constantly taking fresh steps to get tasks done and move toward their goals.

During the Civil War, Abraham Lincoln was frustrated with Union general George McClellan because he wouldn't fight. Lincoln complained that McClellan was too passive and had the "slows."

Don't have the slows. Be action oriented. Seize opportunities quickly. Make requests, promises, and offers frequently. Take the initiative. As productivity expert Brian Tracy says, the faster you move, the better you'll feel.[1]

Use your time efficiently. Develop a reputation for speed and reliability. Take important phone calls immediately. Respond quickly to requests from people with whom you have important relationships (your spouse or partner, your kids, your key colleagues). Move with alacrity.

People don't take action on their goals for three main reasons. First, they are afraid of failing. Second, they have a fixed mindset instead of a growth mindset. And third, they don't exhibit sufficient grit.

Let's explore these three reasons in more detail.

Fear of Failure

We sometimes don't take action because we're afraid to fail. But failure, viewed properly, is an opportunity for learning. Failure is not about our weaknesses, unworthiness, or powerlessness.

When you take on exciting and daunting challenges, it's only to be expected that you won't succeed every time.

Ed Land, the founder of Polaroid, said, "Failure is an event, the full benefit of which has not yet been turned to your advantage."[2] Author Louisa May Alcott said, "I am not afraid of storms, for I am learning how to sail my ship."[3]

It's important to respond well to failure. Be positive. Don't give up. Viewing mistakes, setbacks, and failures as opportunities to learn and grow takes the humiliation out of failing.

Paradoxically, setbacks are to be welcomed, not feared. Through failure, the brain is growing new connections through brain plasticity and is getting smarter.

Failing at something does not mean that you yourself are a failure. Mistakes are a normal part of life. An important life skill is the ability to take risks in a scary world and not be afraid of setbacks.

To fail means that you're trying hard, taking risks, and getting out of your comfort zone—all are important precursors to success.

Too often, schools and parents neglect to teach real-world lessons like these. We need to commend children when they take risks and fail. In her book *The Gift of Failure: How the Best Parents Learn to Let Go So Their Chil-*

dren Can Succeed, Jessica Lahey describes the chance for kids to experience failure as the "opportunity to solve their own problems."[4]

She encourages parents to embrace their children's setbacks along with their successes. She advises them to explain to their children that failure is how a person learns and gets better at something. Lahey says parents should respond in a positive way to failure and demonstrate to their children the value of doing so.

Children need to experience disappointments, setbacks, and failures so they will acquire the ability to be strong, resilient adults in the real world. Psychologist Leonard Sax writes,

> The humility born of failure can build growth and wisdom and an openness to new things in a way that success almost never does.[5]

In pursuing your goals, be bold, try new things, take on challenges, and be a persevering risk taker, knowing that failure is part of the learning process and an inevitable occurrence.

Growth Mindsets

Another reason we don't take action is that we don't have the right mindset. Stanford professor Carol Dweck created the notion of "mindset" and wrote the book *Mindset: The New Psychology of Success*.[6] She draws an important distinction between a "fixed" mindset and a "growth" mindset:

- A "fixed" mindset assumes such basic qualities as intelligence and talent are fixed attributes and can't be changed. People with a fixed mindset tend to stop trying if they don't do well at something because they believe nothing will fundamentally change. They avoid challenges, fearing that they won't look smart.
- In contrast, says Dweck, a "growth" mindset assumes that basic qualities such as intelligence and talent are malleable and can be improved and developed through hard work, smart strategies, and coaching. People with a growth mindset are willing to take risks and wrestle with challenging tasks in a persistent and tenacious way. Such people are not discouraged by mistakes they make but see them as learning opportunities. They are inspired, not intimidated, by smart people and try to emulate them. They know that the more they challenge themselves, the smarter they will become. They value learning more than looking smart. They know that they can strengthen their intelligence by working hard.

Dweck's research shows that it's possible to encourage children and students to have a growth mindset if parents and teachers don't praise ability, talent, or intelligence.

It's far better to praise *the effort* a child makes and her strategies or choices. Praising the process the child used and the diligence she applied will motivate her to persevere—and ultimately better herself.

When a child does well on a test, parents and teachers should say, "You must have worked really hard," rather than, "You must be really smart." Praise effort, not intelligence. Dweck says the ability to learn challenging material comes from the belief that you can.

As a child grapples with difficulties at school, parents should do more than coax her to keep trying. Help her to break a challenge down to smaller, less intimidating components and think through the best strategies and resources for moving forward.

The brain is like a muscle: The more it's used, the stronger it gets. Educator Salman Khan of Khan Academy says, "The brain grows by getting questions wrong, not right."[7] By learning new things, embracing challenges, and being tenacious, a person exercises their brain and makes it more powerful.

Intentional engagement and effort lead to higher intelligence and cognitive ability. There's no limit to what we can achieve if we apply ourselves. Dweck and other scientists are learning that people have more capacity for brain development and lifelong learning than they realize.

The growth mindset is characterized by effort, persistence, a willingness to ask for help, and a deep conviction you can and will get better, more skilled, and smarter. People who have a growth mindset want to be challenged, they want to learn, and they are destined to live successful and meaningful lives.

Grit

The third reason we don't take action is that we lack grit, a virtue like perseverance, drive, endurance, determination, resolve, and fortitude. Angela Duckworth, professor of psychology at the University of Pennsylvania, developed insights on grit that resonate with Dweck's research findings. In her book *Grit: The Power of Passion and Perseverance*, Duckworth shows that grit can be fostered and encouraged.[8] She argues that success has more to do with grit than with intelligence or IQ.

Duckworth's research shows that successful people—whom she defines as those who have overcome disappointments and setbacks to stay focused for a lengthy period on achieving a worthwhile and important goal—have certain traits in common.

All the successful people she studied had specific and highly challenging long-term goals. They persevered through extraordinary challenges and did not give up. And they were driven by a vision and by goals that gave their lives meaning and purpose.

Author Caroline Adams Miller has built on Duckworth's work and uses the term "authentic grit" to mean the "passionate pursuit of hard goals that awes and inspires others to become better people, flourish emotionally, take positive risks, and live their best lives."[9] For Miller, grit isn't a positive unless it is a force for good and creates a valuable legacy.

What are some characteristics of people who lack grit? They may attach more value to status and wealth than to purpose and meaning. They may feel entitled, privileged, and self-satisfied and be unable to absorb constructive criticism and feedback. They may be fragile and quickly quit projects or activities when faced with setbacks and challenges. They may shun hard work. They may be unable to exert prolonged self-discipline to fulfill a commitment, preferring instead the instant gratification of, for example, vegging out in front of a TV.

Duckworth has argued that underachievement in students is often wrongly blamed on poverty, boring textbooks, and large classes. But her research shows that a major reason for students falling short is their failure to exercise self-discipline and grit. They are unwilling to sacrifice short-term pleasure for long-term gain, and they give up too easily when the answer to a problem doesn't come to mind quickly.[10]

To raise kids who have grit, Duckworth encourages parents to pursue what she calls the "Hard Thing Rule." Everyone in the family, including parents, chooses one difficult thing to practice on a regular basis, such as yoga, a foreign language, long-distance running, or playing the violin.

Since all family members make a commitment, they motivate and support each other. Children with grit are willing to practice and are determined to work hard. They learn to believe in themselves, have a sense of purpose, and are not deterred by obstacles.

Scientists such as Dweck and Duckworth believe that grit is a more reliable predictor of success in life than IQ, talent, good looks, health, connections, education, and charm because grit builds character and, as I wrote at the start of this book, success is fundamentally about character development.

Questions and Actions

Based on the concepts and ideas examined in this chapter, consider the following questions and activities:

- Does having a bias for action strike you as a good idea? Why is it advantageous to take initiative?
- Failure is inevitable, and it is critical to know how to bounce back from setbacks and disappointments. How have you recovered from failure in the past?
- Do you have a growth or fixed mindset? Why? What could you do to develop a stronger growth mindset?
- Describe a time in your life when you demonstrated grit—or perhaps failed to demonstrate grit. What did you learn from the experience?

~

CHAPTER NINE

Learn to Say No

The previous chapter stressed the importance of taking action, but there's no point in taking action if it moves your life in the wrong direction. Sometimes the most effective action is to use the word *no*.

Identifying activities in your life that are not important to you (or no longer important to you) and then eliminating them is key to improving your productivity and success.

Learning from Warren Buffett

Billionaire Warren Buffett, the chairman and CEO of Berkshire Hathaway, is nearly ninety and widely admired for being successful. He once said, "The difference between successful people and really successful people is that really successful people say no to almost everything."[1]

On another occasion, he said, "You've gotta keep control of your time and you can't unless you say no. You can't let people set your agenda in life."[2] Buffett says no repeatedly to the unimportant demands that flood his day. This allows him to stay focused on the things that matter to him.

If you don't prioritize your life, other people will. Poet Carl Sandburg wrote, "Time is the coin of your life. It is the only coin you have, and only you can determine how it will be spent. Be careful lest you let other people spend it for you."[3]

If you think that protecting time is selfish, remember how much more giving and loving you can be when you are healthy, rested, and engaged in things that mean a lot to you.

Seven Things Successful People Say No To

Author and leadership expert Marcel Schwantes writes in the magazine *Inc.* that there are seven things successful people like Warren Buffett say no to on a regular basis:[4]

1. They say no to opportunities and things that don't excite them, speak to their values, or further their mission in life.
2. They say no to superficial networking events in which people swap business cards and then rarely hear from one another. (You will learn how to network effectively in chapter 13.)
3. They say no to spending time with uninspiring, critical, or negative people who drag them down. Instead, they spend time with people who energize them and challenge them to be their best.
4. They say no to overworking and workaholism because they don't neglect personal development, self-care, or their loved ones. As we discussed in chapter 5, successful people recognize that if they don't take care of themselves, everything else in their life will suffer.
5. They say no to doing all the work. They delegate as much as they can to others.
6. They say no to giving the steering wheel of their life to anyone else. They exercise agency over their own lives and don't let others set their agenda.
7. They say no to people-pleasing. Successful people don't neglect their deepest wishes to accommodate and yield to the wishes of others.[5]

Saying no to a new commitment honors your existing commitments and allows you to successfully fulfill them. Being overwhelmed, stressed, and exhausted—which is what happens when you don't say no to new requests—makes it much harder for you to meet your existing commitments.

Essentialism

Leadership expert Greg McKeown, in his book *Essentialism: The Disciplined Pursuit of Less*, writes:

> The modern fixation with multitasking and having it all has paradoxically resulted in accomplished, motivated people doing many relatively unimportant things poorly while neglecting their true goals because they are afraid of refusing any request.[6]

McKeown describes "essentialism" as an "approach that emphasizes finding a true, limited set of goals, defining them clearly, setting everything else aside, and not taking on additional responsibilities."[7]

The key, as we discussed in chapter 7, is to distinguish the important from the unimportant and then intentionally ignore the unimportant.

Don't Be a Flake

It's unhealthy to say yes to everything and work yourself frantic trying to meet all the obligations you've taken on. But what's even worse is to say yes, knowing full well that you can't possibly meet the obligation.

That makes you an unreliable flake—and being unreliable is a sure way to destroy trust and damage relationships.

You're a flake if you don't deliver on your promises—if you don't show up when you said you would, or turn up way past the time you agreed to, or fail to fulfill promises and plans that you had committed to.

You want to be one of those people who can be trusted to keep their word and do what they promise to do. Agree only to things you will actually do and do on time. One of the keys to this is learning to say no.

If you tend to be a flake, author Rae Witte recommends you examine *why* you say yes to things you have no intention of following through on. Is it poor time management? Do you have crippling social anxiety? Do you hate disappointing people? Do you just find it hard to say no to people?[8]

Most of us are not flakes. We are simply stressed, overscheduled, and burned out, with no time for thinking, deep work, and solitude.

We must learn to say no when asked to do something so we can limit the number of commitments on our to-do list and maintain some semblance of sanity in our lives.

Only Work on What Matters to You

Saying no can sometimes be hard to do because we're afraid of disappointing people or annoying them. Often, we want to be helpful, even if it means our health and serenity are jeopardized.

Author Elizabeth Scott writes, "Whether you say yes instead of no out of guilt, inner conflict, or a misguided notion that you can 'do it all,' learning to say no to more requests can be one of the biggest favors you can do yourself and those you love."[9]

Even if you have the personal resources to say yes to a request, the most important question to ask yourself is whether, by saying yes, you're going to be working on something that matters to you.

If the answer is no, then say something honest but sensitive, such as "I'm sorry, I'd love to help but my schedule is already packed."

If you're not sure whether to say yes or no, don't get pressured into saying yes. Instead, ask if you can take a day to think about it. This gives you the opportunity to review your existing commitments, as well as your schedule and level of stress, and based on these factors determine whether to say yes or no.

You may want to get back to the person making the request with a counteroffer. Perhaps, for example, you can't do exactly what the person wants, but you're willing to do something less onerous and disruptive to your schedule.

Don't Feel Defensive or Guilty

When you say no to someone, don't feel guilty or defensive. Scott suggests being firm, polite, and clear. You don't have to make excuses or be overly apologetic.

Remember, your time is limited. There are only twenty-four hours in a day. Whatever you commit to limits your ability to do other things. Even if you *can* fit a new commitment into your schedule, if it's not more important than what you would have to sacrifice (including time for personal development), you really *don't* have the time in your schedule.

We say yes to many requests, not out of enthusiasm but because we want to be helpful and supportive to others, and we don't want to disappoint them. Collaboration and cooperation are powerful ways to build relationships with others, but if commitments cause us to become overwhelmed and burned out, then saying yes too much can ultimately damage those relationships.

If you're committing to things that are inconsistent with your personal mission statement and goals, you need to find a way to get back on track, starting with graciously saying no.

Work Hard and Endure

The unwelcome truth is that sometimes you can't say no. For example, in the mid-1980s, executive coach and nonprofit leader Grant Thompson had just taken over as executive director of the League of Women Voters. He was also chair of the board of Sidwell Friends School in Washington, DC.

His plate was full to overflowing, but Thompson was committed to both responsibilities and found them energizing and highly meaningful.

Suddenly two events beyond his control occurred. He was presented with a petition to unionize the employees at the League of Women Voters, and Sidwell Friends School started its first-ever capital campaign.

Thompson couldn't duck either of those obligations because each filled an important dimension of his life. So he persevered and did the best he could, even though he was overwhelmed.

Sometimes saying no is not possible. When that happens, you simply must grit your teeth, work hard, and endure.

Questions and Actions

Based on the concepts and ideas examined in this chapter, consider the following questions and activities:

- What can you stop doing to free up time for things that are important to you?
- Have you encountered flakes in your life—people who don't keep their promises? If so, how has it impacted you?
- Your time is a vital asset, and if you don't guard it carefully, other people will happily take it from you. Describe situations in your life when this has happened—or when you kept it from happening.
- What types of things are you currently saying yes to that should be a no?

CHAPTER TEN

~

Be Choosy about Technology and Social Media

One of the barriers to achieving a meaningful and successful life is the abundance of screens and social media. This chapter unpacks this topic, distinguishing the value of interactive technology from the peril of allowing it to control our lives.

Technology Has Benefits

All of us need to be digitally competent. Much of the work of daily life happens on the internet, so familiarity and comfort with being online is essential.

Many areas of the internet are positive and helpful. It's an extraordinary source of information, education, entertainment, and communications. Podcasts, blogs, and video conferencing can be invaluable.

Online resources provide a healthy and needed community for diverse interest groups. For example, consider people who struggle with gender identity or who have unusual hobbies. They can find support and camaraderie online.

Technology Has a Dark Side

We must be savvy and alert. The online environment includes malicious misinformation, harmful deepfakes, and vicious trolls. It has become a frightening instrument of war, crime, personal intrusion, cruelty, and loss of privacy.

We need to know how to stay safe, and how to distinguish what is real and legitimate from what is fake and malevolent.

The early promise of the internet as an astonishing tool for self-expression, promoting democratic values, and bringing the world closer together has largely fallen flat.[1]

Tech Companies

Tech companies—the companies that are behind social media sites like Facebook and Twitter—have a powerful influence on our emotional, social, and mental development and hence on our success in life and the meaning we find in it. They are spending billions of dollars to attract our attention and time.[2]

The people who run these companies have become some of the world's richest and most influential superstars, "with the power to shift global politics and curate the information diets of billions."[3]

The narrative offered by tech companies about smart phones, social media, and the proliferation of screens is that they improve and enrich our lives by building community and encouraging communication.

For example, Mark Zuckerberg's reformulation in 2017 of Facebook's mission statement says that the company aims to "give people the power to build community and bring the world closer together."[4]

But that impressive and stirring mission statement doesn't reflect what is happening in the real world.

Tristan Harris and the Greed of Tech Companies

Tristan Harris is a Google engineer who became a whistleblower. In a TED talk (seen by more than 2.5 million people), Harris shares how tech companies prey on us psychologically and hijack our attention for their own profit.[5] He wants to make the tech companies behave more ethically and "less like greedy tobacco companies."[6]

Harris argues that tech companies such as Facebook, Twitter, Instagram, Google, and YouTube have been caught in a zero-sum race for our finite time. They must use increasingly persuasive techniques, including artificial intelligence, to grab our attention because they need our attention to make money.

Unfortunately, says Harris, what is best for capturing our attention is not the best for our health and well-being or for our long-term fulfillment and success.

Harris left Google in 2016 and founded the nonprofit Time Well Spent, aimed at fostering more ethical tech-company practices. His goal is to bring attention to unhealthy practices and systems, including the following:

- *YouTube* auto plays the next perfect video, even if it eats into our sleep.
- *Facebook* segregates us into echo chambers, fragmenting our communities.
- *Snapchat* turns conversations into "streaks," redefining how teenagers measure friendship.
- *Instagram* glorifies the picture-perfect life, eroding our self-worth.

All of this is part of a system, argues Harris, that is designed to addict us. He says the desperate race to get our attention is eroding the foundations of our society:

- *Democracy*: Social media rewards outrage, false facts, and deepfake videos because they are good at grabbing our attention. As a consequence, we can no longer agree on what is the truth, and our society has become polarized.
- *Mental health*: The race to keep us glued to our screens 24/7 makes it harder to disconnect. This increases stress, fosters anxiety, and reduces sleep.
- *Social relationships*: We have come to prefer virtual interactions and rewards on screens (such as "likes" and "shares") over face-to-face communication.
- *Our children*: Children are led to replace a healthy sense of self-worth with judgmental likes, insidious comparison with others, and the constant illusion of inadequacy and missing out.

People for centuries have worried that new media technologies will harm society, but Harris points to four dangerous new developments that are different from anything we've faced before:

- *Artificial intelligence*: No earlier media employed incredibly powerful supercomputers to predict—a myriad of steps ahead of our minds—what they could show to keep us glued to the screen.
- *24/7 influence*: No other media steered the thoughts and attention of two billion people from the moment they wake up in the morning until they fall asleep at night.

- *Social control*: No other media redefined the terms of our social lives: self-esteem, when we believe we are missing out on something, and the perception that others agree with us.
- *Personalization*: No other media used a precise, personalized profile of everything we've said, shared, clicked, and watched to influence our behavior at this scale.

Harris describes companies such as YouTube, Facebook, Snapchat, and Twitter as "attention-extraction" companies. He says we cannot rely on these companies to make improvements as this would reduce their revenue.

He concludes that we need to take control of our own lives, moving away from technology that harms society and toward technology that "protects our minds and replenishes society."

Harris issues a clarion call for a cultural awakening that will alert consumers to the problem so they'll demand products that don't harm them or their children.[7]

Digital Minimalism

One cultural awakening that is getting traction is digital minimalism. An astute thinker in this field is Cal Newport from Georgetown University. His book *Digital Minimalism* is about the art of knowing how much personal technology and social media use is just enough to be helpful without causing us to lose focus and attention in our tech-deluged society.[8] Newport defines *digital minimalism* as

> a philosophy of technology use in which you focus your online time on a small number of carefully selected and optimized activities that strongly support things you value, and then happily miss out on everything else.[9]

Digital minimalists start by being clear about their values and goals. Only then do they decide how to live their digital and non-digital lives. The way they use their screens clearly supports their values and goals. They are committed to being highly intentional in the ways they engage with new technologies.

Digital minimalists take deliberate steps to make sure tech companies don't undermine their quest to become the best possible version of themselves. They consciously choose what they pay attention to and avoid being seduced by distracting digital candy on their phones. Author and U.S. senator Ben Sasse writes,

If the ancient Greeks were to anthropomorphize social media as a deity, it would come as the temptress Immediacy. Not nature, patience, or generosity. Not oath, duty, or character. Not service, empathy, or love of neighbor. And definitely not wisdom, self-control, or deferred gratification. Only NOW! Immediacy.[10]

Digital minimalists reject the "temptress Immediacy" and prioritize finding long-term meaning over short-term gratification.

Connections versus Relationships

Newport argues that technology is inherently neither good nor bad. The key, he says, is to use it to support your goals and mission in life rather than letting technology use you.

Tech companies have given us more connection but weakened our real relationships. They've given us loneliness and isolation while flooding us with information. We're less compassionate, less humane, less tolerant, less satisfied, and more aggressive, even while we've become more "connected."[11]

We must become more mindful and intentional about our use of tech-company services. And we need to devote less time to social media. Our lives should be driven by more important things than addictions we've been sucked into.

How to Allocate Limited Time

Even if the internet and social media had no dark side, the fact remains that our attention and time are limited. For the most part, we can only do one thing at a time. To use Mihalyi Csikszentmihalyi's term, our *psychic energy* for experiencing the world is limited.[12]

One of the most important decisions we'll make in our lives is how to invest or allocate our time.[13] Watching screens, following social media, and responding to emails take up a significant amount of our time.

This is a problem because these activities are largely unproductive, and many of them are passive and addictive. They don't particularly challenge us or ask much from us in the way of high-level skills.

Most of the time we're awake, multiple screens are competing for our attention. It's hard to focus on what really matters to us.

Even assuming you've sorted out and decided what your priorities are and what you want to do with your life, it isn't easy to stay focused on your goals when you're distracted by addictive social media like Instagram and Twitter.

You are especially vulnerable to the siren song of screens if you have no plan for your life (that is, no personal mission statement and goals).

How you spend your time and how you choose to allocate your attention will determine your success in life and how fulfilled you feel. As author Nir Eyal points out, our most precious resource—our time—is unguarded and vulnerable, just waiting to be stolen and taken from us.[14]

Breaking Free

As Newport makes clear, many of us have become addicted to our devices. Few of us want to spend so much time online or staring at screens, but these shiny coins suck us into what Newport calls *behavioral addictions*.

Glancing at our smart phones—even when talking with good friends—for fear we may miss something is not only exhausting but damages our ability to hear what those friends are saying. Newport writes,

> The urge to check Twitter or refresh Reddit becomes a nervous twitch that shatters uninterrupted time into shards too small to support the presence necessary for an intentional life.[15]

We must spend less time online and more time focused on the projects and relationships we care deeply about and that are described in our personal mission statements and goals.

In *Digital Minimalism*, Newport gives many examples of digital minimalists who experience major improvements in their lives by reducing their time spent online, focusing instead on a small number of high-value activities.

Being "Indistractable"

Social media as well as other distractions—television, gossip, excessive online shopping—discourage and impede us from achieving our goals. Distractions take us away from what gives our lives meaning and purpose.[16]

Our ubiquitous smartphones interfere with our ability to remain focused on a task. Simply hearing an alert or feeling a vibration is distracting. As soon as you engage with the phone, perhaps to answer a call, your attention can wander to other digital activities, such as answering email or engaging with social media.

Icons, bright colors, and catchy tunes heighten the attraction of digital activities and enhance their ability to draw you away from other tasks.

Research at Harvard University has shown that social media cues, such as "likes" on one of our posts or pictures of our friends laughing, trigger a surge in dopamine, the neurotransmitter associated with pleasure and reward. This may diminish the motivation to pay attention to anything else.[17]

According to a 2018 survey by the technology company Asurion, Americans check their mobile phones an average of eighty times a day, and the range went up to an astonishing three hundred daily checks. But each time we interrupt what we're doing to check our phones, we break our concentration and must start over.[18]

In his book *Indistractable*, Eyal writes, "In this day and age, if you are not equipped to manage distractions, your brain will be manipulated by time-wasting diversions." He adds,

> In the future, there will be two kinds of people in the world: those who let their attention and lives be controlled and coerced by others, and those who proudly call themselves "indistractable."[19]

If we are grappling with a challenging problem, it's natural for us to be triggered into distraction and for our attention to be drawn away from pursuing our goal. We find instant gratification highly tempting.

Eyal, however, points out that the issue is more complex than simply blaming social media and online technology. We ourselves must take responsibility for becoming distracted.

Being indistractable means striving to keep your promises and to do what you say you will do by controlling your attention. Without focus and attention, it's hard to be creative, to achieve your goals, and to find meaning and success. Goethe wrote, "If I know how you spend your time, then I know what might become of you."[20]

Social Media's Bermuda Triangle

Many researchers worry about the possible psychological harm from exposure to social media.[21]

The minimalists Joshua Fields Millburn and Ryan Nicodemus write in their book *Essential: Essays by The Minimalists* that we can get stuck in social media's "Bermuda Triangle," careening from Facebook to Instagram to Snapchat, lost in the meaningless glow of our screens.[22]

They point out that we can "incessantly check email, thumb through an endless stream of status updates, post vapid selfies, or partake in any other number of non-value-adding activities." And they ask, "Is it truly worth your time to obsess over feuding YouTube stars, or whatever is trending on Twitter or Tik Tok?"[23]

But, like Cal Newport and Tristan Harris, Millburn and Nicodemus warn against avoiding the tools of technology that offer possibilities to enrich and better the world. We can use our smartphones to photograph gorgeous landscapes, message loved ones, map out directions to a national park, or to make phone call where we can have actual conversations instead of just collecting likes and other meaningless connections.

We can use Twitter and Pinterest and YouTube to improve our lives and the lives of others and to communicate and share in ways never before available. How can we enjoy the benefits of social media but avoid the dark side? Millburn and Nicodemus underscore that tech tools can be used to harm and damage or to enrich and create. How we use them is up to us.

FOMO versus JOMO

Our media feeds are flooded with snapshots of exciting and seemingly perfect events—the carefully curated moments in our friends' lives. It's stressful, but inevitable, to compare these highs with the conflicts, tedium, banality, and other unglamorous realities in our own lives.

Feelings of self-doubt, inadequacy, and disappointment drag us down rather than move us forward. We need to be energized and motivated to progress toward our goals.

Social media brings pernicious social comparison and fear of missing out (FOMO) into clear focus. FOMO refers to the feeling or perception that others are having more fun, living better lives, or experiencing better things than you are. FOMO involves a deep sense of envy, combined with a sense of helplessness that you are missing out on something big.

The truth is that you're rarely missing out on anything online, but by always being online, you're missing out on life. All the really good things in life get crowded out by addiction to screens.

Some psychologists wisely advocate the joy of missing out (JOMO), the antithesis of FOMO.[24] JOMO means you follow your own drummer, not someone else's, and do your own thing.

We should design our lives to be congruent with our values and goals and depend less on the approval of others.

JOMO is about disconnecting, opting out, and being okay exactly where you are—and spending your time and energy working toward meaningful goals.

Putting Values and Goals in Charge

Having goals and a personal mission statement—an articulated vision for your life that clarifies your values—puts your highest aspirations in charge of your daily life. Goals help you prioritize your search for meaning and purpose over unimportant distractions and pleasures.

We must monitor our digital diet as we would monitor our food diet. Mindless scrolling is the equivalent of eating junk food. Even worse is getting sucked into the poisonous dark corners of social media that can lead to anxiety, stress, confusion, trauma, and despair.

According to Professor James Lang, research suggests that one powerful way to limit distractions in college classes is to set strong goals.[25] We can apply that insight more generally. If you want to shut out distractions, use your personal mission statement to help you articulate inspiring goals so you can more easily pursue things that matter to you.

The more powerful and inspiring the goals you establish, and the more ownership you feel over them, the more you can get done in the face of distraction.

Video Games, Though Addictive, Can Be Beneficial

I want to end this chapter on a positive note relating to video games. I've felt instinctively hostile toward video games for decades but having read researcher Jane McGonigal's book *SuperBetter: The Power of Living Gamefully*, I've come to realize that gamification (including progressively increasing challenges, awarding points or rewards, and adding surprises) can be a potentially useful tool in our quest to be our best selves.[26]

In *SuperBettter*, McGonigal writes, "Playing games is not a waste of time to feel guilty about. It's a skillful, purposeful activity that gives you direct control over your thoughts and feelings."[27]

McGonigal argues that being gameful means applying the strengths and skills you develop during game play to real-life goals and challenges. However, she says that not every gamer is successful in transferring "gameful strengths" to daily life. The biggest obstacle is having an escapist mindset in which the gamer's motivation in playing is to avoid or forget about real life.

McGonigal says that the solution is to play with purpose and to identify the positive effects of playing games (such as increased cognitive skills, stronger relationship skills, the ability to focus, or the experience of positive emotions) and seek them out every time you play. Then look for opportunities to use those strengths, skills, and experiences in everyday life.[28]

The bottom line is that while some video games are alarmingly violent and should be avoided, others could offer benefits, if used the right way.

Questions and Actions

Based on the concepts and ideas examined in this chapter, consider the following questions and activities:

- Was there anything in this chapter that changed your mind about something?
- What are your most frequent distractions? How can you be less distracted and more focused?
- What habits would you like to develop to improve your relationship with social media?
- What do you see as the more pernicious influences of social media in your life?
- During the 2020–2021 pandemic, we relied on social media and apps like Zoom to connect with people. How did social distancing and an expanded reliance on technology make it more challenging for some people to break their addiction to screens?
- Gamer and researcher Jane McGonigal argues that being gameful means bringing the strengths and skills you develop during game play to real-life goals and challenges. How could you put this into effect in your life?
- Monitor your phone usage for a day. Do you glance at the phone a lot? Check for messages? Play games? Look at news bulletins as they come in? How does your phone use affect your work, in-person interactions, or other aspects of your daily life?
- JOMO (joy of missing out) is about disconnecting, opting out, and being okay without comparing yourself to what is on social media. How would you go about shifting toward JOMO in your life?

~

CHAPTER ELEVEN

Be a Successful Parent in Challenging Times

The personal mission statement of every parent surely includes a commitment to be effective, competent, and caring. Most parents are determined to provide a loving environment for their children, teach them well, and set them up for success as they grow into adulthood.

But parents today face more challenges than ever in large part due to the vast influence of interactive technology, screens, and social media.

During the 2020–2021 pandemic, the massive increase in home schooling and online learning increased children's screen time. By some measures, screen time during the pandemic jumped 50 percent overall.[1]

This chapter zeroes in on the problems that today's families may encounter and how parents can overcome them to succeed. We'll cover technology, bullying, our toxic culture, and pornography.

Don't Become a Marginalized Parent

Parents are being edged aside by their kids' screen and social media preoccupations and obsessions. Children's peer-driven and technology-driven lives are making parents feel marginalized.

Instagram, Snapchat, TikTok, YouTube, Facebook, Twitter, and texting encourage children to attach more strongly to their peers than to their parents. Exacerbating the situation is the fact that, in many families, both parents work full time. Kids are on their own more and rely on their peers at a much earlier age than in previous generations.

Digital devices have become co-parents, often supplying children with questionable values and role models. Children need a close, loving, and sympathetic connection with their parents, and they need their parents' attention.

Parents need to be more authoritative (meaning roughly midway between permissive and authoritarian), assert themselves strongly in their children's lives, and form a stronger attachment and be closer to their kids.

In 2015, Common Sense Media, an organization that studies and rates media and technology for kids and families, released a study showing that media use by children is extraordinarily high.[2] Tweens (ages 8 to 12) use an average of *six hours* of entertainment media per day, and teens (ages 13 to 18) use an average of *nine hours* per day. These numbers exclude time spent using media for school or homework.

Don't Become a Distracted Parent

But it's a two-way street. Parents who are glued to their screens marginalize their children, too.

Smart phones have become convenient time fillers. Every time you look at your phone at the store or in the park, you're telling your children that you need to be constantly distracted, and that your phone is more important than they are.

Clinical psychologist Dr. Catherine Steiner-Adair writes in her book *The Big Disconnect* that kids are upset by their parents' screen obsessions. They feel neglected and sidelined when parents are constantly focused on their digital devices. She states,

> We read so much about kids tuning out and living online, but that's only half the problem. More worrisome to me are the ways in which parents are checking out of family time, disappearing themselves, and offering that behavior as a model for their children.[3]

Steiner-Adair says that kids, even those who are obsessed with their iPhones and laptops, complain that "their parents are virtually missing in action, routinely either engaged in cell phone conversation and texting or basking in the glow of the computer screen with work or online pastimes."[4] She adds, "Parents' chronic distraction can have deep and lasting effects on their children."[5] Along the same lines, pediatrician Jane Scott writes,

> The undivided attention that children need from us is in jeopardy. Most people just don't realize how much time they're spending online; what feels like a few minutes is often a half hour or more. When we are with our children, we

need to be with our children—not with them except for the part of us that's reading emails, tweeting, and checking Facebook.[6]

Accepting Media Time, with Limits

Children can easily get addicted to screens and social media. Parents have a responsibility to do more than just monitor what their kids are watching.

They should reduce the time they and their kids spend on cell phones, TV, computers, tablets, video games, and so on so that they can spend more time bonding as a family, reading books, playing outside, engaging in imaginative play, being creative, and socializing face-to-face (post-pandemic) with friends.

Setting screen time and technology limits and boundaries for our children is not easy, partly because parents themselves constantly use electronic devices, and partly because the widespread use of digital technology is relatively new. Parents are dealing with a situation without established standards because no previous generation faced it.

While the ubiquity of technology is new, setting limits and enforcing them consistently and compassionately is something responsible parents have done for generations. But the challenge has been elevated. In his book *Simplicity Parenting*, consultant and trainer Kim John Payne writes, "Our responsibility as gatekeepers is becoming exponentially more difficult even as it's becoming more critical."[7]

Being Conscientious Gatekeepers

Being conscientious gatekeepers is what effective, loving parents do, even if their kids respond with anger, defiance, profanities, or meltdowns.

For example, responsible parents don't allow their children to attend sleepovers where inappropriately violent movies or video games are viewed. Decades of research on graphic violence in movies and video games suggests exposure can foster fear and desensitization.[8]

Setting and enforcing such boundaries is easier said than done because your children might become isolated within friend groups or even mocked. No parent wants that. But good parents are decisive, firm, and strong. They avoid negotiations. There is nothing wrong in having kids experience disappointment because of parents acting in their long-term best interest.

Technology Hijacks Brains

Parenting expert and therapist Meghan Leahy writes,

> Rational and kind boundaries [allow] parents . . . to provide safety. We want to help our children mature into a place where they can better handle their emotional and physical lives. . . . *It's important for parents to remember that technology hijacks brains.* Period. That makes technology boundaries tough to uphold, but even more important to create and keep.[9] (italics added)

You must boldly and unhesitatingly to say to your children, "I love you too much to let you watch a movie (or play a video game, or whatever) that will hurt or harm you."

The report from Common Sense Media concludes that constant attention to devices is making it difficult for kids to have face-to-face conversations or learn empathy.[10] This makes it hard for them to succeed in life.

Multitasking

The report also concludes that excessive use of screens and mobile devices has led to multitasking that children's brains cannot handle. A high percentage of teens admit that they text, use social media, and watch television while doing homework

This hampers their ability to learn how to think and act with patience and perseverance, and it impedes their ability to do deep work. It's difficult to concentrate on a challenging task without getting distracted, especially by social media. Cal Newport reports,

> The more you use social media in the way it's designed to be used—persistently throughout your waking hours—the more your brain learns to crave a quick hit of stimulus at the slightest hint of boredom.[11]

Twelve Guidelines

Interactive technology is here to stay, so here are twelve guidelines for managing it as responsible parents:

1. *Talk with your children about what they're watching and playing.* Teach them to be savvy media consumers by watching their favorite movies and playing video games with them and discussing them, listening respectfully to their views. If you see a video, photo, or post that

is beautiful and inspiring, share it with your children. Gaming as a family, especially engaging in collaborative games where players are required to work together in teams to win, can be fun, while also offering the opportunity for a family to bond.

2. *Monitor what your children are watching and playing and limit screen time.* The American Academy of Pediatrics (AAP) recommends that parents monitor their kids' media diet to help them make wise media choices. AAP recommends (as of May 2018) severely limiting screen time, including television, computers, and video games, for kids age five and under. And for kids six and older, AAP recommends setting consistent limits on screen time, setting limits on types of media, and making sure screen use does not interfere with your children's exercise and sleep. Using screens beyond the AAP-recommended limits encourages behavior problems, sleep problems, diminished school performance, and overeating (because of all the sugary food ads).[12]

3. *Have firm ground rules and boundaries.* Boundaries are important and must be enforced consistently, rigorously, and with kindness. For example, no devices at family dinners, for the first hour after school, and for the last hour before bedtime. No texting after 9 p.m.

4. *Never turn on the TV to provide background noise.* It's better for parents and children to watch specific and agreed-upon shows, and to watch TV together, so that parents can look for teachable moments.

5. *Keep in mind the character and personality of your children.* Sensitive kids can be traumatized by brutal screen violence and need to be appropriately sheltered.

6. *Protect your children.* Kids are at increased risk on social media. Parents have a duty to protect them. You should have full access, with the children's knowledge, to everything they are doing online, and spot check often.

7. *Set a good example and obey the family ground rules.* For example, don't text when driving, at family dinners, or when talking with your children.

8. *Buy high-quality media for your family.* Make them age appropriate by using an established and respected rating system (for example, the one on the Common Sense Media website).[13]

9. *Reach out to experts for help if you need it.* If a child is faltering in school, failing in relationships, or becoming harmed by excessive use of screens and devices, contact the child's doctor or the child's school for help.

10. *Help your children understand the detrimental effects of multitasking.* As mentioned above, children need to learn the importance of focusing on one task at a time. Multitasking—such as texting while doing homework—undercuts a child's capacity for sustained concentration and deep work.

11. *Alert your children to the fact that everything they post online is potentially viewable.* Posts are likely to be open for everyone to see eventually, including malevolent peers, malicious strangers, and curious future employers.

12. *Create family activities with your children.* They need to know that they are your highest priority. Family activities are a valuable substitute for excessive screen time. AAP says that kids need to spend time playing outdoors, reading, pursuing hobbies, and using their imaginations in free play.[14] Family time should be centered on these activities.

Playing Online Games

As I've already suggested, playing online video games may not be all bad for children. As Jane McGonigal makes clear, a love of games can be a strength, not a weakness. (See chapter 10 for more on McGonigal's insights into the benefits of gaming.)

If you have children who love playing, don't make the mistake I once did of assuming that they are wasting their time and heading for trouble. Instead, be open to the strengths they may be developing, such as determination, online research skills, quick thinking, and team leadership.

The War on Childhood

Payne argues that the busyness, stress, and clutter of children's lives, exacerbated by the dominating presence of violence and brutality on screens, are leading kids to have what looks like post-traumatic stress disorder (PTSD).

To Payne, too many kids are fragile, defiant, easily upset, ill at ease, disruptive, fearful, disrespectful, unruly, sullen, and uncooperative.[15] He contends that adult life is flooding unchecked into kids' lives and that the "sanctity of childhood" has been breached. Children are suffering from an "undisclosed war on childhood," Payne says. He urges parents to erect "filters to prevent a child's world from being deluged with adult information, pressures, and concerns."[16]

Similarly, author and psychologist Mary Pipher argued in her 1996 book *The Shelter of Each Other* that, because of TV and other digital devices, children were no longer being socialized by their parents and that technology was destroying families.

She made the case that home life was being displaced by electronics, and that kids were being bombarded by TV and the internet to such an extent that they were being taught to be "self-centered, impulsive, and addicted." They were losing their social skills, exhibiting bad manners, becoming materialistic, and showing low emotional intelligence.[17]

The problems facing families have worsened since Pipher wrote her book in 1996 because of the proliferation of screens.

If parents, who are invariably stressed and exhausted, don't have the time or willingness to teach their children values, the media in which kids are marinating will do it for them—and the results will not be what parents want.

Bullying

You have a major role to play in preventing the bullying of and by your kids. Every year, millions of children are victimized by bullies at school. According to the U.S. Department of Health and Human Services, up to one in five kids is bullied and about the same number admit to bullying.[18] Sadly, bullying is common in school from kindergarten to twelfth grade.

Bullying can be highly damaging to your children. It can adversely affect their ability to succeed in school. What's more, a 2016 study in the *Journal of the American Medical Association* revealed that the effects of being bullied by peers as a child or adolescent are direct, toxic, and enduring. When they reach adulthood, victims were more likely to suffer from anxiety, depression, and feeling unsafe in public places (agoraphobia).[19]

Bullying can be physical (e.g., hitting, punching, and shoving), emotional (e.g., stalking, harassing, and shunning), or verbal (e.g., name calling, hurtful teasing, spreading lies, and gossip). These three types obviously overlap.

Implement the following six ideas to help your children be prepared and strong in the face of bullying:

1. *Teach your children what bullying is and that intentionally aggressive behavior toward another person is wrong.* Teach them the Golden Rule, to treat others as they would like to be treated. Explain the value of empathy. Children who have empathy and emotional intelligence are more likely to speak out against bullying than be bullies, passive bystanders, or victims. Empathy is one of the key markers for finding meaning and success in life.

2. *Model good behavior yourself.* Don't gossip, mock people, be harsh to others, deliberately hurt others, encourage cliques, or try to intimidate other people.

3. *Don't shield your children from difficult and challenging situations.* Shielding them can make them vulnerable to bullies. Instead, let them experience how to deal with difficult people and situations. Overcoming tough challenges helps children learn to be strong, resilient, and self-confident.

4. *Develop good communications with your children.* Talk to them every day about what's going on in school, what went well, and what went wrong. Look for signs they may be bullied. Are they afraid to attend school? Have they become aggressive? Do they appear anxious?

5. *Teach your children what to do if they are bullied or observe bullying.* They should alert the teacher and seek the teacher's advice and guidance. Let your children know that they are not powerless. They have control over how they react and respond to the bully.

6. *Share stories from others (such as friends, siblings, and neighbors) about how they dealt with bullying and what worked for them.* Real-life examples can drive home lessons about techniques for dealing with difficult situations.

Cyberbullying

The internet has worsened bullying by introducing the ugly and abhorrent phenomenon of cyberbullying—bullying that uses electronic media to send intimidating, harassing, or threatening messages, often anonymously. Studies show that one in three teenagers has been a victim of cyberbullying.[20]

Cyberbullying is harder to deal with than traditional bullying for the following reasons:

1. Victims often have no idea who their tormentors are, and it can be hard to determine who is doing the bullying.

2. Cyberbullies often feel anonymous and therefore unrestrained and free to be vicious and hurtful.

3. Victims can never get away from the cruel messages, even after they get home from school.

4. The inability to escape from cyberbullies means the damage and stress felt by victims can be more severe.

5. Usually large numbers of people know about the attacks, and this can lead to profound feelings of embarrassment and hopelessness.

Cyberbullying expert Sherri Gordon writes that the "consequences of bullying and shaming are often unseen online. For this reason, people fail to see they are doing anything wrong online when they hurt other people."[21]

Here are four things you can do to help your children deal with cyberbullying:

1. *Be alert to potential warning signs (such as lower grades or avoiding school activities) that might indicate your child is being cyberbullied.* Such indicators may surface even if the embarrassed victim says nothing.
2. *Talk to your child about what's happening and who may be behind it.* Let your child know it's not their fault and that you'll support and help them.
3. *Document the attack.* Print out or take a screenshot of all the cruel messages so you and your child can show them to school administrators or to lawyers if legal action becomes necessary.
4. *Assist your child in blocking the cyberbully on the phone, email, and social media pages.* Talk to your cell phone provider to find out if it has any tools parents can use to help in this kind of fraught situation (for example, blocking messages from specific senders).

Countering a Toxic Culture

Bullying in its various poisonous incarnations can be a major challenge to you in your mission to help your children flourish. But it's really part of a much bigger problem. Children today are being brought up in a toxic, violent, and sexualized culture.

In 1987, social issues advocate Tipper Gore wrote *Raising PG Kids in an X-Rated Society*, a book about how graphic violence and explicit sex was being fed to children by an immoral entertainment media industry eager to make money at the expense of vulnerable children.[22]

Gore was particularly incensed about how the industry, showing no self-restraint, was glamorizing explicit images of violence and sex to younger and younger kids. Like Payne, she argued that children deserve "vigilant protection from the excesses of adult society."[23]

Unfortunately, the excesses have gotten far worse since Gore's book was published more than thirty years ago. That's because of the relentless invasion of screens into every aspect of our lives and because films and other media have become more graphic and brutal.

A 2013 report from the AAP found that violence in films has more than doubled since 1950, and gun violence in PG-13 films has more than tripled since Gore's book was published.[24] Onscreen violence has also become scarily realistic.

Media violence and graphic sex affect kids in every aspect of their lives, including in the classroom. They distract kids when in school, causing fear and anxiety that hinder their ability to focus and learn and to grow into confident and caring members of society.[25]

The following are four steps you can take to protect your children from inappropriate material:

1. *Watch out for misleading ratings, also known as "ratings creep."* What once might have received an R rating might now get a PG-13 or even a PG rating. That doesn't mean it's going to be suitable for children. Check out Common Sense Media's age ratings as well as its detailed information on the violence and explicit sexual content in a movie or television show.[26] If you're not sure about a particular movie or TV show, watch it yourself before allowing your children to do so.
2. *If your children seem troubled about something, ask if a friend has shared a scary video, movie, or video game.* You may need to talk to the friend's parents or help your children find new friends.
3. *Teach your children about the importance of resisting peer pressure.* The craving to see an inappropriate program or play a violent video game is likely to be because friends are doing so. That's hard to combat, but be firm. Good parents are resolute and authoritative. Parenting expert Dr. Leonard Sax writes in *The Collapse of Parenting*, "It's tough to be a parent in a culture that constantly undermines parental authority."[27]
4. *Look for movies and other media that have positive messages and that can build character.* Again, Common Sense Media and similar sites can help.[28]

Sexual Content and Pornography in the Media

In 1994, Pipher wrote in *Reviving Ophelia*, "The way the media have dehumanized sex and fostered violence should be a topic of a national debate."[29] The need for such a debate has become even more obvious today, when popular culture, exacerbated by an explosion of screens, has worsened and become toxic.

Children today are exposed to massive amounts of sexualized content through advertisements, reality television, movies, music videos, the internet, social media, and video games. Sexually suggestive material encourages sexualized talk and behavior, none of which helps people to succeed and find meaning in life.

When your children reach the age of about ten, you must begin to move from a posture of banning material to explaining why it's harmful. Teaching must replace censorship as your children grow up. Eventually, the education you provide and the judgment you instill in your children must take over.

Pornography deserves special mention because kids are seeing it at shockingly young ages.[30] In her book *American Girls: Social Media and the Secret Lives of Teenagers*, Nancy Jo Sales writes that children are being exposed increasingly to online pornography. And much of the sexual content they see contains violence "in which men dominate and control women, insult them, and sometimes hurt them physically."[31]

Sociologist Gail Dines reports that a 2010 meta-analysis of several studies found an "overall significant positive association between pornography use and attitudes supporting violence against women."[32]

Pornography is an abysmal and inappropriate guide to how the sexes should relate, yet people are growing up marinating in joyless, loveless Pornhub videos. Young people use online pornography as their primary source of sex education. Pornography is becoming the de facto sex educator for them.[33] It has a pernicious effect on boys, girls, and LGBT youth.

Parents must equip their children to deal with sexism, sexual harassment, and sexual abuse. Having the capability and confidence to say no—and the understanding that "no" means "no"—is a vital skill for kids (and grown-ups) to have.

Don't Take a Laissez-Faire Attitude

It's not good enough for you to be passive about your children's exposure to media. Children today routinely access online adult material, attend adult concerts, and watch adult TV programs that glamorize violence, drug use, consumerism, depravity, and promiscuity. You must protect your children from this material and the harm it causes.

Psychotherapist Amy Morin says that media, including movies, glamorize smoking and drugs, normalize violence, glorify casual sex, and romanticize alcohol.[34] It's up to you, as a parent, to protect your children from these damaging influences.

To be a successful parent, you must teach your children to be media savvy and aware that harmful and unhealthy messages can come from movies, TV shows, magazines, online videos, social media, and video games.[35] And you must set a good example by being media savvy yourself.

Questions and Actions

Based on the concepts and ideas examined in this chapter, consider the following questions:

- What are your parenting goals?
- What do your children do online, and how much time do they spend engaged in social media?
- Do you have rules about when you and your children can use devices? Do you enforce them?
- How has social media affected relationships in your family?
- What can you do to instill empathy in your children? How might this change their attitudes to bullying, sexism, racism, misogyny, or other problems that they or their peers might encounter?
- How would you describe yourself as a role model for your children? How might you improve the example you set for them?

〜

CHAPTER TWELVE

Be Organized and Live Simply

Organized space isn't a luxury. It's a necessity if you want to make the most of your life. In this chapter, we focus on the importance of keeping your environment clutter free and organized and the benefits of a less acquisitive lifestyle.

Decluttering and Being Organized

It's frustrating and draining to live in chaos. Getting organized is an energizing, freeing experience. If you're disorganized, you'll find it hard to flourish. Achieving your goals will be difficult because you'll constantly feel stressed, overwhelmed, and distracted by the mess and clutter engulfing you.

You'll find it hard to focus on your top priorities. You'll spend far too long looking for things you can't find. You'll be embarrassed when visitors see how cluttered and chaotic your home and office are.

You'll also find it challenging to keep the place clean, and the problem will keep getting worse because when you get new things, you'll leave them in piles on the floor.

Clutter is an overabundance of possessions that cumulatively create a chaotic environment. Such surroundings negatively affect our well-being and our sense of being in charge of the life we want to lead.

Clutter represents dysfunction—an endless and exhausting to-do list and a future filled with tedious chores. Nonessential possessions drain our bank account, sap our energy, and weaken our attention. They undermine our desire to live in congruence with our values and goals.

When you're organized, your office, desk, kitchen, schedule, and to-do list all work effectively for you as you pursue your goals. Your files, drawers, cabinets, closets, and so on are organized so they enable you to be efficient and successful in becoming the best possible version of yourself.

Decluttering and being organized release deep reservoirs of creative energy. And you have immediate access to the papers and tools you need to do your work effectively.

People who claim they work better from a messy desk are fooling themselves. Studies show that it's best to work from a clean desk and clean workspace.[1] Psychologist Seth Gillihan writes,

> Clutter fills our visual fields and gives our brains endless stimuli to process. As a result, it's harder to focus on tasks, as there are more things to draw our attention. In contrast, tidy spaces let our brains relax, increasing our mental space and concentration.[2]

Don't confuse being organized with being neat or tidy, although that might be a side benefit. Nor is being organized simply getting rid of useless things that fill up the spaces around you.

Getting organized is fundamentally about creating an environment that reflects your character, your values, and what matters to you. It's about expressing yourself effectively and efficiently.

Getting Organized

According to expert and author Julie Morgenstern, the secret to getting organized is "to organize from the inside out."[3] That means creating a system based on your values, goals, and what's important to you.

It doesn't mean buying a few containers and throwing things in them to give the appearance of less mess. That would be organizing from the outside in. Morgenstern says the best way to get organized is, *first*, to determine why you want to get organized. *Second*, to work out what's causing you to be disorganized. *Third*, to create a plan of action to get organized and to transform the look of where you live and work. *And finally*, to take action to clear the clutter, throw junk away, and put what remains in the right place.

The first step: Determine why you want to get organized. The reasons can vary but will likely include some of the following:

- You want to reduce the time you spend looking for things you can't find.
- You want to spend more time on the most important things in your life.
- You want more space for new and important projects.
- You want a calmer and more peaceful environment with less stress and frustration.
- You want to set a better example for your children.
- You want to have a better sense of control and agency over your life.
- You want to make better use of your life.

The second step: Figure out what's causing you to be disorganized. Sometimes the cause is that items have no home (no set place where they are always kept and can always be found). Every item should have a consistent home.

Disorganization can also be caused by having too much stuff and insufficient storage space for it. Or you might have taken on too many projects, have conflicting priorities, or have unfocused goals.

Here's why Morgenstern's organizing "from the inside out" is so important. I urge you to revisit your goals to check that they are in alignment with what really matters to you. It's so easy to get distracted and forget what we really care about. How you're organized should be governed by your goals—those things that make you feel fulfilled and successful and give your life meaning.

The third step: Develop a plan of action. You can dive right into the clutter and disorganization enveloping your life, but it's wiser to come up with an action plan first. What room will you start in? When in the coming week can you schedule time to devote to getting organized? Can you break the job down into smaller subtasks so that you can focus on one at a time and not feel overwhelmed?

The fourth step: Take action and start getting organized. Tidying expert Marie Kondo's book *The Life-Changing Magic of Tidying Up* is helpful, especially her advice to ask a key question when decluttering. She suggests holding up each item and asking, "Does it bring me joy?"[4]

At one level, this might seem silly, but I've found it helpful and you might, too. If not, simply hold up each item and ask, "Do I really need this?" Keep the item only if the answer is yes.

Staying Organized

One way to stay organized is to put everything away at the end of the day. If you don't do this, clutter will quickly return. Ideally the only document left on your desk will be your to-do list for the following day.

Another helpful idea is to handle each piece of paper only once. Don't pick it up and then put it down aimlessly on your desk. Instead, either act on it, refer it to someone else, throw it out, or file it.

One thing I do to organize my study is to draw a map of the space, including all the shelves, cabinets, and closet space. I give every location or space (on average about six to twelve inches) a number. In my study, I have more than seventy "spaces." I think strategically about where things should go, which projects I want near me, and which ones can be farther away and not so easily reachable.

Then I list under each number exactly what's there, so if I'm searching for something, I can simply bring up the "map" document on my laptop, press CTRL-F, and search for it. For example, recently I gave a speech on wildlife filmmaking and was searching for humor. I went to my map and searched for "humor." Up came six locations in my study where I can find jokes and stories.

Getting Things Done

For a deeper look into being organized, I highly recommend the work of author and productivity expert David Allen (see chapter 6). He has written several books on how to be more effective, including *Getting Things Done* and *Making It All Work*.[5]

Allen's goal is to remove stress and anxiety from people's lives, both at work and at home, so they can devote themselves wholeheartedly to pursuing the goals that matter to them. He says that the core to being productive is to "be more creative, strategic, innovative, and simply more present with whatever you're doing."

Allen's Getting Things Done (GTD) method consists of five basic steps: *capture, clarify, organize, reflect,* and *engage.* Capturing means to make a list of everything that is pestering you for attention, thereby getting it out of your head and holding it in a trusted place where you know you can retrieve it. Everything must be inventoried and noted for processing. Open loops, loose ends, and uncompleted promises that stay in your head clutter up your mind and cause stress.

Once you capture all those open loops (i.e., unfinished tasks and projects) in a written list, you can assess them objectively and decide if you're focused on the right things—the things that are consistent with your personal mission statement and goals.

The second step is to clarify what each item in the captured list means. What's the outcome you want? What's the next physical action you should take on it and when? Next-action thinking reduces each new commitment to a series of specific, actionable, concrete steps. Breaking down what we want or need to do into physical actions is the key, Allen says, to getting things done.

The third step is to organize your list of items. For example, put reminders on your calendar for when things must be done. The fourth step is to reflect. This means ruminating on your to-do list and breaking it down into subtasks you either do yourself or delegate. Finally, you engage and take action on what you've listed.

Being organized and having a clear workspace is important, says Allen, because to tackle a challenge or task most productively, you must have the space available to work and spread the tools you need in front of you.

You need an empty head, too, so that you're not distracted by unfinished business. This is why when you're not doing anything else, you should be cleaning up, getting your inboxes emptied, putting your desk in order and cleaned off, and putting things away.

Allen's guidance is based on what he calls "radical commonsense." Inventory all your commitments and open loops—anything that has your attention. Decide the outcomes you want. Decide the next physical, visible actions required to move toward the outcomes you seek. Place reminders of all your commitments, however small, in trusted places that you know you'll check at the right time. Appreciate the value of clear space. Take action and get engaged.

Minimalism and Decluttering

Decluttering and minimalism overlap. Decluttering is removing no-longer-needed items from a room or a space. Minimalism not only removes clutter but also challenges us to discover how little we actually need.

According to minimalist advocate and author Joshua Becker, minimalism is the intentional promotion of the things we most value and the removal of anything that distracts us from it.[6]

It requires an exercise of intentionality because it's a lifestyle choice that contrasts vividly with the conspicuous consumption that typically surrounds us.

Minimalism is not an end in itself but rather a tool to create space and time for what really matters. As we've shown in earlier chapters, what matters ultimately is not money, fame, or possessions but having goals and values that you care deeply about and that give your life meaning.

Minimalism isn't easy to pursue because relentless advertising campaigns tempt us to acquire more and more things that clutter our homes, our offices, and our lives. Marketers and advertisers work diligently to convince us their products are essential for our happiness.

Minimalism is about reducing the number of your possessions until you get to the best possible level for you. It's about owning exactly what you need and no more. Most of us sacrifice energy, time, and money as we accumulate things we don't really need.

These excess things that clutter our lives and distract us may provide temporary pleasure when we first acquire them, but over time they contribute nothing more than stress and deprive us of focus and time.

One of my favorite aspects of decluttering is the space it frees up. Empty bookshelves, space on a desk, space in a closet, and an empty cabinet drawer—all are redolent of new possibilities. Empty space increases your ability to take on new and exciting projects.

Consumerism and Materialism

Our society is afflicted with an excessive preoccupation with consumer goods and luxuries and a sense of need to buy them. But success in life is not measured by how much we consume or acquire. Consumerism does not make life worthwhile.

If you can afford to buy lavish cars, opulent houses, and designer clothes, then you can make more of an impact in life and gain more fulfillment by *not* buying them, living less extravagantly, and donating the money you save to a cause you care about.

Moreover, accumulating excess physical possessions, as we've already discussed, adds stress to your life, takes up space, and brings the demands of maintenance and care.

A meaningful life is not to be found in acquiring as much stuff as possible. Limiting our material aspirations has benefits for ourselves in terms of finding fulfillment, as well as benefits for the environment and the world.

I spent thirty-five years of my professional life producing wildlife films full of jaw-dropping images of bears, wolves, whales, and other amazing creatures.[7] My films did a good job of showing the wonders of nature, but not such a good job of revealing how much damage people are doing to the earth through hyper-consumerism.

Our need to own and possess things has led to deforestation, over-extraction of minerals, waste of natural resources, climate threats, and pollution. Most of us simply own too much stuff—and it's mostly stuff we don't need.[8]

Does Constant Growth Mean Progress?

As already noted, the benefits of living frugally and with less conspicuous consumption accrue beyond one's own life. Since the Industrial Revolution, writes economist David Pilling,

> the whole world has been locked into the idea that one has to grow—either to catch up or to stay ahead or simply to keep in motion the mechanisms of capitalism that depend on endless expansion.[9]

We all tend to strive to earn more disposable income to spend on the goods and services we think will make us happier. Pilling writes, "Turning the planet's resources . . . into things we can consume is pretty much our definition of progress."[10]

The success of our economy is based on constant growth and expansion. We're socially programmed to want more: more money, a better job, a more impressive title, more power, a fancier car, a grander house.

Even those of us who want something done about the threat of global warming find ourselves caught up in a never-ending endeavor to earn more money to spend on the goods and services we have been taught will make us feel happy.

But author and activist George Monbiot asserts,

> Were the poor to live like the rich, and the rich to live like the oligarchs, we would destroy everything. The continued pursuit of wealth, in a world that has enough already (albeit very poorly distributed), is a formula for mass destitution.[11]

Monbiot and Pilling are both arguing that progress, as we currently define it, is not sustainable. We are devouring resources that future generations need and depend on. Endless growth, driven by relentless and ubiquitous advertising, will ruin the planet. Monbiot writes,

> In a society bombarded by advertising and driven by the growth imperative, pleasure is reduced to hedonism and hedonism is reduced to consumption. We use consumption as a cure for boredom, to fill the void that an affectless, grasping, atomised culture creates, to brighten the grey world we have created.[12]

We need to redefine growth and progress away from a focus on maximizing wealth. We need to attach more importance to healthier lives, fewer pandemics, clean air and water, low crime, less bigotry and racism, reduced climate disruption, less inequality, reduced loss of wildlife and biodiversity, more volunteer work and public service, fewer divorces, fewer traffic jams, less onerous commuting, and stronger communities.

Challenging Marketing Messages

It's hard not to be materialistic when we see advertisements everywhere. Corporations even reach out with advertisements directly to children, hoping they will pester their parents to buy them things they don't really need.

In her book *The Shelter of Each Other*, Mary Pipher describes the not-so-hidden messages in advertisements. They include the idea that buying things is important; the concept that "I want what I want now and I am the center of the universe"; the sense that "I am unhappy with what I have now"; and the suggestion that material things will bring happiness. Pipher says these messages help to create an ugly sense of entitlement.[13]

Each of us is exposed to more than three thousand marketing messages every day.[14] We accept this onslaught too passively. We should challenge these messages, be more conscious of their impact, and realize the companies behind them are trying to get our money, not improve our lives. Entire industries depend on our being mindless buyers.

We should do our best to resist the traditional lures of possessions and focus on the goals that bring meaning to our lives. Ben Franklin once told his mother that he preferred his epitaph to be "He died usefully" rather than "He died rich."[15]

Questions and Actions

Based on the concepts and ideas examined in this chapter, consider the following questions and activities:

- Is your desk messy? If so, in what ways does this help or hinder you?
- I wrote, "If you are disorganized, you'll find it hard to flourish." Identify the distractions and frustrations disorganization and clutter cause you. How would you tackle the problem? How would a reduction in clutter help you?
- Draw up map of your workspace. Plan what should go where.
- Do you have too many possessions? What will you do to change that? Can you show that your life is more than your possessions?
- Monitor for a day the marketing and advertisements to which you're exposed. How many of them did you notice? And how many inserted their message into your mind more insidiously? How can you push back?

- In what ways can you try to attach less importance to materialism, acquisitions, and consumerism?
- What would you consider doing to put more emphasis in your life on service and experiences rather than on material goods?

CHAPTER THIRTEEN

~

Network and Find Mentors

Networking is a key skill for those determined to live a full and meaningful life and to become their best selves. And those fortunate enough to find a mentor, either through networking or some other way, have found a person committed to helping them find purpose and success.

Networking

Networking means reaching out to people who can help you meet your goals. Making new friends and nurturing professional relationships can bring you fresh ideas, useful information, and new opportunities.

Effective networking starts with your character. Effective networkers are authentic, unselfish, generous, and honest. The goal is to develop and maintain a reputation as a thoroughly decent person that other people want to work with.

Networking is about building relationships and trust. It is a process of opening doors and getting on the radar of people who might be able to help you.

Treat everyone with respect and courtesy, including those less powerful than you—perhaps *especially* those less powerful than you because that's a test of character. It's easy to be respectful and courteous to people who have more power than you.

Become a resource for other people and help others make useful contacts and network. Although social media sites such as LinkedIn might help you make initial connections, face-to-face conversations are what truly build relationships.

Events and Receptions

Events and receptions are good places at which to network. They give you the chance to meet people who have similar interests and who might be able to help you.

If possible, review the names of the people attending the event or reception before arriving. Identify people who are likely to have relevant insights, ideas, information, and career opportunities to share. Go out of your way to meet them. Ask them specific questions.

You may not often have the opportunity to connect with these people, so make sure you get the most out of these events. Here's how:

1. *Think about your goals before you arrive at the event.* Generate specific goals for a networking event by asking yourself: What are my desired outcomes? Do I want to: Find work? Learn about a specific company? Find a specific kind of job? Find a summer internship? Extend my network of contacts? Gain insight into my career choices? Find career inspiration? Meet people in the industry and get their business cards? Give out my résumé? Sell an idea? Get advice and help? Meet a key person? Be as specific as possible and create a set of goals in writing.

2. *Create a printed business card with your contact information.* If possible, bring printed business cards to any networking event you attend. In addition to your contact information (name, phone number, email address, and website if you have one), add a few words (about your profession, skills, or interests) that will remind the card's recipient who you are. This increases the chance that when he sees your card when he empties his pockets later, he will remember who you are and follow up in some positive way.

3. *Go out of your way to meet people.* Physically move around and work the room. Don't get stuck talking to one person just to be polite. When you're ready to move on, say, "I enjoyed meeting you and learning about your work. I hope to run into you again later." Then shake hands (or touch elbows) and move on. It's likely the other person is ready to move on when you are.

4. *Reach out to people in a warm and sincere way.* Show genuine interest in everyone you meet. Go out of your way to introduce new friends to old friends. Put in a good word for others.

5. *Be curious and listen well.* When you meet someone, smile, shake hands (or touch elbows), make eye contact, and ask open-ended questions. Resist the urge to dominate the conversation. Focus on her interests and concerns, not yours. Listen intently. Be present. Learn her name and use it so you begin to associate the name with the face.

6. *Act with confidence even if you feel shy and intimidated.* You may feel self-conscious and uncomfortable when meeting people more powerful and successful than you are, but effective networking requires you to do it anyway. Do your best to appear self-confident and ignore any negative self-talk. Concentrate on being the best you can be.

7. *When you talk about your work, talk enthusiastically.* Prepare a one-minute profile of what you do or want to do so you're ready to describe your work and ideas in a succinct, clear, and inspiring way.

8. *Take good notes.* During the event, be a sponge and soak up as much learning as you can. Immediately following the event, write down all the key information and ideas you've gleaned.

9. *Don't forget to have fun!* Smile and be happy (or at least act happy). Spread joy, enthusiasm, and goodwill.

10. *Develop an action plan for after the event.* When you get home, write down action items derived from the event—things you're going to do to improve yourself and advance your career and life. Which websites, books, articles, organizations, and people are you going to follow up with?

Once you become comfortable with networking—and this will likely happen with practice and repetition—you'll find it's enjoyable. Networking is key to making new friends, finding new business colleagues, and finding new opportunities.

Mentors

One benefit of networking is the possibility of finding mentors, but networking and mentoring are distinct and should not confused or conflated. A mentor is someone who guides and supports you as you grow professionally. Having a mentor establishes accountability, ensuring you follow up on your commitments.

We all need help and guidance in the different domains of life, from personal to professional. Mentors give you the attention, insight, advice, and candid assessment you need to learn, improve, and succeed.

Effective mentors are focused on you, not on themselves. They encourage you to tap into your own intrinsic wisdom rather than simply telling you what to do.

Mentors help you sort out options and choices and think about them in fresh ways. They don't give advice until and unless they have a full understanding of your situation.

They listen carefully to try to understand the obstacles and aspirations you have. Good mentors inspire you to take constructive action and leave you feeling more resolved.

Sometimes mentors reframe problems so that you can view setbacks and failures with new insight and perspective. They may pose questions for clarification. They challenge and encourage you.

They offer a reality check, instill confidence, and make sure you do what you promise to do. When you create goals and strategies with a skilled mentor, you can often solve your own problems.

Asking Someone to Be Your Mentor

When you identify someone who might be a good mentor, find a way to spend time with him and talk about the areas in which you want guidance. Ask if he would be willing to take on the role of mentor, to help you sort out your thinking and work through challenges.

Remember that asking someone to be a mentor is a significant request, especially if the person is a busy professional with a packed schedule. *New York Times* writer Anna Goldfarb urges people to be "vulnerable." Make it clear why you need help and why the person you have chosen as mentor is distinctly qualified to assist you.[1]

When you ask someone to give you advice and counsel, don't do it by asking if you can "pick their brain." It's a cliché that sounds self-serving and can rub people the wrong way. Instead, ask, "May I get your advice and guidance?" This phrasing sounds more respectful and is more likely to open the door to a candid and productive relationship.

If you're able to schedule a meeting with a potential mentor, bring a prepared list of questions. Show genuine interest in the person. Make it clear you are curious about her personal story.

Try to pinpoint the decisions and actions she made that led to success so you can emulate her. To build the relationship, look for things you might have in common with the mentor, such as schools you attended, areas of the country where you've lived, or causes you both care about.

After the first substantive meeting, send a handwritten thank-you letter. It constantly amazes me that people don't do this and then wonder why, when they ask for a second meeting, their request gets ignored or rejected.

Questions and Actions

Based on the concepts and ideas examined in this chapter, consider the following questions and activities:

- How good are you at networking? What can you do to be a more effective networker?
- List some networking opportunities that would be a good fit for you.
- Do you have a mentor? If not, what steps are you taking to find one?
- In what specific ways might a mentor help you?
- Are their opportunities for you to be a mentor and help others?
- I mentioned the importance of sending a letter of thanks and appreciation, perhaps even handwritten, to a mentor who has helped you. Can you think of someone you could send a letter of thanks or appreciation to?

Epilogue

Design and Create Your Future

By reading this book, you've entertained the idea of examining and designing your life afresh. In this epilogue, I want to give you some final thoughts on mastering life, achieving success, and finding meaning and fulfillment.

Habits of Successful People

How do people live lives full of meaning, purpose, and trusting relationships? In other words, how do people become successful? Being successful starts with successful habits, including the following:

1. *Be organized.* Organization is vital to success. Keeping track of your tasks and commitments using a planner or calendar helps you use your time effectively.
2. *Go the extra mile.* Successful people always make extra effort in their projects and relationships. This is what distinguishes them and makes them extraordinary.
3. *Make a plan with goals.* Successful people envision their futures and how to get there in both their professional and personal lives. Develop a plan that spells out your goals, including deadlines.
4. *Grow from setbacks.* Success is attained by people who have learned to transform setbacks and failures into opportunities for growth and learning.

5. *Welcome criticism.* Successful people welcome criticism gracefully and constructively. They understand that criticism is not meant to tear them down. They use the feedback to improve their professional and personal lives.
6. *Maintain trusting relationships.* Success almost always depends on assistance and support from others. Successful people maintain trusting relationships that help them meet their goals.
7. *Be kind.* Kindness makes collaboration, teamwork, and family get-togethers pleasant and effective. Treating people well offers the dual rewards of uplifting them and building your character.
8. *Look for ways to help others.* Helping others is the key to leading a meaningful and fulfilling life.

Habits to Eliminate from Your Life

We all have bad habits. Some are so commonplace that we don't even recognize them, but these negative practices can become roadblocks to success, including the following:

1. *Allowing clutter.* Mess leads to stress. Keep only the things that serve a useful purpose or bring you delight. Don't get seduced by advertisements encouraging you to buy things you don't need. Clutter is not always physical. Digital clutter is a time-wasting distraction, too. Unsubscribe from useless newsletters and other emails that fill your inbox.
2. *Being a "yes" person.* Don't spread yourself too thin. Avoid getting tied up in obligations that are not important to you. Don't be afraid to say no. Saying no allows you to put your best effort into fulfilling existing commitments.
3. *Being afraid to fail.* You can only succeed if you're willing to fail. Although you won't succeed in everything you attempt, persistence often pays off. Failure is an opportunity for growth and learning.
4. *Indulging in excessive screen time and social media use.* Smartphones have fed a world of instant gratification. We're expected to respond quickly to emails, texts, and social media. To get around this madness, set a schedule for yourself. Don't mindlessly scroll through your feed or flip through channels. Try to check your messages at a designated time. Use common courtesy, and put your phone away when you're in meetings and in conversation with friends or family.
5. *Putting important relationships on the back burner.* Neglecting important relationships is arguably the most important habit to break. Placing

your family members or friends on the back burner leads to unhappiness for everyone, including you. Set aside time each week to reach out to someone you love. Be grateful for the people in your life and find ways to convey this to them.

Things to Never Do

Successful people accomplish tasks efficiently and effectively. They maximize the time available for important things by not wasting precious minutes on activities that don't matter, including the following:

1. *Dwelling on mistakes.* Successful people move past mistakes, assess their shortcomings, and apply this newfound knowledge to achieving future goals.
2. *Getting involved in office politics and conflicts.* Becoming mired in petty activities, such as unimportant workplace conflicts and office gossip, wastes valuable time and energy, not to mention compromising trust and professional relationships.
3. *Waiting for someone to tell them what to do with their time.* One of the best ways to increase your productivity and find success is to take initiative.
4. *Getting trapped by technology.* For most of us, mindless web surfing and preoccupation with phones and other mobile devices hijacks our attention and absorbs an excessive amount of time.
5. *Persevering in unsatisfactory work.* Successful people don't allow themselves to stagnate in disappointing jobs. They either leave dull jobs, look for more fulfilling tasks in the current job, or seek growth opportunities outside the job.
6. *Staying in toxic relationships.* Sometimes you need to end relationships if they are damaging your emotional health. Successful people place a high priority on personal development and don't continue relationships that jeopardize their health.
7. *Being sluggish or languid.* Success cannot be achieved without hard work and having a growth mindset.

How to Overcome Obstacles

When faced with daunting obstacles, many of us lose steam or even give up. Here are five ideas to help you overcome hurdles:

1. *Start with the end in mind.* This concept still holds weight nearly thirty years after author Stephen R. Covey introduced it in his book *The*

Seven Habits of Highly Effective People. Create a personal mission state-ment (see part I of this book) to assist in shaping your life. Identify the most important roles you play—such as parent, spouse, friend, mentor, leader, and executive—and outline in your personal mission statement what it means to succeed in these roles. This will help you organize your priorities, stay focused, and avoid giving up when the going gets tough.

2. *Choose your goals wisely.* Determine what matters most to you. Make a list of your interests and aspirations and align your goals with them. Set inspiring goals because if your goals inspire you, it will be easier to keep reaching for them in the face of adversity.

3. *Anticipate breakdowns.* When working toward your goals, consider the challenges you may face. Ask yourself what problems and breakdowns might arise and get creative in thinking ahead of time about ways around these barriers. Although it's difficult to be prepared for every breakdown, having a plan B will improve your confidence in the jour-ney ahead.

4. *Recognize that success is a step-by-step process.* It can be difficult to stay focused when you are working to meet long-term goals. Instead of wor-rying about how far you still must go, zero in on your next step. Ask, "What is the next action I need to take?"

5. *Ask for help.* The road to achieving your goals can be rough. Surround yourself with a network of people you respect and trust and to whom you can reach out to for support.

A Final Message

I have tried to describe in this book a new kind of success—what I called "slow success" in the introduction—success not tethered to money, status, power, or fame but rather to meaning, purpose, relationships, giving, and generosity.

In his book *Sapiens*, historian Yuval Noah Harari writes,

> Despite the astonishing things that humans are capable of doing, we remain unsure of our goals and we seem to be as discontented as ever. We have ad-vanced from canoes to galleys to steamships to space shuttles—but nobody knows where we're going. We are more powerful than ever before but have very little idea what to do with all that power. Worse still, humans seem to be more irresponsible than ever. Self-made gods with only the laws of physics to

keep us company, we are accountable to no one. We are consequently wreaking havoc on our fellow animals and on the surrounding ecosystem, seeking little more than our own comfort and amusement, yet never finding satisfaction.[1]

After coming to that pessimistic conclusion Harari asks, "Is there anything more dangerous than dissatisfied and irresponsible gods who don't know what they want?"[2]

This book aims to change the world Harari describes. The ideas for success, meaning, and responsibility I've described can move you from drifting and passivity to intentionality and action, so you know where you're going and why.

The following prayer beautifully sums up my message. It's from Shantideva, an eighth-century Buddhist monk:

> May I become at all times, both now and forever
> A protector for those without protection
> A guide for those who have lost their way
> A ship for those with oceans to cross
> A bridge for those with rivers to cross
> A sanctuary for those in danger
> A lamp for those without light
> A place of refuge for those who lack shelter
> And a servant to all in need.

I urge you to dig deeper into yourself to find out what you care about and what matters most to you. Implement a planning system that helps you spend more time on your important relationships, causes, and goals.

Keep working on your personal mission statement and goals, raising them to a higher and higher level, so that when you read them, they excite and inspire you. Your life will be full of fun and joy as you craft yourself into a person who is generous, kind, thoughtful, enthusiastic, bold, productive, and successful.

Four questions that matter are:

1. Did I stay true to my values?
2. Did I make progress toward the vision described in my personal mission statement?
3. Did I pursue worthwhile and challenging goals in a focused and determined way?
4. Will I die with few regrets?

When I was a wildlife filmmaker and spent time filming wolves, I came to recognize the beauty of this wolf credo by Del Goetz:

> Respect the elders.
> Teach the young.
> Cooperate with the pack.
>
> Play when you can.
> Hunt when you must.
> Rest in-between.
>
> Share your affections.
> Voice your feelings.
> Leave your mark.

I wish you luck on your journey to "leave your mark" and to find meaning, fulfillment, and success in your life.

~

Personal Mission Statement and Life Goals

Finishing Strong: Creating a
Fulfilling and Meaningful Life as I Face Mortality

By Chris Palmer
August 14, 2020

Notes:

1. I have one chance at life, so it's crucial I have an accurate map and compass to help me lead a life of purpose, joy, and meaning, and with the fewest possible regrets.
2. The purpose of this document is to be that map and compass. It includes my personal mission statement and my goals. My personal mission statement describes my "true north" and is the foundation for my goals.
3. The level of detail in this document may be unusual, but it encapsulates the totality of my life. It reflects who I am and who I want to be.
4. Getting these goals out of my head and capturing them on paper declutters my mind and gives me peace. As productivity expert David Allen says, "Your mind is for having ideas, not holding them."
5. I review and update this document frequently and plan my day based on it.

Content:

- My personal mission statement
- Core values
- Daily routine
- Goals: community goal, giving back goal, health goal, and growth goal
- New possibilities and aspirations

My Personal Mission Statement

As I approach the end of my days on this earth, I appreciate that I've had a good life and have much to be grateful for. Oliver Wendell Holmes wrote, "Alas for those who never sing, but die with all their music in them." I had the chance to sing. I worked hard and gave life my best shot. I've also been incredibly lucky and extremely privileged, enjoying unearned and unfair social advantages over others because I'm a white male.

I agree with whoever said that the purpose of life is a life of purpose. Living with purpose will make the world a better place and benefit others while also helping me feel fulfilled. I will embrace a purpose-driven life, not a comfort-driven life.

I will find new ways to give my life meaning and purpose. Raising Kimmie, Tina, and Jen gave my life purpose for decades; it still does but to a lesser extent now that they are independent adults and need me less. My primary identities as father, filmmaker, and professor have weakened.

I will nurture new identities. I will still focus on my family and on my role as a husband, father, and grandfather, but I will also build my identity as an author, teacher, speaker, community member, volunteer, health advocate, aging advocate, and death and dying educator.

As I face mortality, I will find joy in designing the meaning and purpose of the last phase of my life. It is my responsibility to find my path and to live my own unique life.

My goal is what MIT's Peter Senge calls "personal mastery." I will clarify the things that matter deeply to me and live my life in the service of my highest aspirations.

I will spend my time on what matters to me. I am what I spend my time on. In historian Will Durant's formulation, I will become what I repeatedly do. Heraclitus wrote, "Day by day, what you choose, what you think, and what you do is who you become." Author Annie Dillard wrote, "How we spend our days is, of course, how we spend our lives."

As *New York Times* columnist David Brooks advocates in his book *The Second Mountain*, I will climb a "second mountain" that is characterized by focusing on what really matters. He distinguishes "eulogy virtues" from "résumé virtues." To move from "résumé virtues" to "eulogy virtues" is to move from activities focused on the self to activities focused on others.

I will work for the greater good. I will give my life meaning and fulfillment by contributing to matters larger than the self and more enduring than my life. William James said, "The great use of life is to spend it for something that outlasts it."

I will set and achieve ambitious goals and be highly active, energetic, and productive. I will design and create a new life with Gail in "retirement" that makes me grateful, purposeful, and excited to be alive. I will align my daily activities with my values and goals. I will find and emulate role models (such as Jimmy Carter) who are flourishing in their end game, despite deteriorating strength and other physical limitations.

I will give my life significance by devoting myself to challenging and worthy tasks. I will have something worth living for—what the Japanese call *ikigai*, which is strongly linked to finding meaning and being optimistic.

I welcome feeling challenged and being outside my comfort zone, especially for a good cause such as fighting an injustice of some kind. It might be stressful to work at the edge of my current capacity, but that is how I learn and grow.

I will not fear setbacks or failures. As psychologist Carol Dweck (the creator of the mindset concept) points out, mistakes help to build character and intelligence. I will savor difficulties, and I will seek out and embrace challenges. I will find out what I am capable of.

If I'm living well, I will always be doing something hard. Philosopher and activist Bertrand Russell said, "When striving ceases, so does life." And Nietzsche believed that embracing difficulty is essential for a fulfilling life. He famously asserted, "What does not kill me makes me stronger." Goethe said, "If you want to make life easy, make it hard."

I will do hard things. Psychologist Angela Duckworth recommends that everyone do at least one hard thing every day. Hard things for me include being a hospice volunteer, learning about death and dying, giving talks, writing books, dancing, playing tennis, juggling, standing on my hands, drawing, and playing the piano.

I will live each day with intention. I will create a life of depth, meaning, and community. I want to make a difference.

I will be, in Adam Grant's formulation, a "giver" not a "taker." I will benefit and help other people. I will strive to make the world a better place. I will be benevolent, farsighted, and generous.

I will optimize my life around growth, challenge, giving, and generosity. I will not prioritize the pursuit of leisure, gratification, enjoyment, and ease. As noted below, my core values are *love, learning, service, trust, gratitude,* and *diligence.*

I will adopt a growth mindset and will seek an abundance of growth experiences. Growth experiences give my life significance and meaning and are the keys to a fulfilled life and a life of learning. T. S. Eliot wrote, "Old men ought to be explorers."

I will create a meaningful legacy that will survive me and will be my gift to the future I will not see. I want "my memory to be for a blessing"—a beautiful Jewish expression. I want to leave more than just money. I hope to ripple into the future, just as my parents have rippled through me. (*Rippling* is psychiatrist Irvin Yalom's word for passing on parts of our self to others. Yalom says it helps to reduce the dread of death.)

I will undertake activities that strengthen my relationship with others, especially with Gail, my family, friends, and neighbors. I will nurture camaraderie and goodwill. As Ken Blanchard puts it, I will "catch people doing things right" rather than focusing on mistakes and errors.

I will cut out all nonessentials from my life and everything of little consequence. I will minimize my use of social media, which can be toxic and dystopian. I will practice "digital minimalism" as described in Professor Cal Newport's book of the same name. I will not blast my free hours into time confetti and so prevent myself from learning new skills and taking on big projects. I will have time for high-quality activities including reading substantive books, writing books, having conversations with friends, and learning to dance and to play tennis. I will be "indistractable" (Nir Eyal's word).

I will pursue a reverse bucket list. Every year, I will jettison obligations, possessions, and relationships that don't advance my life goals.

I acknowledge that I am a beginner in many areas of life. I will relish the role of being a student and lifelong learner. Scientist and author Isaac Asimov said, "The day you stop learning is the day you begin decaying." I will seek mentors and coaches to help me achieve my goals.

I will be open to taking advice and learning from others. I will seek feedback and accept criticism. I know that "feedback is the breakfast of champions." I recognize that the best way to learn is to teach.

I will appreciate the distinction between "doing" and "being." I will relish the chance to watch a bird, admire a flower, and enjoy the moment.

Every day, seven days a week, I will take multiple micro-actions toward my goals. Through consistent daily action I will make major progress. Change is achieved through hundreds of tiny steps.

I will live a life of purposeful action. Action, when matched with specific and inspiring life goals, leads to a meaningful, accomplished, and fulfilling life. Ben Franklin said, "Little strokes fell great oaks." The poet Henry Wadsworth Longfellow wrote, "The heights by great men reached and kept / Were not attained by sudden flight, / But they, while their companions slept, / Were toiling upward in the night." And Robert H. Schuller wrote, "Spectacular achievement is always preceded by unspectacular preparation."

Core Values

I will live by values that are fundamental to an honorable, fulfilling, and joyful life.

They include *love, learning, service, trust, gratitude, diligence, courage, hard work, empathy, kindness, justice, integrity, honesty, patience, self-discipline, compassion, responsibility, fairness, generosity, wisdom, temperance,* and *tenacity.*

These values are timeless, self-evident, self-validating, enduring, foundational, and universal.

I will align my life with my core values of *love, learning, service, trust, gratitude,* and *diligence,* and I will use these values to guide my daily actions.

In living in accordance with these values, I will consistently foster the following twenty-four strengths identified by psychologist Martin Seligman:

1. *Wisdom and knowledge:* curiosity, love of learning, judgment, ingenuity, social intelligence, and perspective.
2. *Courage:* valor, perseverance, and integrity.
3. *Humanity and love:* kindness and loving.
4. *Justice:* citizenship, fairness, and leadership.
5. *Temperance:* self-control, prudence, and humility.
6. *Transcendence:* appreciation of beauty, gratitude, hope, spirituality, forgiveness, humor, and zest.

I will pursue the values and strengths that are most meaningful to me.

Daily Routine

I will keep to the following daily schedule:

- Midnight: Go to bed.
- 8 a.m.: Get up.

- 8:30 to 11 a.m.: Work (take on my most challenging work because in the morning I'm most alert).
- 11 a.m. to 1 p.m.: Exercise for one hour, then play tennis (and swim in the summer).
- 1 to 2 p.m.: Eat breakfast (high-fiber cereal, blueberries, raspberries, flaxseed, nuts, etc.) and read the *Washington Post* and the *New York Times*.
- 2 to 4 p.m.: Write in my gratitude journal, review goals, visit the library, play the piano, practice juggling, practice drawing, meditate, make phone calls, and process emails.
- 4 to 5 p.m.: Eat light lunch (tomatoes, kale, spinach, lentils, black beans, peas, carrots, broccoli, cabbage, etc.). Make this meal for Gail, too.
- 5 to 7 p.m.: Read.
- 7 to 8 p.m.: Eat light dinner with Gail (orange, pear, plum, apple, banana). Start a 17-hour fast.
- 8 to 11:30 p.m.: Write.
- 11:30 p.m. to midnight: Review my mission and goals (this document) and plan the next day.

Goals

I have organized my goals into *four core categories:* **community**, **giving back**, **health**, and **growth**. I recommend to others that they include a fifth core category: "financial." I don't include "financial" in my own goals because we are financially secure and I have little interest in money.

I could have selected other ways to view the totality of my life. For example, by *roles* (husband, father, grandfather, writer, speaker, etc.), or by *life domains* (work, home, community, self, etc.), or by *mission* (to love, to leave a legacy, to laugh, to learn, and to live). They all work equally well and accomplish the same goal of finding a way to organize and examine my life in its entirety.

As already noted, in this last phase of my life, I am comfortable organizing my life in the following way:

1. **Community** includes relationships, social life, a sense of belonging, and engagement in community. I will take the best possible care of Gail, Kim, Sujay, Tina, CJ, Jen, Chase, Kareena, Neal, JJ, Max, Sam, Aiden, Connor, and Dylan. *My community goal is to be an engaged and loving family member and a warm and active community member.*

2. **Giving back** includes sense of purpose, legacy, volunteering, and contributing. Finding meaning is one of the most fundamental needs that I have. *My giving back goal is to live a life brimming with purpose, enthusiasm, and meaning, and to leave a legacy.*
3. **Health** includes diet, exercise, and lifestyle. *My health goal is to be in the best health possible and to invest significantly in personal development.*
4. **Growth** includes lifelong learning, new experiences, overcoming challenges, and adopting a growth mindset. *My growth goal is to embrace challenges and a growth mindset and to devote myself to lifelong learning.*

A healthy, balanced, fulfilling, and active "retirement" requires full engagement in all four of the above overlapping goals. Many activities carry over across multiple areas. They are interrelated and synergistic. Not fulfilling any one of my goals damages and reduces the quality and success of my life.

What follows is more detail on the above goals.

1. *Community goal:* Be an engaged and loving family member and a warm and active community member.

My goals in the "community" core category relate to Gail, Kim, Tina, Jenny, Sujay, CJ, Chase, my grandchildren, my twin brother, my cousins, my nieces and nephews, and a few good friends and neighbors.

Be the best husband possible to Gail. Being a husband is one of the most important roles I have in my life. I appreciate the love and joy I receive from Gail and will do my utmost to return them in spades. I will find ways every day to help Gail proactively. I will strive to make Gail happy and will aim to be a model husband and nurture our marriage. I will build my relationship with Gail *by not taking her for granted* and by doing things together that we both love. I will do fun things with Gail, including grandparenting, dancing, tennis, movies, theater, cooking, travel, playing the piano, taking a drawing class, gardening, birdwatching, road trips, house renovations, and spending time with family and friends. I will prepare for a time when I might need to devote myself full time to caring for Gail.

I'm lucky: I feel deeply cherished and loved by Gail and by my daughters and sons-in-law. Victor Hugo wrote, "The supreme happiness in life is the conviction that we are loved." Warren Buffett says his measure of success is: "Do the people you care about love you back?"

Be the best father possible to Kim, Tina, and Jen—and father-in-law to Sujay, CJ, and Chase—giving them constant love, encouragement, and support. I will *always be there for them*, affirming them, and assisting them as needed. I will spend time in Denver helping Tina and her family, and time in Boise helping Jen and her family.

Having to raise children responsibly had a huge impact on my life. My three daughters re-made me, and I will always be profoundly grateful to them for that. I can thank them by being the best possible father to them, and *I will do my utmost to be an inspiring example*.

One of the legacies Gail and I will leave is a strong family whose members love and care for each other, respect each other, laugh together, have fun together, grow together, enjoy meaningful relationships with each other, and have a deep sense of shared vision around our family's essential meaning and purpose.

Be the best grandfather possible to Kareena, Neal, JJ, Max, Sam, Aiden, Connor, and Dylan, constantly seeking to enrich their lives with exuberant love and affection, as well as exciting projects and adventures. I will introduce them to history, words, language, humor, science experiments, *It's Academic*, family stories, and everything I'm studying and learning. I will help them achieve great things and to lead loving and fulfilled lives.

Strengthen my bonds with my twin brother Jon, all my cousins, all my nephews and nieces, my whole extended family, and Gail's family. I will especially do whatever I can to heal the estrangement between one brother's children.

Strengthen my bonds with our Edgemoor/village friends and neighbors. I want to invest in Edgemoor and the village instead of trying to be every-where in the world. I want a sense of belonging, which can only come from social ties.

Strengthen my bonds with a select group of friends, including: (*names listed in a separate document*).

Honor the fact that relationships are not just vital but are everything. I treasure the family members and friends who bear witness to my life (as I bear witness to theirs) and want to invest in them. I want to feel deeply con-nected, to make real and authentic contact, and *to seek first to understand, then to be understood*.

I will build my relationships with other people, especially the people I am closest to, by being trustworthy and by being sincere. I will do this by small kindnesses and courtesies, keeping promises, making offers, clarifying, and honoring ex-pectations, and displaying integrity and loyalty. I will do these things uncon-ditionally and sincerely, *expecting nothing in return*. I will observe and draw attention to what people are doing right, and I will praise with specificity.

When I have a problem with somebody, I will focus on how I am contributing to that problem, and what I am doing to help create it. Problems are, in fact, opportunities to build relationships with people faster than usual.

I will work on developing the skill and habit of empathy. When I listen to people, I tend to interpret their words and feelings to fit my own opinions and experiences—as if I know the inner terrain of the people when, in fact, I don't. I will recognize this impulse and resist it. I will learn to listen to people's unspoken concerns without making judgments or giving advice. I will place myself within other people's frame of reference to try to experience their feelings as they do. I will try to deeply understand the other person's point of view. *In fact, I will do my best to express the other person's point of view better than they can.*

I will integrate into my communications with people the distinction between "opinions" and "grounded assessments." When I offer opinions, *I will make it clear that they are just opinion. If possible, I will form grounded assessments.* Unlike opinions, grounded assessments are confined to a specified domain, they can be supported by factual evidence, and they are based on clear and articulated standards. They can generate new possibilities for people and lead to action (i.e., a request, an offer, or a promise).

Other goals in the "community" core category include:

1. Be active and engaged in BMAV (village) events, such as the men's lunch, the book club, and the Happy Hour.
2. Host parties at our home for our neighbors, for Aging SIG members, for the BMAV Board, and for Montgomery Hospice fundraising events.
3. Keep a gratitude journal (more on this below under "Health").
4. With Gail, nurture our many family traditions.
5. Create innovative and personal gifts for Gail and the family for birthdays and holidays.
6. With Gail and the family, update our Family Emergency Plan (done).
7. With Gail, plan memorable family vacations.
8. Keep my website www.ChrisPalmerOnline.com updated with help from Jenny.

Actions:

- Focus on Gail.
- Become skilled at telling stories and anecdotes.

- Set up lunches with friends.
- Plan Christmas gifts early in the year.

2. *Giving back goal:* Live a life brimming with purpose, enthusiasm, and meaning, and leave a legacy.
My goals in the "giving back" core category relate to writing books, teaching, giving workshops and talks, using humor, serving on the board of Montgomery Hospice, being a hospice volunteer, leading BMAV's Aging SIG, and serving as president of MFFED.

Write memorable books. These books are the major closing act of my professional career.

My first two published books were on wildlife filmmaking (*Shooting in the Wild* in 2010 and *Confessions of a Wildlife Filmmaker* in 2015).

They were followed by *Raise Your Kids to Succeed: What Every Parent Should Know* in 2017 and *Now What, Grad? Your Path to Success after College* (2nd edition) in 2018.

Then I wrote *College Teaching at Its Best: Inspiring Students to be Enthusiastic, Lifelong Learners* in 2019.

My recent books have all been published by Rowman & Littlefield. Also, Bethesda Communications Group in 2018 published *Love, Dad*, a 700-page book of my letters to my daughters. Books in the works include:

1. *Finding Meaning and Success: Living a Fulfilled and Productive Life.* Published by Rowman & Littlefield.
2. *Dying and Death.* To be published by Rowman & Littlefield.
3. *Science Experiments and Other Games That Grandparents and Other Caregivers Can Do with Kids.* To be published by Rowman & Littlefield. Take drawing classes so I can illustrate the book myself.
4. *How to Age and Retire Successfully.* In development.
5. A book on humor and jokes. In development.

Enlist help on the aforementioned books from key advisors, including (*names listed in a separate document*).

Continue teaching (with TWC, BMAV, and LLB). Be an inspiring and life-changing teacher. Encourage, support, and challenge my students. Relentlessly work to improve my teaching skills.

Give pro bono talks and workshops. Give talks and workshops on how to live successfully and meaningfully, how to age and retire well, how to deal with death and dying, how to write memoirs, and wildlife filmmaking. (*Upcoming talks listed in a separate document.*)

Spend thirty minutes a day absorbing humorous material. While I no longer perform stand-up comedy, I will use more humor in my conversations, speeches, teaching, family journal, and the books I write. I will honor and embrace humor as a major part of my life.

Humor has a power and exhilaration that can accomplish extraordinary things, including bringing people closer together and teaching me to laugh at myself. It can also put challenges into perspective, deflate tense situations, and even activate the immune system. Laughter is an amazing and wonderful phenomenon. I will deepen my understanding of the value of humor and become a more competent observer of the humor in everyday life.

Serve on the board of Montgomery Hospice and chair the Major Gifts & Philanthropy Board Committee.

Serve as a hospice volunteer for Montgomery Hospice. I took the three-day training in September 2019 and started volunteering a few hours a week in October 2019.

Serve as leader of the Bethesda Metro Area Village special interest group on aging, dying, and death. Hold monthly meetings of the Aging SIG at our home. Email to the group weekly with thoughts and ideas.

Serve as president of the MacGillivray Freeman Films Educational Foundation. I became president about ten years ago and will continue in this role, supporting staff, communicating with them often, and chairing quarterly board meetings.

Other goals in the "giving back" core category include:

- Write more children's books with Tina (okeydokeybooks.com) on bullying, health, fitness, morality, and other topics.
- Actively support causes that align with my values and are important to me, including environmentalism, animal rights, and a whole-foods plant-based diet. Financially support the following organizations: (*names listed in a separate document*).

Actions:

- Review and update this goals document daily and plan my day around it so I only focus on essentials.

3. *Health goal*: Be in the best health possible and invest significantly in personal development.

I'm using the word *health* in a broad way to include personal development, which is the vital process of enhancing my capacity to be an effective, giving, and vibrant person. I must take care of myself in order to have the capability to take care of others, including Gail, my family, friends, and neighbors.

Exercise. I will exemplify peak vitality and outstanding health. My 60-minute daily exercise regimen (see my *Dad's Exercise Book* for details) is focused on the five areas of *strength, endurance, flexibility, balance,* and *posture.*

I will find ways not to plateau in my fitness level but to keep raising the bar on my fitness goals. As noted below, in addition to my daily exercise regimen, I will play tennis, swim, do handstands, sprint up and down the stairs, dance, garden, and juggle. *Exercise is medicine.*

Diet. I will continue to eat an organic, whole-foods, unprocessed, plant-based diet to avoid malnourishment and toxic food, as well as for climate change and animal welfare reasons. The standard American diet, or SAD (a diet high in sugar, protein, and unhealthy fats—think hot dogs, hamburgers, French fries, and sugary drinks—SAD indeed and highly inflammatory) shortens lives, promotes disease, encourages cancers, is catastrophic for the health of the planet, exacerbates climate chaos, and causes unspeakable animal cruelty.

My diet will continue to focus on blueberries, raspberries, blackberries, pomegranate seeds, flaxseed, nuts, cruciferous vegetables, tomatoes, carrots, kale, spinach, onion, broccoli, beans, lentils, peas, chickpeas, oranges, apples, and other anti-inflammatory "super" foods that fight cancer, heart disease, and other major health problems.

The SAD diet is typically overly refined and thus low in fiber. Vegetables, fruits, beans, and lentils are terrific sources of dietary fiber. Extensive epidemiological research has been shown a fiber-rich diet to be vital for both intestinal and heart health.

The effectiveness and health of an unprocessed plant-based diet has been proven by many randomized, placebo-controlled, double-blind control trials (the gold standard). Pioneering doctors in this field include Dr. Dean Ornish, Dr. Michael Greger, Dr. Neal Barnard, Dr. Joel Fuhrman, and Dr. Colin

Campbell. Rabbi Moses Maimonides wrote in 1190, "No disease that can be treated by diet should be treated with any other means."

I won't eat anything Little Granny (my father's mother, born in 1890) wouldn't recognize as food. (In doing this, I honor Little Granny's precious memory.) Thus, I will continue to eat foods found in nature (in other words, fresh, unprocessed, and simple whole foods) and that are widely recognized by scientists as nourishing and nutrient-dense. *Food is medicine.*

My father died of prostate cancer (PCa), so I have known for a long time that I'm vulnerable to PCa, despite my healthy diet and lifestyle. Two recent MRIs revealed two cancerous lesions in my prostate. Thanks to doctor friends, John Long and Fred Cantor, I recently enrolled in a protocol for PCa at NIH. While I undergo treatment at NIH, I will maintain an aggressive prostate cancer treatment regimen, through diet and exercise, and in the process reduce my risk for virtually every other age-related disease.

Sleep. I will get a minimum of eight hours of sleep a night. Psychologist Angela Duckworth writes, "Sleep is a miracle drug with no side effects." *Sleep is medicine.*

*In sum, through exercise, diet, and sleep (plus my purpose-driven life and all the love I receive from and give to my family, friends, and neighbors), I will be a super-ager—*someone in his 70s and 80s who has cognitive and physical function equal to that of people decades younger. In the unlikely event that I do not succumb to prostate cancer, I will redefine what 85 looks like.

Other goals in the "health" core category include:

1. *Seek transcendent experiences (shared with Gail).* I will accomplish this by reconnecting with nature and finding glimpses of the sublime. My *goal in this is not to be productive* (in the conventional meaning of that word) but to be connected to nature and to feel recharged, replenished, and inspired by the wonders of the natural world. *I want to give myself the space for contemplation without thinking of time.* Poet William Blake wrote, "To see a world in a grain of sand / And a heaven in a wildflower / Hold infinity in the palm of your hand / And eternity in an hour." And Ralph Waldo Emerson wrote, "Many eyes go through the meadow, but few see the flowers in it." I want to see the flowers. I will find a way to kayak or canoe in wild, pristine areas. I will invite our precious grandchildren! I will make a cross-country road trip to see the American West, including Jackson Hole, the Tetons, and

Yosemite. *I want to feel reverence—viscerally and profoundly—for the ineffable beauty that nature embodies.*

2. *Keep a daily gratitude journal,* not a diary of daily outward events, but a thoughtful chronicling of reflections and ruminations on anything going on that seems important and on especially what I'm grateful for. A journal like that is an *instrument of self-awareness* that can help me watch what I do so I can find out who I am. Such a journal will help me get better at thinking about and savoring what is going well in my life (to offset my natural tendency to focus on what might be going wrong). Our brains, writes Dr. Martin Seligman, have a natural catastrophic bent (for sound evolutionary reasons), but we need to spend more time dwelling on good events to be happier, more optimistic, and less depressed. I will do that through my gratitude journal. Every Christmas, I give each family member a 250- to 300-page bound book of the family gratitude journal for the year that is ending.

3. *Listen to educational podcasts* while doing my daily exercises.

4. *Listen to books on tape* while driving, especially books on American history.

5. *Play the piano and sing daily.* Continue taking piano lessons and teach what I'm learning to my grandchildren. Play duets with Gail and play with Kareena while she plays her clarinet. Write lyrics for songs like *Greensleeves.*

6. *Take weekly dancing lessons* at Bethesda Elementary on Mondays at 7 p.m. and learn to dance well with Gail. Invite friends to join us. In a 1580 essay on aging, Michel de Montaigne wrote, "There is nothing more notable in Socrates than that he found time, when he was an old man, to learn music and dancing, and thought it time well spent."

7. *Juggle balls every day.* Get good enough to entertain people and interject humor. Learn to juggle four balls, learn to juggle by overhand grabbing, and learn to catch balls behind my back. Teach my grandchildren how to juggle.

8. *Do handstands every day.* My goal is to be able to do handstands at age 80. Handstands challenge my whole body, especially my core, my shoulders, and my balance. I enjoy the healthy rush of blood to my head, my legs stretched out gloriously above me, and deftly steadying myself with my hands. It is the epitome of freedom of movement.

9. *Play tennis every day (weather permitting) throughout the year* and have weekly tennis lessons with coach Andy Orben between April and October. I will become a more competitive tennis player. When I

reach 85, I will be a competitive tennis player for that age group. Playing tennis is also a good way of building friendships.

10. *Swim every day in the summer*, doing whole lengths underwater with one breath.

11. *Practice drawing daily*, so I can do the many illustrations needed for my book on games and science experiments. Send drawings to my grandchildren.

12. *Learn to cook a variety of delicious plant-based meals.* I will cook with my grandchildren so they can learn about healthy, unprocessed food. See my file on cooking for ideas. Focus on beans and lentils.

13. *Be a better gardener.* Work with Gail on landscaping our backyard and grow lots of flowers and vegetables. Use our Tower Garden to grow vegetables, especially tomatoes, with our grandchildren.

14. *Be a better birder.* With Gail, learn the names of birds and learn about their lives by observing them in our garden. Learn all we can from David Moulton. Teach what we learn to our grandchildren.

15. *Meditate daily* using Sam Harris's Waking Up app.

4. *Growth goal:* Embrace challenges and a growth mindset and devote myself to lifelong learning.

My goals in the "growth" core category include studying books on key topics; being organized for meaning and fulfillment; creating a meaningful legacy; and preparing and planning for old age, dying, and death. I am committed to lifelong learning and improvement, and thus to continually opening new possibilities for myself and others.

Actively study books for at least two hours daily and practice deep reading. Only read books that are so meaningful to me that I want to read them again and again to uncover and learn their essential messages. Ralph Waldo Emerson said, "You become what you think about all day long." I will read biographies and autobiographies of people who have lived courageous, inspiring, and generous lives. I will constantly improve and enrich my vocabulary and my ability to write.

Be organized for meaning and fulfillment. *Reduce my worldly possessions and move toward minimalism and simplicity.* Rigorously declutter and "death-clean" my study and the house so that I don't unfairly dump that onerous work on my family when I die. Purge unimportant and out-of-date papers, files, and books. Keep my study highly organized so I can think, read, and write productively.

Create a meaningful legacy that will survive me and, as I noted earlier, will be my gift to the future I will not see. I want "my memory to be for a blessing." I want to leave more than just money. I hope to "ripple" into the future and to enlarge the lives of others who survive me. Psychologist Erik Erikson wrote, "I am what survives me."

I want to be remembered by my family, friends, and colleagues as a person grounded in decency, simple goodness, infectious vitality, and inspiring enthusiasm; as someone with a lasting and wonderful marriage, a great sense of humor, and a strong work ethic; as a person who made his role and responsibilities as a father and grandfather one of his highest priorities; as a person who committed himself to learning and education and who pursued his goals with passion; and as a person who left the world a better place.

As I think about my legacy, I will focus on my non-financial assets, including love, wisdom, beliefs, stories, and values that I want to pass on when I die. An African proverb says, "When an old man dies, a library burns to the ground."

I will produce an "ethical will." An ethical will (sometimes called a "legacy letter") is a way to convey wisdom and love between the generations. It contains personal reflections, values, aspirations, and expressions of love. I want to say what is in my heart that might otherwise be left unsaid.

My ethical will consists of the following:

1. An "heirlooms" letter dated March 31, 2020, to the family on non-financial family assets. To accompany that letter, Tina and I have created a shared google drive, in which we are collecting non-financial family assets, including books, letters, photos, stories, videos, and other heirlooms, as described in the March 31, 2020, letter to the family. That letter acts as a "Table of Contents" for the shared google drive. Please go to drive.google.com and see the shared folder called "Shearer-Palmer Family Essentials."
2. A five-page "goodbye" letter (or "gratitude" letter) dated January 11, 2019, thanking Gail and my family in case I die suddenly and don't have a chance to say goodbye in person.
3. A letter dated June 20, 2020, to Kimmie, Tina, and Jenny expressing why I feel so proud of them.
4. Books, journals, and letters to provide a loving and enduring gift—a legacy—to my grandchildren and great grandchildren. For example, my book on how to achieve a meaningful and successful life was written with my grandchildren very much in mind.
5. A goodbye video (in development).

6. A 50-page book of family stories, my 120-page family history, our family mission statement, the 320-page book Gail and I wrote for Kim on our lives, my 700-page book of letters to my Kim, Tina, and Jenny, and many other items collected in the shared google drive.

The idea behind creating an ethical will and a meaningful legacy is to capture my essence as a person and my vision for the future, so that future generations (my heirs) can benefit from it. In this way, I hope to live beyond my death (so to speak) and continue to support my family even after I am gone.

After I die, I hope to be thought of as a great ancestor. My death does not end my responsibility to those I leave behind. I want to be a light that shines through our family for generations. I will support my family after I have died.

When I am no longer here, you can find me in my daughters and grandchildren, and in my friends. Historian Doris Kearns Goodwin writes that Eleanor Roosevelt often quoted the simple lines, "They are not dead who live in lives they leave behind: In those whom they have blessed they live a life again." In other words, after I die, I can live in others by what I gave.

Prepare and plan for old age. As a secular humanist, I need to find a meaning in life that is not annulled or destroyed by the inevitable death awaiting me. If death means extinction and oblivion (which I believe it does), then does life have any meaning? When I accept that I have a finite life, how do I not despair?

The answer is that I will create something that will be significant enough to make my life worthwhile. I will live a life that matters. I will do more than simply survive. Death will not lead to nothingness, even though I concede that my life is a brief transition between two oblivions (or in Vladimir Nabokov's phrasing in his autobiography, "a crack of light between two eternities of darkness").

I will fight stagnation. At 72, I am officially old (what I would call young old age because I'm still vigorous). Old age does not have to be—as it is for so many—depressing, boring, and lonely. Annie Dillard warned that "the surest sign of age is loneliness." I will do my utmost to combat isolation, despair, and feelings of worthlessness.

I will retain a zest for life until I die. My goal is to age successfully and to remain independent for as long as possible. Sadly, people over 65 watch on average nearly 50 hours of television per week. I will not be one of them because my many challenging and exciting projects (outlined in this document) make watching television for hours impossible.

I will set an example of successful aging to my daughters and friends by living to my full potential and not prematurely withering. In a sense, I'm scouting the territory of "old age" for my daughters and sons-in-law to help them when it is their turn to enter this new and forbidding land. I'm finding out what to expect and teaching those I love the wisest way to navigate the treacherous waters of elderhood.

I will fight marginalization. Unlike in Japanese culture and in Native American tribal communities, elders are not revered in Western culture. I will fight ageism and the disrespect, invisibility, and marginalization usually afforded old people. I will oppose the negative stereotypes that portray old people as useless, feeble, and contributing nothing.

I will retain some agency over aging, even as my body ages. According to the Pew Charitable Trust, 25 percent of aging is genetic while 75 percent is environmental and behavioral. We now know, says Professor Linda Fried of Columbia University, that "at least half of the chronic health concerns of older age can be prevented." It is possible to be younger (i.e., healthier) longer.

I should not—will not—be afraid of aging, even though it is scary, and my horizons and interests will inevitably shrink. My own decline will be offset by the blossoming of others through my mentoring and coaching.

As I grow old, I will engage in continual development, learning, growth, and discovery. I want to be a role model for dealing competently and gracefully with the challenges of old age. I will not be complacent, sluggish, or disengaged. The writer Gabriel García Márquez wrote, "It is not true that people stop pursuing dreams because they get old; they grow old because they stop pursuing dreams."

I will study and become knowledgeable about end-of-life issues. I will study death and dying and deepen my understanding of it. As already noted, I will write a book on this topic.

I realize that death is my constant companion—as it is for us all. I will let this awareness guide me to make the best use of my time and live life to the fullest every moment. Irvin Yalom wrote, "The way to value life, the way to feel compassion for others, the way to love anything with greater depth is to be aware that these experiences are destined to be lost."

There will come a time when the last living person who remembers me dies (likely one of my grandchildren). Then I will move from the "remembered dead" to the "truly dead." It is futile, even vacuous, to dwell on such a melancholy thought. The better response is for me *to redouble my efforts now to live a full life.* When I die, Little Granny (my father's mother born in 1890) will become truly dead. No one alive will have any memory of her.

Prepare and plan for my death. I will plan the end of my life in detail, working closely with Gail, so that the stress on Kim, Tina, and Jen (and Gail if she survives me) is minimized.

I have written a four-page memo (dated April 2, 2020) entitled "In Case of My Death" to help Gail (and Kim, Tina, and Jenny) when I die.

One of my greatest gifts to my family will be to gently usher them through the process of my death, *so it is a positive, loving, and inexpensive experience for them.*

My goal is to set an example of how to have a good death. This goal will imbue my life with meaning to the very end. I will face death with courage and dignity.

I want to die with the minimum of regrets, open loops, and loose ends. My goal is to "walk through the valley of the shadow of death" with stoicism and courage, bringing cheer and comfort to those around me.

I always want to know the truth about my condition, treatment options, and the chance of success of treatments. I do not want to be deceived or misled.

My *advance directive (or living will)*, supplemented with discussions I am having (and will continue to have) with Gail, describes how I want my final days to unfold. Gail is my health care agent (or proxy) and will speak for me if I cannot. Kim, Tina, and Jen will be my health care agents if Gail dies before I do.

The following is important to me: being able to talk with my family, being mentally alert and competent, preserving quality of life, having autonomy and independence, being comfortable and free of pain, leaving good memories for my family, dying quickly rather than lingering in agony, and avoiding expensive care.

What is not important to me (indeed, is repugnant to me) is living as long as possible, regardless of quality of life. If the prognosis is grave, my physical state is dire, and there is little chance that I will ever regain mental or physical function, then I want to be allowed to die peacefully. Being assigned to an ICU and hooked up to multiple machines would be worse than death for me. The pain, discomfort, isolation, lack of autonomy, and hopelessness would be unbearable.

The following are all anathema to me, and I firmly reject them: mechanical breathing and artificial ventilation, tracheotomy, CPR, artificial nutrition and hydration (through a nasogastric tube or a PEG tube), hospital intensive care, electroshocks to my heart, medications to stimulate heart function, dialysis, chemotherapy or radiation therapy, and surgery. I would include antibiotics in this list but am happy to leave that decision to Gail. She may decide a short trial period is warranted.

I believe that if I have an irreversible illness or intractable pain, I have the right to end my life in any way I choose—a right to death with dignity. I want a good death if I can no longer enjoy a good life. I want to extend my health span, not my life span. *I support medical aid-in-dying (MAID) and want access to MAID medications,* so I have the option of taking a lethal dose of medicine. *I do not want my life prolonged artificially after it has ceased to be the life I want as captured in this goals document.*

If I'm in pain or am breathless or in any way discomforted, I want those symptoms relieved fast and vigorously with morphine, even if the treatment unintentionally advances the time of my death or even causes my death. With intense pain, I welcome palliative sedation and (as already noted) medical aid-in-dying.

I do not want life-sustaining interventions if I am permanently unconscious (i.e., in a coma) and terminally ill. By terminally ill, I mean having an incurable and irreversible illness that is likely to cause death within a few months. I see no purpose in prolonging my dying if it is painful, miserable, and hopeless.

If I have lost all cognitive ability, then I request that I not be spoon-fed. I do not want my life to be prolonged by artificial means (medicines, machines, CPR, tube feedings, etc.) if I'm totally bedridden, or if I cannot smile, recognize and communicate with my family, swallow, bathe, or use the bathroom.

I don't want my family to suffer by watching me suffer. I do not want to be seen and remembered in a sad, pitiful state. I want to die before I become a stranger to my family through the cruel ravages of old age.

Please make sure that my doctors and nurses know about the kind of person I was before getting sick and senile. For example, I want my family to show them a photo of me doing a handstand in my 70s!

I want to be protected from well-meaning religious folk who want to convert me before I die.

How I want to die. *Before I get to the "waiting room for death," I'd like lots of visitors and to be surrounded by Gail, my daughters, sons-in-law, grandchildren,* and *great-grandchildren*. I want my loved ones to make space to grieve, but to combine that with celebratory food, wine, music, stories, roasting, and toasting. I want my death to release love. My death is not a tragedy. I didn't die young.

As I die, I would love to have family members tell me about their plans as well as their happy memories. I would like to have photos of loved ones in my room near my bed. I would love to have my hand held and to be talked to when possible, even if I don't seem to respond to the voice or touch of others. I would like to be kept fresh and clean at all times, and I would like my lips and mouth kept moist to stop dryness.

I far prefer hospice care to hospitalization. I'd like my doctor to make a referral to hospice as soon as I am eligible. And if I'm in hospital, I'd like a referral to palliative care at the earliest opportunity, even if undergoing curative treatment.

Casey House. I'd love to die at home with hospice care but realize that at some point, this may impose too big a burden on members of my family. If that is the case, then it is okay for me to spend my last few days in Casey House (a beautiful inpatient facility with Montgomery Hospice, www.montgomeryhospice.org).

If necessary, I will use VSED (voluntarily stopping eating and drinking) to die. When there is no hope for recovery, my life is near an end, and I am no longer enjoying being alive, and assuming MAID is unavailable, I will intentionally hasten my death by stopping all non-palliative medicines and by using VSED. I will initiate VSED *before* I stop recognizing loved ones and am unable to communicate.

I favor VSED, which causes death by dehydration within 8 to 14 days, because it is peaceful and causes little suffering when properly supported by good oral care and pain-relieving analgesics. The slowness of it also provides time for reflection, family interactions, and mourning. I believe that VSED is justified when the burdens of my life outweigh the benefits.

I would rather end my life using VSED than suffer the despair of a lengthy stay trapped in an ICU on mechanical life support, being overmedicalized and in pain, intubated, trached, given electric shocks for cardiac resuscitation, and wasting absurd amounts of money while feeling miserable and fearful. I want to avoid ICUs and nursing homes, both of which are tantamount to something akin to torture.

I plan to obtain a DNR (do-not-resuscitate) order (i.e., no CPR) and a MOLST (Medical Orders for Life-Sustaining Treatment) from my doctor. DNR is also called DNAR (do-not-attempt-resuscitation) or AND (allow-natural-death). MOLST will support my advance directive. The difference between an advance directive (AD) and a MOLST is that an AD is a legal document while a MOLST is a medical order. A MOLST provides a new tool for patients near the end of life to control their medical treatment better than advance directives alone, though both are important.

In sum, I don't want my death to be over-medicalized. I do not want to endure the pain of futile medical procedures. *I want it driven by quality of life issues and palliative care* rather than invasive and painful medical care. I do not want my life extended by any medical interventions if my death from a terminal condition is imminent, or if I am in a persistent vegetative state, or if I am in an end-state incurable condition that will continue its course until death. *If I'm seriously ill, it is more important to me to enhance my quality of life, even if it shortens my life.* My advance directive codifies these instructions. *If I become demented*, please follow the directions in the letter on pages 127–29 of Katy Butler's book *The Art of Dying Well.* I do not want to survive the end stages of dementia.

Prepare and plan for my immediate post-death. As already noted, I have written a four-page memo (dated April 2, 2020) entitled "In Case of My Death" to help Gail (or Kim, Tina, and Jenny if I survive Gail) when I die.

I will prepare a draft obituary as well as details of my memorial service. I will meet with funeral director Will Pumphrey to pre-plan what happens after I die, so that the burden on Gail and the girls is minimized.

In a way, it makes more sense to have my memorial service *before* I die while I am still cognitively functioning, so that I can thank people. This is called a "living funeral" or "living wake."

I abhor embalming and firmly reject it. I want to minimize expenses, request *not* to be embalmed, and I prefer not to waste money on a coffin. If I need one, then I want it to be the cheapest one possible.

I will plan for the disposal of my remains in as green a way as possible. I will research alternatives to cremation. Water cremation or alkaline hydrolysis (also called "green cremation" and "bio-cremation") is one appealing option.

Another (newer) option is for my body to become compost (soil) through legalized human recomposition. In May 2019, Washington became the first state to legalize human composting. No coffin, no chemicals, no fossil fuels, and no wasteful cemetery plot. Recomposition offers an alternative to embalming and burial or cremation that is natural, safe, sustainable, and will result in significant savings in carbon emissions and land usage. Folk singer Peter Seeger, a supporter of recomposition, sings, "When radishes and corn you munch, you may be having me for lunch."

Having said all that, if green alternatives are not available for whatever reason, I will reluctantly agree to cremation. If I'm cremated, I want my ashes mixed with

Gail's and then, if Gail agrees, buried under a beautiful tree. I like the idea of my body (minus organs given to others) helping to nurture a magnificent tree.

Other goals in the "growth" core category include:

1. Deepen my knowledge of what makes a successful "retirement."
2. Deepen my knowledge of death and dying issues.
3. I wrote an article on fathering for the January 2020 issue of *Legacy Arts Magazine*, and will write another article, this one on success, this year.

Actions:

1. Read voraciously every day.
2. Work on getting my legacy organized and created. Continue creating my ethical will (legacy letter).
3. Update my January 11, 2019, "goodbye" letter (or "gratitude" letter) to my family.
4. Update my March 31, 2020, "heirlooms" letter (on non-financial family assets).
5. Update my April 2, 2020, memo, "In Case of My Death."
6. Draft my memorial service and help Gail draft hers. Select music.
7. Draft my obituary and help Gail draft hers.
8. Update our wills and draft a financial power of attorney.
9. Make decisions on donating organs (done—I included this decision in my advance directive) and on giving my body to the Maryland Anatomy Board.
10. Research alternatives to cremation.
11. Hold a pre-planning funeral meeting with funeral director Will Pumphrey.

I warmly embrace, with profound enthusiasm, all the goals in this document. I will be the best person I can be, so I can die feeling at peace and with few regrets.

I will end this goals document with a list of ideas, aspirations, and possibilities I'm mulling over and considering.

New Possibilities and Aspirations

1. Teach at The Writer's Center (TWC) on a regular basis. Also give more lectures at Live & Learn Bethesda (LLB), Leisure World, Asbury Village, OASIS, and villages like Little Falls Village.
2. Write letters of gratitude to friends and family who have helped, inspired, and supported me during my life.
3. Develop a workshop on how to retire, age, and die successfully.
4. Start a blog or podcast on retirement, aging, dying, and death.
5. Become a certified death doula.
6. Get a tattoo on my chest over my heart saying, "No Code." Buttress this with a MOLST and DNR. ("Full code" status means "do everything possible to keep me alive," so "No Code" means the opposite: Let me die.)
7. Find a drawing class to do with Gail.
8. Write a letter of advice to Kareena, who is entering her second decade and faces so many challenges not of her own making.
9. Every week write a letter (via snail mail) to my grandchildren with stories and life advice. Tell them inspiring stories that show them their strengths. Tell them vivid stories from family history.
10. Create a new nonprofit to combat entertainment that is toxic, reckless, harmful, and traumatizing to children. Broadcasters, to their everlasting shame and disgrace, are incorporating terrifying violence and graphic sex in programs they know young children watch.
11. Study the American West and Native Americans. Visit key historic sites (e.g., the battle of Little Bighorn), especially now that Tina and Jenny live out west.
12. Explore the cottage three miles north of the White House where Abraham Lincoln spent his summers in 1862, 1863, and 1864. Also explore Civil War forts and battlefields and the D-Day beaches at Normandy.
13. Create a book club focused on biographies and autobiographies (for example, books about Ambrose Bierce and Oscar Wilde).
14. Create a village book club devoted to the Civil War.
15. Update my family history with all the new material I've learned and collected since I wrote my 120-page book in 1991.
16. Write a book on humor and jokes.

Recommended Reading

Albom, Mitch. *Tuesdays with Morrie: An Old Man, a Young Man, and Life's Greatest Lesson*. Doubleday, 1997.

Allen, David. *Making It All Work: Winning at the Game of Work and the Business of Life*. Penguin, 2008.

Allen, David. *Getting Things Done: The Art of Stress-Free Productivity*. Penguin, 2015.

Applewhite, Ashton. *This Chair Rocks: A Manifesto against Ageism*. Celadon Books, 2016.

Autrey, James. *Life and Work: A Manager's Search for Meaning*. Avon, 1994.

Barabási, Albert-László. *The Formula: The Universal Laws of Success*. Little, Brown and Company, 2018.

Becker, Joshua. *The Minimalist Home: A Room-by-Room Guide to a Decluttered, Refocused Life*. Penguin Random House, 2018.

Bennis, Warren. *On Becoming a Leader*. Addison Wesley, 1989.

Bennis, Warren. *An Invented Life: Reflections on Leadership and Change*. Addison Wesley, 1993.

Brooks, David. *The Second Mountain: The Quest for a Moral Life*. Random House, 2019.

Budd, Matthew, and Larry Rothstein. *You Are What You Say: The Proven Program That Uses the Power of Language to Combat Stress, Anger, and Depression*. Crown, 2000.

Burnett, Bill, and Dave Evans. *Designing Your Life: How to Build a Well-Lived, Joyful Life*. Knopf, 2016.

Covey, Stephen. *The Seven Habits of Highly Effective People*. Simon & Schuster, 1989.

Covey, Stephen, A. Roger Merrill, and Rebecca Merrill. *First Things First: To Live, to Love, to Learn, to Leave a Legacy*. Simon & Schuster, 1994.

Csikszentmihalyi, Mihaly. *Flow: The Psychology of Optimal Experience.* Harper, 1990.

Csikszentmihalyi, Mihaly. *Finding Flow: The Psychology of Engagement with Everyday Life.* Basic Books, 1997.

Currey, Mason. *Daily Rituals: How Artists Work.* Knopf, 2013.

Dweck, Carol. *Mindset: The New Psychology of Success.* Ballantine, 2016.

Eyal, Nir. *Indistractable: How to Control Your Attention and Choose Your Life.* BenBella Books, 2019.

Eyre, Linda, and Richard Eyre. *LifeBalance: Bringing Harmony to Your Everyday Life.* Ballantine, 1987.

Frankl, Viktor. *Man's Search for Meaning.* Simon & Schuster, 1959.

Franklin, Ben. *Autobiography.*

Freedman, Marc. *How to Live Forever: The Enduring Power of Connecting the Generations.* Public Affairs, 2018.

Gardner, Howard, et al. *Good Work: When Excellence and Ethics Meet.* Basic Books, 2001.

Goleman, Daniel. *Emotional Intelligence: Why It Can Matter More Than IQ.* Bantam, 1995.

Greiff, Barrie. *Legacy: The Giving of Life's Greatest Treasures.* HarperCollins, 1999.

Hall, Edith. *Aristotle's Way: How Ancient Wisdom Can Change Your Life.* The Bodley Head, 2018.

Harari, Yuval Noah. *Sapiens: A Brief History of Humankind.* HarperCollins, 2015.

Harvard Business Review. *On Managing Yourself.* Harvard Business Review Press, 2010.

Hillman, James. *The Force of Character: And the Lasting Life.* Random House, 1999.

Holiday, Ryan. *Stillness Is the Key.* Portfolio/Penguin, 2019.

Jenkins, Jo Ann. *Disrupt Aging: A Bold New Path to Living Your Best Life at Every Age.* PublicAffairs, 2016.

Johnson, Sue. *Hold Me Tight: Seven Conversations for a Lifetime of Love.* Little, Brown Spark, 2008.

Kaag, John. *Hiking with Nietzsche: On Becoming Who You Are.* Farrar, Straus and Giroux, 2018.

Kondo, Marie. *The Life-Changing Magic of Tidying Up: The Japanese Art of Decluttering and Organizing.* Ten Speed Press, 2016.

Kusher, Harold S. *Living a Life That Matters: Resolving the Conflict between Conscience and Success.* Knopf, 2001.

Lee, Blaine. *The Power Principle: Influence with Honor.* Simon & Schuster, 1997.

Levitin, Daniel J. *Successful Aging: A Neuroscientist Explores the Power and Potential of Our Lives.* Dutton, 2020.

Loehr, James. *Toughness Training for Life: A Revolutionary Program for Maximizing Health, Happiness, and Productivity.* Penguin, 1993.

May, Rollo. *The Discovery of Being.* Norton, 1983.

McGoldrick, Monica. *You Can Go Home Again: Reconnecting with Your Family.* Norton, 1995.

McGonigal, Jane. *SuperBetter: The Power of Living Gamefully.* Penguin, 2015.

McKeown, Greg. *Essentialism: The Disciplined Pursuit of Less.* Crown Business, 2014.

Meacham, Jon. *The Soul of America: The Battle for Our Better Angels.* Random House, 2018.

Miller, Caroline Adams. *Getting Grit: The Evidence-Based Approach to Cultivating Passion, Perseverance, and Purpose.* Sounds True, 2017.

Mohr, Tara. *Playing Big: Practical Wisdom for Women Who Want to Speak Up, Create, and Lead.* Penguin Random House, 2014.

Morgan, Edmund S. *Benjamin Franklin.* Yale University Press, 2002.

Morgenstern, Julie. *Organizing from the Inside Out: The Foolproof System for Organizing Your Home, Your Office, and Your Life.* Henry Holt and Company, 1998.

Newport, Cal. *Digital Minimalism: Choosing a Focused Life in a Noisy World.* Portfolio/Penguin, 2019.

Nozick, Robert. *The Examined Life: Philosophical Meditations.* Simon & Schuster, 1989.

Ornish, Dean, and Anne Ornish. *Undo It! How Simple Lifestyle Changes Can Reverse Most Chronic Diseases.* Ballantine, 2019.

Palmer, Chris. *Raise Your Kids to Succeed: What Every Parent Should Know.* Rowman & Littlefield, 2017.

Palmer, Chris. *Now What, Grad? Your Path to Success after College,* 2nd ed. Rowman & Littlefield, 2018.

Palmer, Chris. *College Teaching at Its Best: Inspiring Students to Be Enthusiastic, Lifelong Learners.* Rowman & Littlefield, 2019.

Peters, Tom. *Thriving on Chaos: Handbook for a Management Revolution.* Knopf, 1987.

Puddicombe, Andy. *The Headspace Guide to Meditation and Mindfulness.* St. Martin's Press, 2011.

Robbins, Anthony. *Unlimited Power: The New Science of Personal Achievement.* Fawcett, 1986.

Rohn, Jim. *The Five Major Pieces to the Life Puzzle: A Guide to Personal Success.* Jim Rohn International, 1991.

Roser, Laura. *Your Meaning Legacy: How to Cultivate and Pass on Non-Financial Assets.* Golden Legacy Press, 2018.

Sagan, Carl. *The Demon-Haunted World: Science as a Candle in the Dark.* Ballantine, 1996.

Schwartz, Tony. *What Really Matters: Searching for Wisdom in America.* Bantam, 1995.

Seligman, Martin. *Flourish: A Visionary New Understanding of Happiness and Well-Being.* Simon & Schuster, 2011.

Senge, Peter M. *The Fifth Discipline: The Art and Practice of the Learning Organization.* Doubleday, 1990.

Smith, Emily Esfahani. *The Power of Meaning: Finding Fulfillment in a World Obsessed with Happiness.* Crown, 2017.

Solomon, Sheldon, Jeff Greenberg, and Tom Pyszczynski. *The Worm at the Core: On the Role of Death in Life.* Random House, 2015.

Steiner-Adair, Catherine. *The Big Disconnect: Protecting Childhood and Family Relationships in the Digital Age.* HarperCollins, 2013.

Tracy, Brian. *Maximum Achievement: Strategies and Skills That Will Unlock Your Hidden Powers to Succeed.* Fireside, 1993.

Yalom, Irvin. *Becoming Myself: A Psychiatrist's Memoir.* Basic Books, 2017.

Zander, Rosamund, and Benjamin Zander. *The Art of Possibility: Transforming Professional and Personal Life.* Penguin, 2000.

~

Syllabus for
Design Your Life for Success

Design Your Life for Success

Email: christopher.n.palmer@gmail.com

Phone:

Chris's website is www.ChrisPalmerOnline.com

This three-part workshop is sponsored by the Bethesda Metro Area Village and by the Connie Morella Library.

It is designed and led by **Chris Palmer,** a passionate advocate of personal growth. Chris loves helping people find meaning, success, and fulfillment.

In addition to being a former professor, he is an author, film producer, speaker, father, and grandfather.

The workshop is open to the public, and *it is free.* By all means bring a friend!

Please register on line (Click here to register.)

"I created this workshop because I believe we all need to spend more time reflecting on how to find more purpose, meaning, and passion in our lives, and focusing on what really matters to us."

Dates and Location

- Wednesday, April 15, 6 to 8 p.m.: "Developing a Vision for Your Stage of Life"
- Wednesday, April 22, 6 to 8 p.m.: "Making Your Vision Operational"

- Wednesday, April 29, 6 to 8 p.m.: "Taking Action and Raising Your Productivity"

All classes are at the Connie Morella (Bethesda) Library at 7400 Arlington Road, Bethesda, MD 20814. *Come to all three sessions if you can.*

The workshop is free, but *registration is required.* Please click here to register. If you have any trouble registering, please email or call Chris Palmer.

Bethesda Metro Area Village is a nonprofit working to help you stay in your home as you age—safely, independently, and in the community you love. We offer volunteer-provided services and robust social programs to enrich the social lives of our members. If you are interested in learning more about membership or how to volunteer, check us out at http://www.bmavillage.org or email director@bmavillage.org.

Workshop Description

The workshop will explore the goals, strategies, and tactics necessary to live a successful, fulfilled, and productive life. We will reflect on our lives, discuss what really matters to us, consider how we find purpose and meaning in our lives, explore our life goals, think about our values, produce personal mission statements, examine how to take better care of ourselves, and learn effective time-management skills.

The workshop will focus on the following types of questions:

1. What are my goals? How can I bring more purpose, focus, and meaning to my life? What is the best way for me to shape the person I want to become so I can contribute in a meaningful way to society and helping other people?
2. Is there a dissonance between how I spend my time and what is most important to me?
3. How can I take better care of myself (physically, mentally, spiritually, socially, and emotionally)?
4. What is the best way to draft a powerful and inspiring personal mission statement so that I can begin to see my life in a fresh, focused, and revitalized way?
5. What do the words *success, happiness,* and *fulfillment* mean? How are they distinct?
6. What are the best ways of integrating the vision I have for my life, the plan I need to achieve it, and the actions to make things happen?

7. What are the benefits of taking more risks and getting outside my comfort zone?

This workshop is about actively designing our lives rather than simply drifting forward, reacting to what happens to us. It is important to periodically sit back, quietly reflect, and ask if our lives are headed in the right direction. It is healthy to look at the person we have become and ask if this is really who we want to be. We should proactively shape our character, decide our future, and create a rewarding life of meaning and purpose.

We want to behave in ways that are true to our most honorable, generous, and best selves. This workshop gives you the chance to design and shape the kind of person you want to be and to articulate the goals you want to achieve in your life, both professionally and personally.

Delivery

This workshop consists of three, two-hour discussion sessions on three consecutive Wednesday evenings. We will strive for class sessions that are interactive, lively, engaging, creative, and fun.

The workshop will be discussion-based and often involve working on your own quietly thinking and writing or working in pairs or small groups.

Workshop Learning Outcomes

By the end of the workshop, you will be able to do the following:

1. Formulate what really matters to you and what values are important to you.
2. Create and develop a personal mission statement that reflects the best possible life you want to lead, a life that is passionate, honorable, focused, purposeful, and meaningful.
3. Include in your personal mission statements changes you plan to make to your life to bring it into closer alignment with your life goals.
4. Apply essential time-management skills to your life.

How the Workshop Is Taught

I will encourage an active learning environment. Please bring a notebook to class so you can write and take notes. The room we are using does not have desks or tables to write on.

For homework, the class may read excerpts from books by Tara Mohr, Jane McGonigal, Edith Hall, Carol Dweck, Julia Cameron, Martin Seligman, Laura Roser, Irvin Yalom, Emily Esfahani Smith, Stephen Covey, Marie Kondo, David Allen, Ben Franklin, and Victor Frankl.

Instructor's Bio

Chris Palmer is a teacher, speaker, author, and environmental film producer. He served on American University's (AU) full-time faculty as a professor and as Distinguished Film Producer in Residence until his retirement in 2018. In 2004, he founded AU's Center for Environmental Filmmaking at the School of Communication. Over the past thirty years, Chris has spearheaded the production of more than 300 hours of original programming for primetime television and the IMAX film industry.

He has written five books: *Shooting in the Wild: An Insider's Account of Making Movies in the Animal Kingdom* (Sierra Club Books, 2010); *Confessions of a Wildlife Filmmaker: The Challenges of Staying Honest in an Industry Where Ratings Are King* (Bluefield Publishing, 2015); *Raise Your Kids to Succeed: What Every Parent Should Know* (Rowman & Littlefield, 2017); *Now What, Grad? Your Path to Success after College*, 2nd ed. (Rowman & Littlefield, 2018); *College Teaching at its Best: Inspiring Students to be Enthusiastic, Lifelong Learners* (Rowman & Littlefield, 2019). His website is http://www.ChrisPalmerOnline.com.

Thank you for your interest in the workshop.
Please call or email me if you have questions.

~

Fifty Ways to Improve Your Personal and Professional Life, Increase Your Productivity, and Feel Fulfilled

A Handout by Chris Palmer
www.ChrisPalmerOnline.com

All successful people are fulfilled and productive. They are good time managers and are well organized. They get a lot more done than the average person. This handout focuses on fifty ways to improve your success and productivity (i.e., to get your life in balance, to focus on what's important, to get more done, and to get it done faster).

I. Rethink Your Life
II. Create a Personal Mission Statement
III. Set Goals and a Plan
IV. Take Action
V. Some Final Thoughts

I. Rethink Your Life

1. *Rethink your life.* Improving your success involves more than ridding your life of time wasters like poorly run meetings, interruptions, and gossip. Radical gains in success and productivity come from ceasing to pursue a course of action (a job, a contract, a career, or a relationship) that is wrong for you. Don't waste years of your life working at something that you don't particularly enjoy or that you consider trivial. If

you are unhappy or feel unhealthily stressed, you may need to rethink your whole life rather than trying to make superficial improvements.

2. *Find out who you really want to be and what you really want to do.* Then *align that with work you truly love.* This is the key to having a happy and successful career. It will unleash untapped creative powers within you and lead to a leap in productivity that will astonish you.

3. *Don't let time, money, and fear stop you. What could you imagine doing if time, money, and fear were not obstacles? What would you do if you knew you could not fail?* If you had all the money in the world, what would you do for free? What are you passionate about? What fascinates you? What drives you onto your soapbox?

4. *Focus on what matters most to you in your professional and personal life. Is there alignment between how you spend your time and what is important to you?* Or are you spending time on projects and relationships that in the long run don't matter to you? When there is congruence between how you spend your day and what matters most to you, you increase both your inner sense of peace as well as your productivity. You feel happier, more effective and more fulfilled. You will have both ambition and serenity.

5. *Identify the challenges you face in achieving your goals. To repeat, do you see a significant gap between how you spend your time and what is most important to you?* What are the things in your personal and professional life that are stopping you from spending time on the issues, relationships, and projects that you care most deeply and passionately about? What is missing from your life right now?

6. *Create a list of the steps you can take to begin to overcome the challenges you identified in answering the last question.* Possibilities include: get a coach, identify a role model, stop smoking, eat more vegetables, combat anxiety, have a weekly date with your spouse, exercise every morning, enrich your vocabulary, read deeply, be more patient with your kids, get home every night for family dinners, join a cycling club, clear the mess off your desk, be more loving, get out of debt, lose weight, watch less TV, be more curious and creative, speak up more in staff meetings, get more sleep, eat less junk food, volunteer for a local nonprofit, stop to smell the roses, spend more time outside, take art lessons, smile more, keep the promises you make, make more offers, and seek help more often.

7. *List the things that deeply matter to you and that are most important to you.* Possibilities include: values like kindness and consideration for others, certain relationships, your health, having enough money to

support your family, feeling useful and appreciated, living to your full potential, finding a partner, increasing your knowledge, changing the world in some positive way, changing yourself in some way, working with decent, moral, and trustworthy colleagues, saving the environment for future generations, having more fun, being more playful, developing your sense of humor, feeling more joy in living, feeling safer and more secure, balancing your work and personal life, getting in better shape, securing a qualification of some kind, discovering something you feel passionate about, being better organized, transforming an embittered relationship into a loving one, caring for someone you love dearly, getting out of the rut you feel you're in, feeling less lonely and isolated, being more expressive and demonstrative, and feeling more grateful for all you have.

II. Create a Personal Mission Statement

8. *Make one of the roles in your life "self-development/renewal."* You have to take care of yourself before you can take care of anybody or anything else. Self-development/renewal is the vital process of enhancing your capacity to make you a more effective and fulfilled person. There are four dimensions to self-renewal: physical, social/emotional, mental, and spiritual:
   - *Physical* includes fitness, exercise, strength, flexibility, endurance, eating healthily, getting enough sleep, and deep relaxation.
   - *Social/emotional* includes love, friendship, connecting with others, volunteering, helping someone, and having a sense of belonging.
   - *Mental* includes learning, studying, reading, visiting museums and science centers, solving puzzles, writing, and developing intellectually.
   - *Spiritual* includes finding a purpose and meaning in your life through: service to others, art, contemplation, poetry, going on a personal retreat to reflect on your life, creating a personal mission statement, being at one with nature, identifying long-range goals, studying your family history, leaving a legacy, or whatever ways that create joy and passion for you personally.

9. *Identify your most important roles. By roles, I mean your key responsibilities and relationships.* For example, sister/brother, husband/wife/ life partner, mother/father, son/daughter, grandparent, friend, mentor, role model, team member, communicator, educator, volunteer, manager, lobbyist, community activist, yoga instructor, soccer coach, learner, artist, athlete, entrepreneur, environmentalist, and so on.

Pick about seven. By identifying your roles, you create a variety of perspectives from which to examine your life to ensure balance.

10. *For each of your roles, identify the people who are most important to you. Nothing is more important in our lives than the relationships we build with other people.* Relationships are more than important. They are everything.

11. *Select one person with whom you have a critically important relationship.* What are the assessments you would like this person to make about you at your funeral? What character traits and behaviors would you like them to praise and be grateful for?

12. *Keep your life in balance. The main reason for becoming more productive is so you can spend more time on what is really important to you.* It is tempting to become so preoccupied with work that we lose sight of why we wanted to become successful at work in the first place. Keep your life in balance by being aware of all your important roles in your life (not just your roles at work). Having a happy home life should be among your highest goals in life. However important your work is to you, there are things in your life outside of your work that need a lot of your time, including your spouse, kids, and health. Restorative rest, relaxation, and leisure are important. Athletes don't train all day, every day.

13. *Give your life purpose and meaning.* Having a personal mission statement that is deeply meaningful to you will give you a sense of purpose and meaning. It will help you figure out what you want to do and then integrate it into your daily life and decisions. Don't expect an epiphany as you think about your purpose in life. It often takes time to find the words for a personal mission statement that inspire and excite you.

14. *Write the story of your life.* In creating your personal mission statement, you are beginning to write the story of your life. What gives your life meaning? What should you do with your life? Whom do you want to become? Who are you? What do you stand for? What is your life fundamentally about? What matters deeply to you?

15. *Create your own unique personal mission statement.* Your personal mission statement helps you decide at critical moments in your day what to do with your time and energy. It describes what kind of person you want to be and what you want to achieve in your life. It can be as short as one sentence, and it doesn't have to be perfect. There is no "correct" way of doing it, and you can revise it as often as you want. Without a personal mission statement, our lives can sometimes seem chaotic, overly busy, and adrift.

III. Set Goals and a Plan

16. *Set goals. This is a powerful process. Without goals, our lives are essentially drifting without focus.* Goals turn our dreams into reality. They cause us to stretch and grow in new ways. In fact, what you *get* by achieving a goal is less valuable than what you *become* by achieving that goal.

17. *Put your goals in writing. Your goals are of little help unless they are in writing.* Putting your plans on paper makes a goal more concrete, meaningful, and real. It is much more likely that you will exercise integrity and fulfill the promises you make to yourself and to others when your goals are in writing.

18. *Articulate your long-range goals in your professional life, your personal life, and in the four self-development/renewal areas (physical, social/emotional, mental, and spiritual).* This is a critical step if you are to align your daily activities with what is most important to you. Incorporate your long-range goals into your personal mission statement.

19. *Subdivide each of your long-range goals into more manageable shorter-range goals. Begin to think of these short-range goals as commitments; that is, goals you are committed to achieve.* These commitments must be expressed in such a way as to meet the SMART test (i.e., they must be specific, measurable, achievable, relevant, and time bound). For example, if one of your long-range goals is to write a book on your family history, then a few of your commitments could be: interview your mom and dad by June 1, find a coach who can help you by July 1, find all the photos in your parents' home relating to your grandparents and their parents by August 1, and so on.

20. *Plan weekly, not daily.* Planning daily is problematic because it is too easy to get caught up in the minutiae of urgent activities and lose the connection between your commitments (your important strategic goals) and the daily rush of meetings, phone calls, email, and so on. Have a regular time once a week (I do it on Sunday evening) to review your personal mission statement and your commitments, and block off time on your calendar for you to commit yourself to work on them. In this way, you put the "big rocks" on your calendar first so they don't get squeezed out by the unimportant "pebbles." For example, if one of your commitments is "to repair a strained relationship with a colleague," then at the start of the week you would schedule time (perhaps for lunch) to meet with that person. In this way, you can begin to spend more time on those relationships, projects, and goals that matter most to you.

21. *Incorporate your commitments (including those relating to renewal) into your weekly schedule.* I am repeating the previous point but it needs to be repeated because so many people underestimate its importance. What are the commitments you want to add to your schedule as you do your weekly planning? Select commitments from each of your roles (including "self-development/renewal") and make a specific appointment with yourself during the week with a determination to make massive progress on the task/relationship/project you've selected. These "rocks" will form a solid foundation on which to build your weekly activities and help keep your life in balance. As things come up during the week, prioritize and schedule around your goals.

22. *Get a planner or notebook in which you can keep your personal mission statement, your roles and key relationships, your long-range goals, your commitments, and your schedule.* Identifying what you are passionate about and committed to achieving in your life and then keeping those commitments is deeply satisfying. A planner or notebook of some kind can help. Label your notebook or planner "My Life Plan." Mastery of the principles taught in this workshop can be applied to any productivity tool of your choice.

23. *Don't be a slave to your plan.* It isn't always necessary to follow a plan exactly. A plan is there to keep you *headed in the right direction*, not to deprive you of all spontaneity. In fact, one of the benefits of planning is to free you up to be more spontaneous and to enjoy life more. A plan gives you an option to choose from.

24. *Remember that each day is important and should not be wasted. Each day that passes means you have one day less to live. The secret of your life and your future lies hidden in your daily routine.* Derive what you are committed to do on a daily basis from your commitments in your personal mission statement rather than from the torrent of emails, meetings, interruptions, and so on, that tend to distract you from staying focused on what matters most to you. In this way, you can live each day by being true to your values, goals, and passions. Your goal is to make daily decisions consistent with your commitments. You have integrity when your daily actions are consistent with your personal mission statement.

25. *Strengthen your self-respect and integrity by making and keeping promises to yourself and others.* Making promises that are kept (or at a minimum effectively managed) is a characteristic of successful people. Take all your commitments very seriously, however small. When you agree to do something, do it, and do it when you said you would in the way

you agreed to do it. Develop the habit of attaching great importance to the commitments you make to yourself and to others.

26. *Don't let urgent matters displace important matters.* A personal mission statement helps prevent this from happening. Unimportant but urgent matters (e.g., interruptions, some meetings and phone calls, other people's minor issues, and so on) should never be given priority over important yet not urgent matters (e.g., planning, preparation, preventing crises, getting feedback, building relationships, reflection, learning, personal development, seizing new opportunities, and so on).

27. *To repeat, don't confuse urgent tasks with important tasks.* Occasionally, urgent tasks are important. More often, urgent tasks are not important, and important tasks are not urgent. This is why important tasks, such as building a relationship with your spouse, often get neglected.

IV. Take Action

28. *Relentlessly take new actions.* To be successful in any field, you must relentlessly take new actions. Your enthusiasm can energize you to take action, but taking action can also increase your enthusiasm. Many of us are stuck in "inaction" because of fear or some other reason. Overcoming fear and taking action can change our mood from one of resignation and despair to one of ambition and serenity.

29. *To repeat: overcome fear and take action, no matter how small.* Taking action, even if it is only calling a friend for advice or visiting a website, gets you out into the world where good luck is more likely to be. Thomas Jefferson observed that the harder he worked, the more good luck he seemed to have.

30. *To repeat yet again (because of its importance), take initiatives constantly. Highly productive people are intensely action oriented.* Be constantly in motion. Relentlessly take initiatives to get the job done and to move continuously toward your goals. Remember Lincoln's frustrations with General George McClellan in the Civil War. Lincoln complained McClellan had the "slows." Don't have the slows. Be action oriented. Seize opportunities quickly. Make requests, promises, and offers as often as possible. Take the initiative. The faster you move, the better you will feel.

31. *Move quickly, and develop a reputation for speed and reliability.* Take important phone calls immediately. Complete all small jobs (under a couple of minutes) immediately. Respond quickly to requests from people with whom you have important relationships (your spouse,

your boss, your kids, and so on). Pick up speed. Hustle. Do it now. Develop a fast tempo.

32. *Ask yourself the following question over and over again: What is the best use of my time right now?* This is a key question if you are interested in improving your productivity. Discipline yourself to work only on the answer to that question. Remind yourself that the answer is not "refreshing my Facebook newsfeed" or some other time-sucking activity.

33. *Apply the 80/20 rule (i.e., 20 percent of the things you do will account for 80 percent of the value of all the things you do).* Your job is to identify those few activities that are so vitally productive and spend more time on them.

34. *Always think on paper. Don't work out of your mind. Work from written lists.* Whenever you have a new task, add it to your list. Don't keep it in your head. This will sharpen your thinking and increase your effectiveness and productivity. Crossing off items one-by-one will motivate you to keep going, give you energy, and elevate your mood.

35. *At the start of each day in the office, don't check your email (or if you feel impelled to, check in very quickly). Instead, select the most important and valuable strategic task you are facing and work on that until it is finished.* This will energize you for the whole day and make you feel like a winner. By starting your day tackling the biggest challenge you face, you will set yourself up to storm through the rest of the day brimming with self-confidence and enthusiasm.

36. *Don't waste time starting and restarting a task. Select the most important thing you have to do on your list (the task that will make the biggest difference to your life and career), then focus on it with energy and concentration.* Keep only that task, and nothing else, in front of you. Discipline yourself to stay with it until it is complete. When it is complete, you will feel a rush of good feelings (high self-esteem, joy, optimism, tranquility, and high energy) that will reward you for your self-discipline.

37. *Learn to decline requests from others. Sometimes the best time-saver of all is the word "no." Learning how to decline a request without damaging a relationship is a valuable skill.* Identifying activities in your life that are not important to you (or no longer important to you) is key to improving your productivity and happiness. What can you stop doing so you can free up time to do more of the things that are really important to you?

38. *Organize your workspace. People who claim they work better from a messy desk are deluding themselves. Studies show this not to be true at all.* Work from a clean desk and clean workspace.

39. *Handle each piece of paper once. Don't pick it up and then put it down aimlessly on your desk. Toss it, refer it to someone else, act on it, or file it.* When in doubt, throw it out. If you haven't read it within six months, it is junk and should be tossed. The same rule applies to emails: respond, file, or delete. Do not let emails accumulate.

40. *Listen attentively and actively to other people. Most of us have never learned how to listen well enough to deeply understand a person from their frame of reference.* Listening in this way is hard work. It means listening to understand rather than reply. Listening empathetically in this way doesn't necessarily mean you agree but simply that you understand. Because the other person's need to be understood is satisfied, you are more likely to be listened to and understood in return.

41. *Don't blame others when things go wrong, but instead focus on how you contributed to the breakdown. Take responsibility.* When something goes wrong, it is tempting to look for someone or something to blame. A better first step is to ask, "How did I contribute to this breakdown? What did I do to help bring about this state of affairs?"

V. Some Final Thoughts

42. *Use travel time productively. Too many of us squander travel time needlessly.* Turn your car into a learning machine (i.e., a college on wheels) by playing tapes that teach you skills you need to succeed in your relationships or some other area in which you are striving to do better. On a plane, don't drink alcohol or waste time reading the junk in the seat pocket in front of you. Rather, make every minute count by preparing for your upcoming presentations and meetings or by working on a high-priority strategic goal.

43. *Resolve to be efficient and to not waste time. Commit to be highly productive and efficient in everything you do.* Become an expert in time management and personal productivity. Learn and practice the fifty suggestions in this workshop so they become habits. Become a model of self-discipline—the ability to make yourself do what you should when you should, whether you feel like it or not.

44. *Make a commitment to deepen your understanding of success and fulfillment. They are not the same.* Success and happiness are not goals to capture and hold. They happen incidentally while you are living out your own vision of life and living a life built on integrity, trust, courage, love, fairness, service, patience, self-discipline, responsibility, generosity, hard work, and tenacity. Happiness is not a goal but rather a consequence of pursuing something deeply meaningful to you.

45. *Commit to dig deeper into yourself to find out what you care passionately about and what matters most to you.* Implement a planning system for yourself that helps you spend more time on those relationships and projects that matter most to you.

46. *Twice a year, keep a time diary for a week.* Review how you are actually spending your time and compare it to how you would *like* to be spending your time.

47. *Keep a personal journal.* This will help you become a more skillful observer of yourself and become more self-aware of the identity you create for yourself with other people. If you are unhappy about something or if you are pleased by something you have accomplished, write about it. When you gain an insight, put it on paper. Keeping a personal journal encourages you to constantly improve, to raise your standards, to live more purposefully, and to observe with fascination how much of behavior is "automatic" rather than intentional. Keeping a journal helps you to design and invent your own life rather than drift along under the influence of your genes and environment.

48. *Rid yourself of any duplicity in your life.* Fulfillment and duplicity are mutually exclusive.

49. *Reach out to friends and colleagues for feedback and coaching.* Everyone needs a coach. We all need help and guidance in the different domains of our life, including our personal lives. Without feedback, we stop learning and can become arrogant, isolated, and prone to errors of judgment. Your coach (or a good friend) can hold you accountable for the promises you make. A coach is someone who poses questions for clarification, challenges and advises you, provides a different and fresh perspective, listens and understands you, offers a reality check, instills confidence, and ensures that you follow up on your commitments.

50. *Reinvent yourself every year when you rigorously reevaluate and revise your personal mission statement.* Thinking periodically about how you would reinvent your life is crucial to radically improving your success, fulfillment, and productivity. Do you want to continue doing what you are doing? You are getting older, and time is running out. Be bold in your thinking.

Question: What specific steps are you committed to take in the next 48 hours to start making changes in your life to implement what you have learned in this workshop?

~

Notes

Introduction

1. For more on slow medicine, see Victoria Sweet, *Slow Medicine: The Way to Healing* (Riverhead Books, an imprint of Penguin Random House, 2017). Also see Dennis McCullough, *My Mother, Your Mother: Embracing "Slow Medicine," the Compassionate Approach to Caring for Your Aging Loved Ones* (Harper Perennial, an imprint of HarperCollins, 2009). Katy Butler, *Knocking on Heaven's Door: The Path to a Better Way of Death* (Scribner, 2013) is another excellent introduction to slow medicine.

2. For more on slow food, visit Slow Food USA, https://www.slowfoodusa.org/frequently-asked-questions. "Slow Food is food that's good for us, good for our environment and good for the people who grow, pick, and prepare it. In other words, food that is good, clean, and fair. In many ways, Slow Food is the opposite of fast food. Slow Food is fresh and healthy, free of pesticides and chemicals, and produced and accessed in a way that's beneficial to all—from the farmer to the eater. It's a way of saying no to the rise of fast food and fast life. Slow Food means living an unhurried life, taking time to enjoy simple pleasures, starting at the table."

3. A few others have used the term "slow success," but it isn't widely used.

4. James Stavridis, *Sailing True North: Ten Admirals and the Voyage of Character* (Penguin, 2019).

5. Quoted by George Sheehan in his book *Running and Being: The Total Experience* (Simon & Schuster, 1978), 18.

6. Dave Ellis, *Creating Your Future: Five Steps to the Life of Your Dreams* (Houghton Mifflin, 1998), 3.

7. I still teach the workshop free of charge, and if you are interested in taking it, please write to me at christopher.n.palmer@gmail.com.

8. I came across this wonderful quote from Lorde in mortician Caitlin Doughty's coruscating book *Smoke Gets in Your Eyes: And Other Lessons from the Crematory* (Norton, 2014) about death and dying.

9. By "wisdom literature," I am referring to the classic and philosophical books of our society, sometimes going back more than two thousand years, that deal with the art of living wisely and productively.

10. Isaac Asimov, *Asimov Laughs Again: More Than 700 Favorite Jokes, Limericks, and Anecdotes* (HarperCollins, 1992), 145.

11. I highly recommend Liesl Johnson's daily email on words, "Make Your Point," http://www.hilotutor.com/.

Chapter One

1. Chris Palmer, *Raise Your Kids to Succeed: What Every Parent Should Know* (Rowman & Littlefield, 2017).

2. Peter F. Drucker, "Managing Oneself," *Harvard Business Review*, January 1999.

3. Albert-László Barabási, *The Formula: The Universal Laws of Success* (Little, Brown and Company, 2018).

4. Barabási, 12.

5. Chris Palmer, *College Teaching at Its Best: Inspiring Students to Be Enthusiastic, Lifelong Learners* (Rowman & Littlefield, 2019).

6. Arthur C. Brooks, "In the Age of a Reality-TV President, Americans Are Saying No to Fame," *New York Times*, October 18, 2019.

7. A. C. Brooks.

8. Dr. Catherine Steiner-Adair, *The Big Disconnect: Protecting Childhood and Family Relationships in the Digital Age* (HarperCollins, 2013), 221.

9. Bill Burnett and Dave Evans, *Designing Your Life: How to Build a Well-Lived, Joyful Life* (Knopf, 2016).

10. Burnett and Evans, xvi.

11. Speech by New York governor Theodore Roosevelt, Chicago, April 10, 1899; see https://en.wikipedia.org/wiki/The_Strenuous_Life.

12. David Brooks, *The Second Mountain: The Quest for a Moral Life* (Random House, 2019).

13. D. Brooks, 301.

14. Jon Meacham, *The Soul of America: The Battle for Our Better Angels* (Random House, 2018), 40.

15. Meacham, 40.

16. Edith Hall, *Aristotle's Way: How Ancient Wisdom Can Change Your Life* (The Bodley Head, 2018).

17. Hall, 41.

18. Martin E. P. Seligman, *Flourish: A Visionary New Understanding of Happiness and Well-Being* (Atria paperback, Simon & Schuster, 2011), 2.

19. Seligman, 2.

20. Seligman, 24, 241.

21. Seligman, 24, and throughout his book.

22. For example, see https://www.ncbi.nlm.nih.gov/pmc/articles/PMC3122271/.

23. Winston Churchill, "Painting as a Pastime" in *Amid These Storms* (Charles Scribner's Sons, 1932).

24. The quote is from Arianna Huffington's 2015 book, *Thrive: The Third Metric to Redefining Success and Creating a Life of Well-Being, Wisdom, and Wonder.* See http://ariannahuffington.com/thrive.

25. Huffington.

26. Bill Gates's blog, December 29, 2018, https://www.gatesnotes.com/About-Bill-Gates/Year-in-Review-2018?WT.mc_id=12_29_2018_21_YIR2018_BG-EM_&WT.tsrc=BGEM.

27. Seligman, *Flourish*, 10, 11.

28. See https://en.wikipedia.org/wiki/Ralph_Waldo_Emerson.

29. See https://stevemaraboli.net/.

30. Emily Esfahani Smith, *The Power of Meaning: Finding Fulfillment in a World Obsessed with Happiness* (Crown, 2017).

31. For example, see https://positivepsychology.com/parenthood-paradox/.

32. Palmer, *Raise Your Kids to Succeed*, xix.

33. Bronnie Ware, *The Top Five Regrets of the Dying: A Life Transformed by the Dearly Departing* (Hay House, 2019).

34. Ware.

Chapter Two

1. Walker Percy, *The Moviegoer* (Knopf, 1961).

2. I'm grateful to Christiane Wiese, former director of Volunteer Services at Montgomery Hospice in Rockville, Maryland, for introducing me to this poem by Rabbi Alvin Fine.

3. Irvin Yalom, *Becoming Myself: A Psychiatrist's Memoir* (Basic Books, 2017).

4. Cal Newport, *Digital Minimalism: Choosing a Focused Life in a Noisy World* (Portfolio/Penguin, 2019), 85.

5. Albert Camus, *The Myth of Sisyphus and Other Essays* (Knopf, 1955), 4.

6. Rabbi Harold Kushner, *When Bad Things Happen to Good People* (Random House, 1981).

7. Yuval Noah Harari, *Sapiens: A Brief History of Mankind* (HarperCollins, 2015), 391.

8. Viktor Frankl, *Man's Search for Meaning* (Simon & Schuster, 1959), 117.

9. Frankl, 93.

10. Emily Esfahani Smith, *The Power of Meaning: Finding Fulfillment in a World Obsessed with Happiness* (Crown, 2017), 24.

11. Chris Palmer, *College Teaching at Its Best: Inspiring Students to Be Enthusiastic, Lifelong Learners* (Rowman & Littlefield, 2019), 67.

12. Bill Gates, "What Are the Biggest Problems Facing Us in the 21st Century?," *New York Times Book Review*, September 4, 2018, https://www.nytimes

.com/2018/09/04/books/review/21-lessons-for-the-21st-century-yuval-noah-harari .html.

13. See https://www.nightingale.com/articles/success-a-worthy-destination/.

14. See http://www.bbc.co.uk/radio4/history/inourtime/greatest_philosopher_ludwig _wittgenstein.shtml.

15. Smith, *The Power of Meaning*, 5.

16. See https://en.wikipedia.org/wiki/Steven_Pinker.

17. Bill Burnett and Dave Evans, *Designing Your Life: How to Build a Well-Lived, Joyful Life* (Knopf, 2016), 184.

18. John Kaag, *Hiking with Nietzsche: On Becoming Who You Are* (Farrar, Straus and Giroux, 2018), 220.

19. See https://existentialstoic.wordpress.com/2018/07/21/the-untamed-tongue/.

20. See https://en.wikipedia.org/wiki/Johann_Wolfgang_von_Goethe.

21. Quoted in James Stavridis, *Sailing True North* (Penguin, 2019).

22. Anu Garg (born April 5, 1967) is an American author and speaker. He is also founder of Wordsmith.org, an online community comprising word lovers from an estimated 200 countries. I highly recommend his free daily email about words.

23. Thomas H. Naylor, William H. Willimon, and Magdalena R. Naylor, *The Search for Meaning* (Abingdon Press, 1994), 8.

24. See https://www.thejoandidion.com/.

25. Stephen R. Covey, *The Seven Habits of Highly Effective People* (Simon & Schuster, 1989).

26. Visit https://www.newyorker.com/science/maria-konnikova/struggles-psychol ogist-studying-self-control.

27. See https://www.jimrohn.com/.

28. See https://en.wikipedia.org/wiki/Simon_Wiesenthal.

29. See https://www.scientificamerican.com/article/the-american-economy-is -rigged/.

30. Jon Meacham, *The Soul of America: The Battle for Our Better Angels* (Random House, 2018).

31. See https://www.jordanbpeterson.com/12-rules-for-life/.

32. Frankl, *Man's Search for Meaning*, 135.

33. I'm grateful to quotation expert and author Dr. Mardy Grothe for bringing this Thomas Mann quote to my attention. See www.drmardy.com.

Chapter Three

1. John Kaag, *Hiking with Nietzsche: On Becoming Who You Are* (Farrar, Straus and Giroux, 2018), 219–21.

2. See https://en.wikipedia.org/wiki/Simon_Sinek.

3. See https://www.becomingminimalist.com/.

4. Cal Newport, *Digital Minimalism: Choosing a Focused Life in a Noisy World* (Port-folio/Penguin, 2019), 125, 126.

5. Anthony de Mello, *Awareness: The Perils and Opportunities of Reality* (Random House, 1990), 3.

6. See http://www.powertalk.se/about/.

7. An excellent article on personal mission statements is from Tara Parker-Pope, "In with the New Mission Statement," *New York Times*, January 5, 2015.

8. See https://plato.stanford.edu/entries/nietzsche/.

9. See https://medium.com/publishous/the-only-difference-between-successful -unsuccessful-people-b9e70f952f66.

10. See https://en.wikipedia.org/wiki/Linus_Pauling.

11. Epictetus, *A Manual for Living: A New Interpretation by Sharon Lebell* (Harper-Collins, 1994), 60, 61.

12. Bill Burnett and Dave Evans, *Designing Your Life: How to Build a Well-Lived, Joyful Life* (Knopf, 2016), xxix.

13. Burnett and Evans, xxix.

14. Peter M. Senge, *The Fifth Discipline: The Art and Practice of the Learning Organization* (Doubleday, 1990), 7.

15. Senge, 142.

16. Stephen R. Covey, *The Seven Habits of Highly Effective People* (Simon & Schuster, 1989).

17. Nir Eyal, *Indistractable: How to Control Your Attention and Choose Your Life* (BenBella Books, 2019), 191.

Chapter Four

1. Jane McGonigal, *SuperBetter: The Power of Living Gamefully* (Penguin, 2015), 2–8.

2. McGonigal, 2–8.

3. Anne Lamott, *Bird by Bird: Some Instructions on Writing and Life* (Anchor Books, 1994), 19.

4. See http://www.tonyrobbins.com.

5. Cyn Meyer is the founder of Second Wind Movement and helps seniors have richer, more fulfilling "retirements." I have worked with her and highly recommend her coaching. Visit http://secondwindmovement.com/about-cyn-2/.

6. Tim Herrera, "Don't Waste Your Time with Bad Resolutions: This Is How to Do Them Right," *New York Times*, December 18, 2017.

7. See https://www.briantracy.com/.

8. Mihaly Csikszentmihalyi, *Finding Flow: The Psychology of Engagement with Everyday Life* (Basic Books, 1997), 301.

9. Caroline Adams Miller, *Getting Grit: The Evidence-Based Approach to Cultivating Passion, Perseverance, and Purpose* (Sounds True, 2017), 201.

10. I'm indebted to Dr. Mardy Grothe for bringing these quotes from William Sloane Coffin and James Russell Lowell to my attention. His website is http://www .drmardy.com.

11. See http://www.drmardy.com.

12. Martin Seligman, *Flourish: A Visionary New Understanding of Happiness and Well-Being* (Simon & Schuster, 2011), 221–23.

13. Edith Hall, *Aristotle's Way: How Ancient Wisdom Can Change Your Life* (The Bodley Head, 2018), 60.

14. The quote can be found in Clayton Christensen, "Managing Oneself," *Harvard Business Review*, January 1999, 3.

15. Thomas Friedman, "Owning Your Own Future," *New York Times*, May 10, 2017.

16. Chris Palmer, *Confessions of a Wildlife Filmmaker* (Bluefield, 2015).

17. Megan Greenwell, "Ignore the Career Blogs (and Listen to Me)," *New York Times*, October 13, 2019.

18. Chris Palmer, *Now What, Grad? Your Path to Success after College*, 2nd ed. (Rowman & Littlefield, 2018).

19. Bill Burnett and Dave Evans, *Designing Your Life: How to Build a Well-Lived, Joyful Life* (Knopf, 2016), 49.

20. Nicholas Kristof has an excellent e-newsletter. The quote about careers in finance and consulting comes from his December 5, 2019 issue: https://mail .google.com/mail/u/0/#inbox/WhctKJVjPdrkLzhHLkHDJwljqtPprFpvgkQWsfkBrdfncr GtZNfSkbCTxgFbjHhWlQZwdLB.

21. David Allen, *Getting Things Done: The Art of Stress-Free Productivity* (Penguin, 2015).

Chapter Five

1. See https://simonsinek.com/.

2. Aline Holzwarth, "How Self-Care Fits into a Model of Generosity," *Give and Take blog*, February 6, 2019, http://www.giveandtakeinc.com.

4. Stephen R. Covey, *The Seven Habits of Highly Effective People* (Simon & Schuster, 1989), 288.

5. Covey, 288.

6. George Sheehan, *Running and Being: The Total Experience* (Simon & Schuster, 1978).

7. See https://www.health.harvard.edu/staying-healthy/obesity-in-america-whats -driving-the-epidemic.

8. See https://aubreyreinmiller.com/info/.

9. Dean Ornish and Anne Ornish, *UnDo It! How Simple Lifestyle Changes Can Reverse Most Chronic Diseases* (Ballantine, 2019), 6.

10. Moses Maimonides, *The Guide for the Perplexed*, published ca. 1190.

11. Jane Brody, "Behind Health-Robbing Ailments: Inflammation," *New York Times*, December 24, 2019.

12. Mandy Oaklander and Heather Jones, "7 Surprising Benefits of Exercise," *Time*, September 1, 2016.

13. Daniel J. Levitin, *Successful Aging: A Neuroscientist Explores the Power and Potential of Our Lives* (Dutton, 2020), 256–79.

14. Michael Pollan, *In Defense of Food: An Eater's Manifesto* (Penguin, 2008).

15. Andy Puddicombe, *The Headspace Guide to Meditation and Mindfulness* (St. Martin's Press, 2011).

16. See also Sam Harris, *Waking Up: A Guide to Spirituality without Religion* (Simon & Schuster, 2014).

17. See https://www.healthline.com/health/science-sleep-why-you-need-7-8-hours-night.

18. See https://angeladuckworth.com/.

19. Thanks to psychologist Angela Duckworth for the idea from neuroscientist Matthew Walker. See Duckworth's e-newsletter of January 5, 2020, titled "Sleep Success," published by Character Lab, 3401 Market Street, Suite 202, Philadelphia, Pennsylvania, 19104.

20. See also Irvin D. Yalom, *Staring at the Sun: Overcoming the Terror of Death* (Jossey-Bass, 2008), 119.

21. Martin Seligman, *Flourish: A Visionary New Understanding of Happiness and Well-Being* (Simon & Schuster, 2011), 20.

22. Seligman, 20, 21.

23. Ben Sasse, *Them: Why We Hate Each Other and How to Heal* (St. Martin's Press, 2018), 11.

24. Sasse, 67.

25. Bruce Feiler, "Here's How to Ask for Forgiveness," *New York Times*, September 27, 2015.

26. Dr. Emma Seppala is the associate director of the Center for Compassion and Altruism Research and Education at Stanford University. Visit http://ccare.stanford.edu/.

27. George Will, "Our Epidemic of Loneliness," *Washington Post*, October 14, 2018.

28. See https://en.wikipedia.org/wiki/Mother_Teresa.

29. Jim Rohn, *The Seasons of Life* (Jim Rohn International, 1981).

30. David Brooks, *The Second Mountain: The Quest for a Moral Life* (Random House, 2019), 300.

31. See http://www.HealthLetter.MayoClinic.com, September 2016, 6.

32. See http://www.HealthLetter.MayoClinic.com, 6.

33. David DeSteno, "The Only Way to Keep Your Resolutions," *New York Times*, December 29, 2017.

34. "Wish I'd Said That," WIST, wist.info/other/39380/.

35. I highly recommend Dr. Mardy Grothe. His website is http://www.drmardy.com.

36. Dr. Sue Johnson, *Hold Me Tight: Seven Conversations for a Lifetime of Love* (Little, Brown Spark, 2008), 9.

37. See http://bowlingalone.com/.

38. Johnson, *Hold Me Tight*, 14.

39. Dr. Mary Pipher, *The Shelter of Each Other: Rebuilding Our Families* (G. P. Putnam's Sons, 1996).

40. Seligman, *Flourish*.

41. Johnson, *Hold Me Tight*, 26.

42. Johnson, 6.

43. See https://en.wikipedia.org/wiki/Solitary_confinement.

44. Seligman, *Flourish*, 67.

45. J. R. Storment's wrenching LinkedIn post can be found at https://www.linkedin.com/pulse/its-later-than-you-think-j-r-storment/.

46. Cal Newport, *Digital Minimalism: Choosing a Focused Life in a Noisy World* (Portfolio/Penguin, 2019), 141–44.

47. Newport, 141–44.

48. Covey, *Seven Habits*.

49. Mardy Grothe has written many books, including the entertaining *I Never Metaphor I Didn't Like: A Comprehensive Compilation of History's Greatest Analogies, Metaphors, and Similes*, and his website is www.drmardy.com. He is one of the world's foremost experts on quotations.

50. See https://en.wikipedia.org/wiki/Simone_de_Beauvoir.

51. See https://en.wikipedia.org/wiki/Isaac_Asimov.

52. Peter Senge, *The Fifth Discipline: The Art and Practice of the Learning Organization* (Doubleday, 1990), 14.

53. Samuel Smiles, *Self-Help: With Illustrations of Character and Conduct* (John Murray, 1859).

54. See https://en.wikipedia.org/wiki/Shonda_Rhimes.

55. Grace Fleming, "Introduction to Critical Thinking," Thought Company, September 24, 2018, https://www.thoughtco.com/introduction-to-critical-thinking -1857079.

56. Thomas L. Friedman, "Online and Scared," *New York Times*, January 11, 2017.

57. Kendra Cherry, "How to Identify a Pseudoscience," Thought Company, February 13, 2019, https://www.thoughtco.com/what-is-a-pseudoscience-2795470.

58. Carl Sagan, *The Demon-Haunted World: Science as a Candle in the Dark* (Ballantine, 1996), 22.

59. I'm grateful to Rabbi Gary Fink, senior vice president of counseling and family support at Montgomery Hospice in Maryland (I serve on its board) for helping me think through these spiritual issues.

60. See note 58.

61. See https://en.wikipedia.org/wiki/Felix_Adler_(professor).

62. David Brooks, "The Moral Bucket List," *New York Times*, April 11, 2015.

63. Edmund S. Morgan, *Benjamin Franklin* (Yale University Press, 2002).

64. See https://en.wikipedia.org/wiki/H._L._Mencken.

65. Again, I highly recommend the excellent work of Dr. Mardy Grothe, who has written many books. His website is http://www.drmardy.com.

Chapter Six

1. John C. Maxwell, *Intentional Living: Choosing a Life That Matters* (Hachette Book Group, 2015), 5.
2. See https://www.briantracy.com/.
3. David Allen, *Making It All Work: Winning at the Game of Work and the Business of Life* (Penguin, 2008).
4. David Brooks, *The Second Mountain: The Quest for a Moral Life* (Random House, 2019), 52–59.
5. Brooks, 59.
6. See https://www.dominican.edu/directory-people/gail-matthews.

Chapter Seven

1. Edmund S. Morgan, *Benjamin Franklin* (Yale University Press, 2002).
2. See https://en.wikipedia.org/wiki/Robert_Schuller.
3. Jim Rohn, *The Seasons of Life* (Success Books, 1981).
4. See https://en.wikipedia.org/wiki/Will_Durant.
5. See https://plato.stanford.edu/entries/heraclitus/.
6. See http://www.anniedillard.com/books-annie-dillard.html.
7. Nir Eyal, *Indistractable: How to Control Your Attention and Choose Your Life* (BenBella Books, 2019), 54.
8. Rohn, *Seasons of Life.*
9. See https://www.famousphilosophers.org/bertrand-russell/.
10. See https://plato.stanford.edu/entries/nietzsche/.
11. See https://en.m.wikipedia.org/wiki/Johann_Wolfgang_von_Goethe.
12. Visit https://angeladuckworth.com/.
13. Mason Currey, *Daily Rituals: How Artists Work* (Knopf, 2013).
14. Visit https://gretchenrubin.com/blog/.
15. Visit http://www.anniedillard.com/.
16. Jim Rohn, *The Five Major Pieces to the Life Puzzle* (Jim Rohn International, 1991).
17. See https://www.poetryfoundation.org/poets/henry-wadsworth-longfellow.
18. See Monday.com and also their excellent article on time blocking at https://monday.com/blog/increase-your-productivity-with-time-blocking-a-step-by-step-guide/?utm_source=mb&utm_campaign=pockettab.
19. Visit Professor Cal Newport's website: https://www.calnewport.com/.
20. https://www.webmd.com/fitness-exercise/news/20140407/sitting-disease-faq#1.
21. "Navy Seal Admiral Shares Reasons to Make Bed Everyday," *Be Better Than Average channel*, January 19, 2015, YouTube video, 1:41, https://www.youtube.com/watch?v=KgzLzbd-zT4.
22. "What It Means to Eat the Frog," *Noisli blog*, March 4, 2016, https://blog.noisli.com/what-it-meansto-eat-the-frog/.

23. Susan Moon, *This is Getting Old: Zen Thoughts on Aging with Humor and Dignity* (Shambhala, 2010), 158.

24. Chris Palmer, *Now What, Grad? Your Path to Success after College*, 2nd ed. (Rowman & Littlefield, 2018), 73.

25. https://careeradvancementblog.com/disadvantages-multitasking/.

26. https://wakingup.com/.

27. https://www.mentalfloss.com/article/60632/11-scientific-reasons-why-being -nature-relaxing.

28. Ashley Yeager, "Evening Screen Time Can Sabotage Sleep," *Science News for Students*, November 1, 2017, https://www.sciencenewsforstudents.org/article/ evening-screen-time-can-sabotage-sleep.

29. Mihaly Csikszentmihalyi, *Finding Flow: The Psychology of Engagement with Everyday Life* (Basic Books, 1997), 127.

30. See https://www.briantracy.com/.

31. Kara Cutruzzula writes a useful newsletter on work, life, and productivity: https://us14.campaign-archive.com/home/?u=b1819370f078f7aaea854586f&id=985 443e86d.

32. See note 31.

33. I'm grateful to Professor Cal Newport for the concept of "deep work," and I highly recommend his podcast "Deep Questions."

34. Palmer, *Now What, Grad?*

35. See https://www.funkypenguin.co.nz/review/what-is-attention-residue-and-how -do-i-defeat-it/.

36. See note 35.

37. Palmer, *Now What, Grad?*

38. See https://www.briantracy.com/.

39. Mihaly Csikszentmihalyi, *Finding Flow: The Psychology of Engagement with Everyday Life* (Basic Books, 1997).

40. Cal Newport, *Digital Minimalism: Choosing a Focused Life in a Noisy World* (Portfolio/Penguin, 2019), 177.

41. Stephen Covey, A. Roger Merrill, and Rebecca Merrill, *First Things First: To Live, to Love, to Learn, to Leave a Legacy* (Simon & Schuster, 1994).

42. Emily Esfahani Smith, *The Power of Meaning: Finding Fulfillment in a World Obsessed with Happiness* (Crown, 2017), 172.

43. Dr. Christina Karns, "There's a Deep Neural Connection between Gratitude, Giving, and Values," *Washington Post*, December 25, 2018.

44. E. J. Dionne Jr., "What Gratitude Requires," *Washington Post*, November 28, 2013.

45. See https://www.huffpost.com/entry/stephen-colbert-anderson-cooper-grief_n _5d563c44e4b0d8840ff0d466.

46. Martin Seligman, *Flourish: A Visionary New Understanding of Happiness and Well-Being* (Simon & Schuster, 2011), 30–31.

47. Seligman, 30–31.

48. Jeff Durham, "Taking Responsibility for Your Actions," *Life Coach Expert*, November 7, 2019, http://www.lifecoachexpert.co.uk/TakingResponsibility YourActions.html.

49. Durham.

Chapter Eight

1. See https://www.briantracy.com/.

2. Peter Senge, *The Fifth Discipline: The Art and Practice of the Learning Organization* (Doubleday, 1990), 154.

3. See https://en.wikipedia.org/wiki/Louisa_May_Alcott.

4. Jessica Lahey, *The Gift of Failure: How the Best Parents Learn to Let Go So Their Children Can Succeed* (HarperCollins, 2015).

5. Leonard Sax, *The Collapse of Parenting: How We Hurt Our Kids When We Treat Them Like Grown-Ups* (Basic Books, 2016), 191.

6. Carol Dweck, *Mindset: The New Psychology of Success* (Ballantine, 2016).

7. Salman Khan, "Let's Use Video to Reinvent Education," *TED Talk*, March 2011, https://www.ted.com/talks/salman_khan_let_s_use_video_to_reinvent_education.

8. Angela Duckworth, *Grit: The Power of Passion and Perseverance* (Scribner, 2016).

9. Caroline Adams Miller, *Getting Grit: The Evidence-Based Approach to Cultivating Passion, Perseverance, and Purpose* (Sounds True, 2017), chapter 4 starting on page 57.

10. From Martin Seligman, *Flourish: A Visionary New Understanding of Happiness and Well-Being* (Simon & Schuster, 2011), 117.

Chapter Nine

1. Marcel Schwantes, https://www.inc.com/marcel-schwantes/warren-buffett-says-this-is-1-simple-habit-that-separates-successful-people-from-everyone-else.html.

2. See https://en.wikipedia.org/wiki/Warren_Buffett.

3. See https://en.wikipedia.org/wiki/Carl_Sandburg.

4. See note 1.

5. See note 1.

6. Greg McKeown, *Essentialism: The Disciplined Pursuit of Less* (Crown Business, 2014).

7. McKeown.

8. Rae Witte, "Quit Being the Flaky Friend," *New York Times*, December 24, 2018.

9. Elizabeth Scott, "Say No to People Making Demands on Your Time," June 2, 2019, VeryWellMind, https://www.verywellmind.com/say-no-to-people-making-demands-on-your-time-3145025.

Chapter Ten

1. Robert Samuelson, "Dealing with the Internet's Split Personality," *Washington Post*, June 1, 2020, A21.

2. Chris Palmer, *Raise Your Kids to Succeed: What Every Parent Should Know* (Rowman & Littlefield, 2017), chapter 11, starting on page 75.

3. "Trump vs. Mods: Old Fight Goes Nuclear," *New York Times*, May 20, 2020, B8.

4. See https://fortune.com/2017/06/22/mark-zuckerberg-facebook-mission-groups/.

5. Tristan Harris's TED talk, https://www.ted.com/talks/tristan_harris_how_a _handful_of_tech_companies_control_billions_of_minds_every_day.

6. See note 5.

7. See Tristan Harris's website, https://www.tristanharris.com/.

8. Cal Newport, *Digital Minimalism: Choosing a Focused Life in a Noisy World* (Portfolio/Penguin, 2019).

9. Newport, 28.

10. Ben Sasse, *Them: Why We Hate Each Other and How to Heal* (St. Martin's Press, 2018), 198.

11. Newport, *Digital Minimalism*.

12. Mihaly Csikszentmihalyi, *Finding Flow: The Psychology of Engagement with Everyday Life* (Basic Books, 1997), 6.

13. Csikszentmihalyi, 8.

14. Nir Eyal, *Indistractable: How to Control Your Attention and Choose Your Life* (BenBella Books, 2019), 54.

15. Eyal, xi.

16. For an enlightening TED talk by Professor Adam Alter on why our screens make us less happy (given in April 2017), see https://www.ted.com/talks/adam_alter _why_our_screens_make_us_less_happy?language=en.

17. Eyal, *Indistractable*.

18. Eyal.

19. Eyal, 2, 3.

20. See https://en.m.wikipedia.org/wiki/Johann_Wolfgang_von_Goethe.

21. See https://www.ncbi.nlm.nih.gov/pmc/articles/PMC4183915/.

22. See https://www.theminimalists.com/ee/.

23. See note 22.

24. For example, see https://www.psychologytoday.com/us/blog/happiness-is-state-mind/201807/jomo-the-joy-missing-out.

25. James M. Lang, *Small Teaching: Everyday Lessons from the Science of Learning* (Jossey-Bass, 2016).

26. Jane McGonigal, *SuperBetter: The Power of Living Gamefully* (Penguin, 2015).

27. McGonigal, 51.

28. McGonigal, 117–19.

Chapter Eleven

1. Brian X. Chen, "Doom Scrolling Again? Snap Out of It," *New York Times*, July 16, 2020, B5.

2. Common Sense Media, *Landmark Report: U.S. Teens Use an Average of Nine Hours of Media per Day, Tweens Use Six Hours*, November 2, 2015, https://www.commonsensemedia.org/about-us/news/press-releases/landmark-report-us-teens-use-an-average-of-nine-hours-of-media-per-day.

3. Catherine Steiner-Adair, *The Big Disconnect: Protecting Childhood and Family Relationships in the Digital Age* (HarperCollins, 2013), 11.

4. Steiner-Adair, 11.

5. Steiner-Adair, 16.

6. Jane Scott, "Parenting by Siri," *New York Times*, August 10, 2014.

7. Kim John Payne, *Simplicity Parenting: Using the Extraordinary Power of Less to Raise Calmer, Happier, and More Secure Kids* (Ballantine, 2009), xi.

8. Anya Kamenetz, "I Was a Screen-Time Expert. Then the Coronavirus Happened," *New York Times*, August 9, 2020.

9. Meghan Leahy, "Creating a Good Boundary," *Washington Post*, June 4, 2015.

10. Common Sense Media, *Landmark Report*.

11. Cal Newport, "Career Tip: Quit Social Media," *New York Times*, November 20, 2016.

12. American Academy of Pediatrics, "American Academy of Pediatrics Announces New Recommendations for Children's Media Use," October 21, 2016, https://www.aap.org/en-us/about-the-aap/aap-press-room/pages/american-academy-of-pediatrics-announces-new-recommendations-for-childrens-media-use.aspx.

13. https://www.commonsense.org/.

14. See note 12.

15. Payne, *Simplicity Parenting*.

16. Payne, 8.

17. Mary Pipher, *The Shelter of Each Other: Rebuilding Our Families* (G. P. Putnam's Sons, 1996).

18. U.S. Department of Health and Human Services, "Who Is Affected and How Many Are at Risk for Bullying?" January 21, 2017, https://www.nichd.nih.gov/health/topics/bullying/conditioninfo/Pages/risk.aspx.

19. "Association of Bullying Behavior at Eight Years of Age and Use of Specialized Services for Psychiatric Disorders by Twenty-Nine Years of Age," *Journal of the American Medical Association*, February 2016, http://jamanetwork.com/journals/jamapsychiatry/article-abstract/2472952.

20. Chris Palmer, *Raise Your Kids to Succeed: What Every Parent Should Know* (Rowman & Littlefield, 2017).

21. Sherri Gordon, https://www.verywell.com/sherri-gordon-bullying-expert-460467.

22. Tipper Gore, *Raising PG Kids in an X-Rated Society* (Bantam Books, 1987).

23. Gore, 27.

24. American Academy of Pediatrics, "Gun Violence Trends in Movies," November 2013, http://pediatrics.aappublications.org/content/early/2013/11/06/peds.2013 -1600.

25. Palmer, *Raise Your Kids to Succeed.*

26. https://www.commonsense.org/.

27. Leonard Sax, *The Collapse of Parenting: How We Hurt Our Kids When We Treat Them Like Grown-Ups* (Basic Books, 2016), 23.

28. https://www.commonsense.org/.

29. Mary Pipher, *Reviving Ophelia: Saving the Selves of Adolescent Girls* (Ballantine, 1994).

30. Peggy Orenstein, *Boys and Sex: Young Men on Hookups, Love, Porn, Consent, and Navigating the New Masculinity* (Harper, 2020).

31. Nancy Jo Sales, *American Girls: Social Media and the Secret Lives of Teenagers* (Knopf, 2016).

32. Gail Dines, "Is Pornography Immoral? That Doesn't Matter: It's Now a Public Health Crisis," *Washington Post*, April 10, 2016.

33. Orenstein, *Boys and Sex.*

34. Amy Morin, "Four Reasons You Should Pay Close Attention to Your Teen's Movies," *Very Well Family*, February 23, 2021, https://parentingteens.about.com/four-reasons-you-should-pay-close-attention-to-your-teens-movies. See also https://amymorinlcsw.com/ecourse/.

35. See note 34.

Chapter Twelve

1. For example, see the *Harvard Business Review*, https://hbr.org/2019/03/the-case -for-finally-cleaning-your-desk.

2. Seth J. Gillihan, PhD, "The Mental Health Benefits of Tidying Up," *WebMD blogs*, January 25, 2019, https://blogs.webmd.com/mental-health/20190125/the-mental-health-benefits-of-tidying-up.

3. Julie Morgenstern, *Organizing from the Inside Out: The Foolproof System for Organizing Your Home, Your Office, and Your Life* (Henry Holt and Company, 1998), 13.

4. Marie Kondo, *The Life-Changing Magic of Tidying Up: The Japanese Art of Decluttering and Organizing* (Ten Speed Press, 2014).

5. David Allen, *Getting Things Done: The Art of Stress-Free Productivity* (Penguin, 2015). Also, David Allen, *Making It All Work: Winning at the Game of Work and the Business of Life* (Penguin, 2008).

6. Visit https://www.youtube.com/channel/UCBMKymQczkDxCpE1R2vvA4Q. Also see Joshua Becker's blog, https://www.becomingminimalist.com/.

7. Chris Palmer, *Shooting in the Wild* (Sierra Club Books, 2010). Also see Chris Palmer, *Confessions of a Wildlife Filmmaker* (Bluefield Publishing, 2015).

8. John Vidal, "The Seven Deadly Things We're Doing to Trash the Planet (and Human Life with It)," *London Guardian*, December 19, 2016.

9. David Pilling, "Against GDP: We Need to Rethink Economic Growth to Save the World," *Time*, December 12, 2019. Pilling is also the author of *The Growth Delusion: Wealth, Poverty, and the Well-Being of Nations* (Tim Duggan Books, 2018).

10. Pilling, "Against GDP."

11. George Monbiot, "Embarrassment of Riches," *Monbiot.com*, September 20, 2019, https://www.monbiot.com/2019/09/20/embarrassment-of-riches/.

12. George Monbiot, "The Kink in the Human Brain: Pointless, Joyless Consumption Is Destroying Our World of Wonders," *Monbiot.com*, October 2, 2014, https://www.monbiot.com/2014/10/02/the-kink-in-the-human-brain/.

13. Mary Pipher, *The Shelter of Each Other: Rebuilding Our Families* (G. P. Putnam's Sons, 1996), 15.

14. Brooke McAlary, *Slow: Simple Living for a Frantic World* (Sourcebooks, 2018), 84.

15. Rick Atkinson, *The British Are Coming: The War for America, Lexington to Princeton, 1775–1777* (Henry Holt and Company, 2019), 28.

Chapter Thirteen

1. Anna Goldfarb, "Forget 'Can I Pick Your Brain?' Ask for Advice," *New York Times*, March 18, 2019.

Epilogue

1. Yuval Noah Harari, *Sapiens: A Brief History of Humankind* (HarperCollins, 2015), 415–16.

2. Harari, 416.

Index

~

About the Author

Chris Palmer is an author, speaker, wildlife filmmaker, and retired professor. He serves on the Board of Montgomery Hospice; is writing a book on aging, death, and dying; is a hospice volunteer; and runs an "aging well" group for the Bethesda Metro Area Village.

During his filmmaking career, he swam with dolphins and whales, came face-to-face with sharks and Kodiak bears, camped with wolf packs, and waded hip-deep through Everglade swamps.

For more than thirty-five years, Palmer spearheaded the production of more than three hundred hours of original programming for prime-time television and the IMAX film industry, work that won him and his colleagues many awards, including two Emmys and an Oscar nomination. He has worked with Robert Redford, Paul Newman, Jane Fonda, Ted Turner, and many other celebrities. His IMAX films include *Whales*, *Wolves*, *Dolphins*, *Bears*, *Coral Reef Adventure*, and *Grand Canyon Adventure*.

He has authored seven books on a variety of subjects, including wildlife filmmaking, parenting, and teaching, and he has written a memoir. Proceeds from his books go to fund scholarships for students at American University (AU).

Starting in 2004, Palmer served on AU's full-time faculty as Distinguished Film Producer in Residence until his retirement in 2018. While at AU, he founded and directed the Center for Environmental Filmmaking in the School of Communication. He also created and taught a popular class called *Design Your Life for Success*.

Chris and his wife Gail have lived in Bethesda, Maryland, for almost fifty years and raised their three daughters there. They now have nine grandchildren. Palmer was a stand-up comic for five years. He has jumped out of helicopters and worked on an Israeli kibbutz, and was a high school boxing champion. Palmer is currently learning to juggle, draw, dance, play tennis, and play the piano. He loves to stand on his hands for exercise and keeps a daily gratitude journal.

Palmer currently serves as president of the MacGillivray Freeman Films Educational Foundation, which produces and funds IMAX films on conservation issues. MacGillivray Freeman Films is the world's largest and most successful producer of IMAX films.

Palmer was honored with the Frank G. Wells Award from the Environmental Media Association and the Lifetime Achievement Award for Media at the 2009 International Wildlife Film Festival. In 2010, he was honored at the Green Globe Awards in Los Angeles with the award for Environmental Film Educator of the Decade. In 2011, he received the IWFF Wildlife Hero of the Year Award for his "determined campaign to reform the wildlife filmmaking industry." In 2012, he received the Ronald B. Tobias Award for Achievement in Science and Natural History Filmmaking Education. He received the 2014 University Faculty Award for Outstanding Teaching at AU, the 2015 University Film and Video Association Teaching Award, and the 2015 Lifetime Achievement Award at the International Wildlife Film Festival.

In his twenty years before becoming a film producer, Palmer was an officer in the Royal Navy, an engineer, a business consultant, an energy analyst, an environmental activist, chief energy advisor to a senior U.S. senator, and a political appointee in the Environmental Protection Agency under President Jimmy Carter.

Palmer holds a BS with first-class honors in mechanical engineering from University College London; an MS in ocean engineering and naval architecture, also from University College London; and a master's degree in public administration from Harvard University, where he was a Kennedy Scholar and received a Harkness Fellowship.

Chris can be reached at christopher.n.palmer@gmail.com. His website is www.ChrisPalmerOnline.com. Proceeds from the sale of this book will go to fund scholarships for students at the American University School of Communication.

CPSIA information can be obtained
at www.ICGtesting.com
Printed in the USA
LVHW081619250721
693634LV00002B/19

9 781475 850536